CURRENCIES OF
IMAGINATION

CURRENCIES OF IMAGINATION

Channeling Money and Chasing
Mobility in Vietnam

Ivan V. Small

CORNELL UNIVERSITY PRESS   ITHACA AND LONDON

First published 2018 by Cornell University Press

Printed in the United States of America

Library of Congress Cataloging-in-Publication Data

Names: Small, Ivan Victor, 1972– author.
Title: Currencies of imagination : channeling money and chasing
    mobility in Vietnam / Ivan V. Small.
Description: Ithaca [New York] : Cornell University Press, 2018. |
    Includes bibliographical references and index.
Identifiers: LCCN 2018016486 (print) | LCCN 2018017641 (ebook) |
    ISBN 9781501716904 (pdf) | ISBN 9781501716898 (epub/mobi) |
    ISBN 9781501716874 | ISBN 9781501716874 (cloth ; alk. paper) |
    ISBN 9781501716881 (pbk. ; alk. paper)
Subjects: LCSH: Vietnamese—United States—Economic conditions. |
    Vietnamese—United States—Social conditions. | Emigrant Remittances—
    Vietnam. | Vietnam—Economic conditions—1975– | Immigrants—Family
    relationships—Vietnam. | Immigrants—Family Relationships—
    United States. | Money—Social aspects—Vietnam. | Money—
    Social aspects—United States. | Families—Economic Aspects—
    Vietnam. | Families—Economic aspects—United States. |
    Transnationalism—Social aspects—United States. |
    Transnationalism—Social aspects—Vietnam.
Classification: LCC E184.V53 (ebook) | LCC E184.V53 S63 2018 (print) |
    DDC 973/.0495922—dc23
LC record available at https://lccn.loc.gov/2018016486

Contents

Illustrations

Foreword

In the spirit of anthropological reflexivity (Marcus and Fischer 1999; Clifford and Marcus 2010), I begin this book by acknowledging that this project has been in part framed and motivated by my personal observations and experiences with remittances to Vietnam in my own American family. As a child growing up in New Jersey in the 1970s and 1980s, I often watched my mother, a Vietnamese immigrant who came to the United States in the 1960s as a student, pack boxes full of goods to send to family members in Vietnam who were living under harsh and largely unknown political and economic conditions. These material goods were often laced with hidden dollars, foreshadowing some of the stories that the informants in the present study relate, for my grandfather, uncle, cousins, and other members of my extended family in Vietnam. Sometimes my mother would ask me to write a short note to my grandfather, whom I had not met since I visited Vietnam at the age of one, to slip into the box. The financial, material, and emotional flows between our family and distant kin in Vietnam continued as the years went by. As I grew up, I saw family relationships revived but also some deterioration in the wake of transnational family sponsorships, trips back to Vietnam and remittance obligations—all of which involved various degrees of emotional expectation and exhaustion.

In 2003, between getting a master's degree in international affairs and starting work on my PhD in cultural anthropology, I spent five months in Vietnam looking for a research topic that would allow me to apply a grounded social and cultural lens to my long-standing interest in macro-level issues related to the global political economy. I was accompanied by my bà ngoại (maternal grandmother), who had emigrated from Vietnam to the United States in 1981 to live with our family but had often been dissatisfied in her new environs and frequently expressed a longing to return to her homeland and extended family. Carrying a bag full of thousands of crisp dollar bills earmarked for various relatives, I traveled to Vietnam with my grandmother to explore what options she might have were she to return to live there. We explored and feasted, traveling to visit family members, tourist sites, and temples. Together we celebrated Tết (the lunar new year) in her home village (quê) and delivered much money and many gifts. Over the course of the trip, I was exposed to the complexities and complications of money in cementing and eroding social relations. Eventually I realized that the doctoral research topic I was searching for had been right in front of me, and that I had been participating in it all along. Intriguing stories from my family's past that had been unknown to me were recounted by relatives on multiple occasions, making me increasingly aware of a side of my heritage that I had largely put aside when I was growing up. My grandmother eventually returned to the United States, somewhat tired and occasionally wary of some of the relatives, friends, and neighbors whom we had visited and given presents to, but also relieved and grateful to have reestablished relationships with her extended kin network and appreciative of the hospitality they had shown us.

I returned to Vietnam in 2007 for an extended period of time to conduct the present study on the social dynamics of migration and remittances across a broad spectrum of families and communities. During this period I based myself in Ho Chi Minh City, which, under the name of Saigon, had been the capital of South Vietnam. Many Vietnamese left their country from that city and now are returning to it, with the ongoing economic and political opening of the country. From there, I followed remittances to what I term in this book "remittance geographies," including the central coast and the Mekong Delta. I use this term because each location had unique features in which remittances played an important role, but that role varied depending on context, as I will describe in the chapters that follow. I spent eighteen months in Vietnam during this first period of fieldwork, without returning to the United States. When I finally did return, I went to California, home to the largest Vietnamese American communities in the United States. I lived in the greater San Francisco and Los Angeles metropolitan areas, to better understand the other side of the trans-Pacific migration and remittance equation. In all, I spent nearly two uninterrupted years conducting multi-sited fieldwork and examining a host of angles to consider how remittances have facilitated and complicated transnational kin and community relations among Vietnamese in Vietnam and the United States since the end of the Vietnam War. In deconstructing what remittances are and what they represent, I interrogate the roles, symbolisms, and affects of the movement of money and gifts, as well as the global and state infrastructures that facilitate their transfer and exchange.

In the summer of 2015, after completing my first year in a tenure-track faculty position, I returned to Vietnam for three months to follow up on my earlier investigations as well as begin new research. I spent a portion of this summer traveling in Vietnam for the first time with my mother, who had stayed away from the country for nearly twenty years in part due to the exhaustion that extended family obligations and memories had caused her. For me it was a remarkable opportunity to see my mother rediscover and experience the land of her birth together with my father, who had spent his formative post-college years in Vietnam working with agricultural development initiatives. Together we reflected on all that had changed since the 1960s and participated in reestablishing relationships with places and people from which our family had long been disconnected.

This book is not an auto-ethnography, and my purpose is not to tell this story here. However, in the spirit of reflexivity I relate it briefly to offer the reader some transparency and insight into the motivations and frameworks that may have influenced my interests in and orientation toward this study. The chapters that follow relate stories of money, things, and people, some of which may be pieced together and some that simply stand on their own. If I came to this study with an interest in clearly understanding the patterns by which remittances shape and manage social relations, influenced perhaps by my own complex experiences with them, I come away from it not necessarily more informed—able to offer an interpretive or predictive framework or blueprint of how remittances work—but rather even more intrigued by the *many* ways they work and are repeated even when they do not work. The question of work itself, and how money reveals the connections we often implicitly weave between conceptions of identity and labor, will also be addressed in this study. If anthropological analysis can be understood as a dialectic between ethnography and theory (Boyer, Faubion, and Marcus 2015), this book offers the reader a journey that engages both, and both with each other. I can only hope that the experience of reading this book will be as compelling and thought provoking as my own unforgettable journey researching and writing it, and that it may inspire more inquiries and voyages in turn.

Acknowledgments

The writing of this book has been a remarkable academic, personal, physical, and intellectual journey back and forth across the Pacific on multiple occasions, and I have many people to thank for inspiring and sharing the voyage.

First of all, I carry a great debt of gratitude to my graduate school advisers, who helped guide me through the initial stages of this project while earning a PhD at Cornell University. I could not have asked for a more patient, encouraging, and inspirational mentor than Andrew Willford. I can only hope to emulate his compassion, kindness, humility, and brilliance in my own professional and personal trajectory. James Siegel was a guiding inspiration, teaching me to appreciate the intellectual apprehension that comes at the limits of comprehension, where thinking and seeing begins anew. Shelley Feldman was a dynamic interlocutor, offering an important intellectual bridge between anthropology and development sociology, a field this book also seeks to address. Keith Taylor pushed me to conduct careful scholarship informed by deep geographical, literary, and historical understanding, and I appreciate his commitment to speaking across disciplinary boundaries.

During a trip to Vietnam in 2003 I met two graduate students in the field whose spirited conversations motivated me to pursue doctoral research in Vietnam-related studies in the first place, Erik Harms (now at Yale University) and Matt Masur (now at Saint Anselm College). At Cornell, I fondly remember my colleagues in the Anthropology Department. It would be impossible to name them all, but Reighan Gillam from my initial graduate cohort started and continues this academic journey with me, and we meet annually at the national anthropology meetings but also outside of them to celebrate all of life's professional and personal milestones. Cornell's Southeast Asia Program was also formative in helping me think comparatively about Vietnam within Southeast Asia, and I will always be nostalgic about the close-knit scholarly community I belonged to there. I thank Claudine Ang, Samson Lim, John Phan, Joe Pittayaporn, Andrew Johnson, Jane Ferguson, Tyrell Haberkorn, Nina Hien, Doreen Lee, Rick Ruth, Becky Butler, Pamela Corey, Tim Gorman, Trais Pearson, Chika Watanabe, Eileen Vo, Hong Bui, Martin Loicano, Courtney Work, and Mirabelle Yang, among others, for their conversations and company over long working days and nights in the Kahin Center.

In Vietnam, where I conducted ethnographic fieldwork, I thank the Anthropology Department at Vietnam National University in Ho Chi Minh City (HCMC) for sponsoring my research and giving me an opportunity to present my findings to a Vietnamese academic audience for feedback. In particular I wish to thank Nguyễn Văn Tiệp, Trương Thị Kim Chuyên, Trần Thị Minh Giới, and the late Đặng Phong (in Hanoi) for helping me establish research contacts and advising and supporting my work. There were other scholars in the field who also shared the excitement, explorations, frustrations, and reflections of field research in Vietnam. I fondly remember motorbike adventures with Chris Schweidler; ethnographic explorations with Khai Thu Nguyen; *bia hoi* in the alley with Mitch Aso and Christine Tran; and outings to various holes in the wall with Van Ly, Allen Tran, and others.

I also thank the Vietnamese American Non-Governmental Organization Network, and particularly Diep Vuong, which invited me to participate in its humanitarian initiatives that span Vietnam and the United States. In Vietnam and California countless friends and colleagues have helped me navigate field research, and I humbly thank the many organizations, families, and individuals who generously invited me into their lives and offered me their time and insights so that I might better understand the complexities of remittance economies and the emotions they produce. Many institutions assisted and advised me during my time in Vietnam, including the Vietnamese Ministry of Foreign Affairs; the Department of Anthropology, Department of Vietnamese Studies, and Office of International Relations at Vietnam National University Ho Chi Minh City; the Binh Đinh Provincial People's Committee; the HCMC District Four Fatherland Front; the HCMC Overseas Vietnamese Liaison Office; the International Organization for Migration; Asia Foundation; Ford Foundation; Asian Development Bank; United Nations Development Programme; School for International Training; Council for International Educational Exchange; Vietnam State Committee for Overseas Vietnamese Affairs; Vietnamese Academy of Social Sciences; École française d'Extrême-Orient in Hanoi; the Ho Chi Minh City National Library; and the U.S. consulate in Ho Chi Minh City.

Over the past five years I have benefited from fresh perspectives and experiences that have informed the revision of this book. Ashok Gurung at the New School's India China Institute offered me a unique opportunity to think about my work in Vietnam through the lens of China and India—two regional powers that continue to profoundly shape Southeast Asia. Through work with the Smithsonian I have had the chance to lead study trips to Vietnam on additional occasions to share and expand my research. At the University of California, Irvine (UCI), where I did my postdoctoral work, I thank Bill Maurer for his support and mentorship. I also thank everyone at UCI's Institute for Money, Technology, and Financial Inclusion—including Smoki Musaraj, Jenny Fan, and John Seaman—and the Department of Anthropology for pushing me to further think through concepts of money and acts of payment in a broader comparative and infrastructural light. I thank Linda Vo at UCI's Department of Asian American Studies for introducing me to the wonderful Vietnamese American Arts and Letters Association in Orange County, California, where I enjoyed participating in a dynamic community dedicated to promoting Vietnamese American and Vietnamese transnational cultural production. The members of my Southern California Southeast Asia reading and writing group—Sarah Grant, Sylvia Nam, Duy Lap Nguyen, Lilly Nguyen, and Ma Vang—were a refreshing source of cross-institutional and -disciplinary intellectual support and inspiration. I also appreciated invitations from Mariam Lam at UC Riverside and Nguyen-Vo Thu Huong and George Dutton at UCLA to present my research in colloquium settings while in California, the feedback from which was very helpful in developing my analysis. Since I came to Connecticut, I have enjoyed participating in a collegial department at Central Connecticut State University, whose members are committed to reflecting on the broader picture of anthropological, humanistic and social scientific inquiries and their applications. I thank Abigail Adams, Kenny Feder, Warren Perry, Evelyn Phillips, Tom Rein, Sylvia Jalil-Guttierez, and Stephanie Waldman for their camaraderie. I have taught classes with remarkable students whose honest, humble, and open inquiries constantly inspire me to revisit my research questions and theoretical orientations with new eyes. In Connecticut I have also benefited from a robust Asian and Asian American studies intellectual community, in particular thanks to the strong representation of Vietnamese studies across the four Connecticut State campuses as well as through faculty affiliations with the Yale University Council for Southeast Asian Studies and the University of Connecticut (UConn) Asian and Asian American Studies Institute. I thank the other members of the Connecticut Vietnam Studies group—Erik Harms, Michele Thompson, Wynn Wilcox, Bradley Davis, Ben Kiernan, Marguerite Nguyen, Quang Phu Van, Quan Tran, and Nu-Anh Tran—for their friendship and collaboration. I owe a deep debt of gratitude to Cathy Schlund-Vials at UConn for arranging a book workshop for this manuscript before I submitted it to publishers, and to Christina Schwenkel from the University of California, Riverside, for flying out to facilitate the workshop. The detailed feedback and thoughtful discussions on the manuscript during the workshop were invaluable in moving this book toward publication. And of course, heartfelt thanks to the anonymous reviewers who took the time to carefully read the manuscript and offer thoughtful advice and insights on how to make the final revisions.

Most of all I thank my family for their nurturing encouragement and for inspiring me to be an anthropologist by exposing me to travel and different cultures from an early age, including living in the Philippines and Sri Lanka. My parents, Leslie Small and Loan Anh Nguyen thi Small; my sister, Irene; my brother-in-law, Tumelo; and my niece, Kha-ai; have been an unwavering source of support, love and joy. Thank you also to my family in Vietnam for their deep and genuine hospitality over the years, including Câu Diệu, Hạnh, Nguyên, Ba Ta, and the many others who welcomed me and have helped me think of Vietnam as a second home. This project was in part inspired by my grandmother, Lê Thị Điệp, whose memory I will cherish. Deep love, thanks, and gratitude go to my wife, Na-Rae Kim, whom I had the wonderful and life-changing fortune to meet while presenting material from this book at the Association for Asian American Studies.

Finally, I gratefully acknowledge the support for my doctoral studies at Cornell University, the Fulbright-Hays Doctoral Dissertation Research Award that took me to Vietnam, and the American Association of University Professors grant that funded my follow-up research to complete the writing of this book. Much gratitude goes to Cornell University Press, Westchester Publishing Services, and my editor, Jim Lance, who showed sincere enthusiasm about this project from the beginning and helped guide it into the world with the vision that it might interest anthropologists and development economists but also many others. I hope that the audiences who read this book are diverse, and that the stories and analyses in it will inspire further reflection about the remarkably complex, yet ever intimate, sociocultural and infrastructural dynamics of international migration and remittance economies.

CURRENCIES OF IMAGINATION

FIGURE 1. Navigating out to sea, south central coast of Vietnam.

MONEY, GIFTS, AND FLOWS

This is a book about remittances and migration. It is also about money and gifts; memory; value and relationships; and the vicissitudes of financial, material, and bodily flows in a global economy. It is a book about Vietnam and the United States.[1] It is not about the Vietnam War. Nonetheless, the stories told here originate with war and the devastations of its aftermath.

On April 30, 1975, the twenty-year-old government of the Republic of Vietnam (RVN, commonly known as South Vietnam) capitulated to the Democratic Republic of Vietnam (North Vietnam) and southern Viet Cong forces. In the days prior to the RVN's collapse, key officials from the Saigon government and their families who feared the consequences of a communist victory had already begun an exodus out of the country. The United States, South Vietnam's military, political, and economic ally, was the destination for many of these early refugees. Camp Pendleton in San Diego County, California, was designated as the first camp to receive refugees as they fled the turmoil of the U.S. Cold War interventions in Asia. Indeed, as the anthropologist Heonik Kwon (2008) has pointedly argued, the Cold War experienced by Americans and Russians was in fact, for most of the world, not a cold one at all. The proxy wars supported by the rival superpowers and China that brutally played out from Korea to Vietnam and El Salvador remind us of the violent reality that much of the world's population experienced the confrontational half-century following World War II as very much a hot war.

Following the end of what the United States called the Vietnam War, American policies aimed to punish and isolate the new government of the unified Socialist Republic of Vietnam, formally established in 1976.[2] This was in part a

1

response to Vietnamese military intervention in and eventual occupation of Cambodia, as the Sino-Soviet split created new proxy wars in the region—this time between Soviet and Chinese communist client states. The United States imposed an embargo on Vietnam and withheld diplomatic recognition of the Hanoi government for twenty years. Meanwhile, mismanaged attempts to impose command-economy socialism on a reunified yet economically embargoed country still reeling from more than thirty years of war (a period that began during World War II) led to mass material shortages and poverty.[3] This tragic situation would continue for a generation. In the mid-1980s, Vietnam was classified as one of the poorest countries in the world (World Bank Vietnam). Refugees, usually (and always technically) political but increasingly economic, streamed out of the country, many in rickety fishing boats not meant for long sea voyages.[4] Many Vietnamese who stayed in the country were forced by the government to relocate to New Economic Zones, while thousands of former Saigon government collaborators disappeared into reeducation prison camps. Wars with Cambodia and China in the 1970s led to further casualties. In the end, hundreds of thousands of Vietnamese perished in the generation following the Vietnam War, whether trying to flee at sea or under the harsh economic and punitive political conditions of the new fully Communist-controlled Vietnam.

Vietnamese who had managed to flee the country—often going first to refugee camps in Southeast Asia and then settling in Western countries including the United States, Australia, Canada, France, and Germany—looked back at the homeland from which they were now exiled with consternation. Many had deep political reservations about the new regime and worried about how relatives and friends left behind were faring under its isolation from the West and the failing internal management of the economy. As just one indicator of the disastrous economic conditions at the time, Vietnam (which is now one of the largest exporters of rice in the world) in the 1970s could not even produce enough rice to feed its own population (Beresford and Dang 2000; Kerkvliet 2005).

Given such dire living conditions, the Vietnamese refugees who had settled abroad began to send aid to their family members left in Vietnam. Officially known as remittances (*kiều hối*), such informal aid flows from migrants often settled in developed countries to families and home communities in developing countries are widespread in many migrant communities and indeed a motivating factor for migration.[5] In the case of Vietnamese refugees in the 1970s and 1980s, however, sending international remittances was not easy, particularly between the United States and Vietnam. The lack of official diplomatic and economic relations between the United States, where most members of the Vietnamese diaspora had resettled and from which two-thirds of the remittances are sent, and Vietnam meant that there were no readily available financial channels for sending money. Nonetheless, Vietnamese found creative ways to send aid to relatives, skirting official value-transfer infrastructures while producing new informal ones. Starting in the late 1970s, Vietnamese in the diaspora began to ship boxes of material goods to relatives. With the embargo, Vietnamese had a difficult time accessing supplies to meet basic needs, from food and shoes to medicine. Family members resettled overseas would carefully collect such items and ship them in boxes to Vietnam, similar to the practice of sending *balikbayan* boxes to the Philippines (Rafael 2000; Lee and Nadeau 2011) but without equivalent transnational communication flows that could quickly confirm their reception. When a shipment arrived in Vietnam, recipient households would be notified, and a household member then typically traveled to the airport or, in more remote areas, the local People's Committee to collect it. It was not uncommon for officials and middlemen to take a share of the goods received.

The basic purpose of sending these goods from abroad was twofold. First, they provided recipients with much-needed items. From clothes to soap, people in Vietnam were in desperate need of basic material needs. Second, such goods provided a form of exchangeable value. They could be traded for other items, including those that would meet immediate subsistence needs such as perishable foodstuffs, which could not be sent but were nonetheless constantly in short supply in postwar Vietnam. A black market in material goods emerged in Vietnam, supplementing or even bypassing the local currency that had become prohibitively inflationary (before 1986, inflation was at times over 700 percent). People exchanged material goods such as electronic calculators, radios, and watches sent from abroad for needed foodstuffs such as rice, vegetables, and meat. Black markets that facilitated such exchanges had the added effect of conjuring up nostalgia for the capitalist lifestyle of the bygone pre-1975 era. This was especially true in Saigon, which had been a cosmopolitan city with economic and cultural linkages to the United States and other capitalist Western countries prior to reunification. In particular, the Commodity Import Program to provide American aid to South Vietnam through consumer goods had fueled a material consumption pattern that Saigon society had become accustomed to but that came to an abrupt halt after the Communist victory in the Vietnam War (Hunt 2014).

As Vietnam's inflation began to stabilize following the *Đổi Mới* ("renovation") economic reforms after 1986, and as Vietnam and the United States moved to normalize relations in the 1990s, channels for sending money from the United States and receiving it in Vietnam began to open. Increasingly, money returned to its regular functions of storing and exchanging value. The Vietnamese government, desperately short of foreign currency reserves, actively encouraged monetary remittances and moved to ease policy restrictions and taxes that were impeding them. Vietnam experimented with legalizing the use of dollars and gold as alternatives to state currency in the late 1980s and early 1990s, and eventually there was a general consensus that tolerating an informal dual currency system would be beneficial for economic growth (Van Arkadie and Mallon 2003). Material remittances continued, but financial remittances grew rapidly. By the time the United States finally restored diplomatic relations in 1995, during the administration of President Bill Clinton, twenty years had passed since the end of the Vietnam War. While many former refugees in the Vietnamese exile community still felt uncomfortable about returning to Vietnam or feared that they would be unwelcome there, they generally remained firmly committed to supporting family members who were still in Vietnam. In the meantime, a new diasporic generation was coming of age whose experience of extended family relations had been largely shaped by remittances, letters, and photos from physically distant and often unmet relatives. In such a situation, monetary and material remittances along with their personalized accompaniments took on important symbolic meanings. They represented the more proximate and physical relations that had been far more common within families before exodus and exile. In filling both the spatial and the growing temporal gap between separated kin, remittances took on an increasingly affective character that heightened specters of migration but also imaginaries of migrants and the worlds they inhabited. The geographies and societies that migrants had departed to and in which they were being transformed were of increasing curiosity to those who stayed in Vietnam. While the affective dimensions of money sent by migrants have been observed in other case studies—from the Philippines (Parreñas 2001; Mariano 2017) to Haiti (Glick-Schiller and Fouron 2001)—in Vietnam's situation a generation of refugee exile heightened the scope and intensity of monetary affect.

Money and the Affective Infrastructure of Exchange

What is money, and why do we place value in it? When faced with such questions, we often turn first to the material manifestation of money we are most familiar with: cash. According to a common American expression, "cash is king"—which implicitly assumes the universality of money's value and form. We use cash to pay for things, we collect and store it to save, and we often come to believe that material cash itself has intrinsic value. Of course, in most cases a government designates the value of the cash we hold, printing it as currency and managing policies to maintain its worth and exchangeability. Although in many cases in the contemporary world money is only paper, the fact that so many people steadfastly believe in the value of our materially ephemeral cash speaks to our inherent trust in the state that stands behind it. When we have a surplus of cash, we put it in the bank, and our money is transformed into a record. Our faith in the banking system, also backed by the state, to hold our cash and convert it to an accounting record that can be transferred or one day be turned into cash again also speaks to the importance of the financial and political infrastructure behind money.[6] Without a competently managed monetary infrastructure, a formal economy and market will devolve and eventually dissolve. The material symbol of such an economy (money) will quickly become worthless through inflation, as we have seen in cases ranging from the German Weimar Republic in the early twentieth century to Zimbabwe in the early twenty-first century.

The classic definition of working money is that it effectively serves as a means of exchange, a method of payment, a measure of value, and a unit of account. As the anthropologist Paul Bohannan (1955) observed in the case of British Nigeria in the 1950s, modern money makes exchanges and transfers across distance possible because it purportedly holds universally recognized and accepted exchangeable value that is easily portable and not perishable. Of course, money intersects with and may disrupt localized manifestations of value and rituals of exchange, as Bohannan documented.[7] However, money is not simply a utilitarian tool that replaces cultural valuation systems. It can also elucidate them. Economic anthropologists have long maintained that money is more than merely a facilitator of economic management and exchange.[8] As the anthropologist Bill Maurer argues, beyond the classic economic definition, "money is also a system of relationships, a chain of promises, and a record of people's transactions with each other" (2015, 46). These include overtures and transactions of generosity, as well as indebtedness (Mauss 1967; Graeber 2011). Money is a technology for managing the economic realm, but it is also an apparatus for mediating social relations. Indeed, the entangled realms of the social and economic betray the artificiality of the categorical and analytic divide. Money may appear to stand outside of us (we might adamantly and even ethically maintain that it does not define us), yet subjectively we know that money is intimately caught up in countless of our motivations and behaviors.

Does money shape us? Does it reflect us? Georg Simmel, one of the early theorists of money, asserts in *The Philosophy of Money* that money's usefulness is in creating a medium of exchange by which individual subjective desires articulated via particular material things are objectively and universally mediated. Two individuals agree on a price, which quantifies a thing that might be differently valued by each individual in isolation. Yet the seeming simplicity of this monetary function is not as simple as it seems, and its effects are not necessarily contained in the mere process of exchange. Money mediates between individuals and the objects they desire, value, and consume, but it also seeps into those relationships, entangling as well as elucidating them. Simmel reflects:

The philosophical significance of money is that it represents within the practical world the most certain image and the clearest embodiment of the formula of all being, according to which things receive their meaning through each other, and have their being determined by their mutual relations . . . the projection of mere relations into particular objects is one of the great accomplishments of the mind; when the mind is embodied in objects, these become a vehicle for the mind and endow it with a livelier and more comprehensive activity. The ability to construct such symbolic objects attains its greatest triumphs in money. For money represents pure interaction in its purest form; it makes comprehensive the most abstract concept; it is an individual thing whose essential significance is to reach beyond individualities. (2004,129)

Money attempts to assign a singular objective valuation to things that are diversely and subjectively desired and that may be exchanged between people who subjectively desire each other. In this function and process, money confronts the rela-

FIGURE 2. Man with dollar bill from overseas relative.

tional entanglement of value. As Karl Marx (1992) reminds us, the engaging of two parties in a transaction reveals that value is produced only through exchange and is not inherent in things themselves. Money represents a relationship between two parties, but in doing so it entraps them, connecting them to each other but also to money as an expression of that connection. This ability to imagine a connection through symbolic objects, Simmel says, is the great "triumph" of money. A materially tangible medium, it reaches "beyond individualities," one of the effects of which is that it becomes "a vehicle for the mind and endow[s] it with livelier and more comprehensive activity." Money, then, is as much a channel for the lively activity of the mind (the imagination, if you will) as it is a way of objectively mediating value. Money both shapes and reflects us. This occurs not only in the material conditions of its exchange and use, but also in the imagined hypotheticals of its transformative possibilities. Money is practical, but it is also very much affective.

Remittances as Money

We now return to the topic of remittances and connect it to this expanding understanding of what money is and does. Remittances are most commonly defined as the transfer of money between individuals and families in the diaspora to their counterparts in the homeland. As discussed, the desire to send remittances is a common motivation for international migration, as people move from peripheral to core countries in the global economy to earn money in places with more opportunities and send it home to places with fewer. Remittances have become a topic of widespread interest in public policy circles, particularly since the start of the twenty-first century. Following the September 11 attacks on the United States in 2001, governments and international organizations realized that transnational terror had in part been enabled by cross-border financial support, and they became paradoxically both interested in and anxious about international capital flows. In October 2001 the Financial Action Task Force made recommendations about terrorist financing that extended oversight requirements designed to prevent money laundering to remittance providers. However, increased attention to the regulations governing cross-border remittances also increased awareness of the significance of their flows. International migrant money flows were foregrounded, and development practitioners started to seriously analyze their potential for reducing poverty. Samuel Maimbo and Dilip Ratha's edited volume, *Remittances: Development Impact and Future Prospects* (2005b), one of the first major comparative studies of the topic, enthusiastically highlights the quantities of informal aid sent by migrants to their home communities. Maimbo and

Ratha celebrate the "recent revival in interest in migrant remittances" due to the "sheer size these flows have acquired" (2005a, 3), second only to foreign direct investment and higher than overseas development assistance, and reflect on their potential for poverty reduction. Over the past fifteen years, studies on remittances have multiplied, mostly within the analytic framework of development economics. For example, the applied economists Richard Adams and John Page (2005) estimated that a 10.0 percent increase in remittances can reduce poverty in the receiving country by 3.5 percent. Increased policy attention to and tracking of remittances generally exaggerated their quantitative increases, now globally estimated at over $600 billion annually (World Bank 2016), well over four times the amounts recorded by Maimbo and Ratha (2005a).[9] Remittances have in many ways become a silver bullet for policy makers, leading to inflated hopes for global development and long-term poverty solutions in the Global South.

The burden of earning and sending those remittances, of course, has been on the backs of migrants, whose stories have often been backgrounded even while their money is foregrounded by states, international organizations, and development NGOs. As Ester Hernandez and Susan Coutin (2006) have pointed out, the exuberant development discourse on remittances ignores important issues such as migrants' hardship, risk, and bodily absence as externalities. Dangerous working conditions, unsavory labor contracts, trafficked labor, unsustainable debt, absent parents who miss out on their own children's upbringing, and in situ displacement are just a few of the associated costs overlooked in economic calculations of the benefits of remittances. Not only are the costs rendered external and invisible, but migrant monies themselves come to be seen as public goods, leveraged by states to guarantee foreign reserves and as collateral to secure loans. In the case of diaspora bonds, migrants are even solicited to provide loans to governments (Ketkar and Ratha 2010). At a local level, migrant families are expected to invest their hard-earned remittances in a so-called productive manner that benefits the long-term development of their communities and countries. Hernandez and Coutin note that state and development discourses surrounding issues of remittances and migrants "contribute to producing the enterprising subjects of neoliberalism" (2006, 201), whereby states put the burden of development on migrants rather than administering effective policies to provide sustainable livelihoods for their populations. Remittance-led development schemes can result in long-term dependency on migration. Countries like the Philippines, a pioneer in promoting state-facilitated international labor migration schemes since the 1980s, have come to depend on migration as a way of securing foreign reserves. Ten percent of the population of the Philippines is estimated to reside outside the country at any given time. Filipino programs to train nurses and nannies have exploded, all with an intention of sending graduates out of the country rather than of finding them gainful employment in the local economy.

All of the development discourses surrounding the poverty-reducing potential of remittances generally reflect a classic economic take on money. Remittances are primarily understood to be just money, and even when they are in nonmonetary form they are seen as still having material value that is convertible to money. As such, they can be analyzed according to money's functional capacity to transfer and mediate value from places and people in the world system where it can be accumulated to places and people where it is scarce. Money fulfills its objective function of facilitating exchange and payment, and of measuring and quantifying value. In a globalized world, money is the most convenient tool for facilitating payment and channeling universally accepted value across distance and borders. The International Monetary Fund defines remittances as "household income from foreign economies arising mainly from the temporary or permanent move of people to those economies. Remittances include cash and noncash items that flow through formal channels, such as electronic wire, or through informal channels, such as money or goods carried across borders" (2009, 18).

When we take a closer look at what motivates these value transfers, however, analyses of remittances become more complicated. The sociologist Luin Goldring (2004) disaggregates remittances into three primary subcategories: family, investment, and collective remittances. The first subcategory is the most familiar. People send aid to kin, a recognizable activity in any familial situation but here easily visualized due to the cross-border nature of the support. However, extending the definition of remittances to investment and collective transfers expands the category beyond family obligations. This expanded definition betrays an implicit assumption that there is a natural connection between these remittance categories in which affective and emotional motivations may override individualistic economically rational ones. In the case of Vietnam, Dang Nguyen Anh (2005), a Vietnamese sociologist who has examined the development impact of primarily domestic but also international remittances, argues that "remittances" is an umbrella term covering money sent by migrants to relatives in their places of origin, personal investment transfers, collective transfers, and charitable remittances. In this case, the last two subcategories parallel Goldring's category of collective remittances. But what element across these disparate subcategories unifies them? Certainly, they are all transnational capital transfers between members of the same national or ethnic group. But why is the ethnic link the key to understanding these particular capital transfer phenomena? What distinguishes diasporic investment remittances from foreign direct investment, a categorically separate

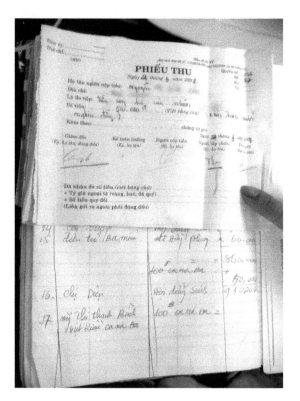

FIGURE 3. Remittance accounting.

realm of financial analysis? Why are diasporic collective and charitable remittances distinct from overseas development assistance or other humanitarian aid from international NGOs? At the root of this tripartite remittance grouping of family, investment, and collective is a sense of what motivates the sending of such monies: ethnic and emotional ties. It is precisely at this point where notions of affect clearly re-enter the monetary picture. The transfer of value between kin and members of a particular ethnic group assumes an affective motivation that goes beyond the standard economic caricature of a rational choice actor whose behavior is solely based on self-interest. And it is here that an additional category of remittances, also analyzed as connected with the previous categories of family, investment, and collective, further reveals the effect of remittances, symbolized most significantly by money but expanding the category far beyond it.

The sociologist Peggy Levitt identifies a fourth type of remittance practice called social remittances (1998, 2001). These include "ideas, practices, identities, and social capital that flow from sending to receiving country communities" (1998, 926). Social scientists have taken a keen interest in this additional subcategory of remittances. Social remittances have also been incorporated into development-economic frameworks as what has come to be known as gray matter, or knowledge transfers: the idea that diasporic subjects learn valuable skills abroad that can be reinvested or returned (remitted) to the home country for purposes of development. The assumption is that among diasporic populations one can always find altruistic and nationalistic motivations connected to homeland, family, roots, and so on that drive "home" bound return. Value, in multiple forms but most apparently as money, appears to be transferred because of selfless motivations. In this sense, remittances can be money and continue to be widely materially symbolized by it, but they are also undoubtedly gifts with all of their affective trappings.

Remittances as Gifts

As an anthropologist, I find the issue of remittances compelling and deserving of focused analytical attention, but from a slightly different perspective than a general economic one. My interest is in digging further into the question of how remittances affect and reflect sociality and relational identities. The notion of social remittances and its analytical linkage to, but also clear separation from, other migrant monetary transfers betray the facts that money is always more than money, and that migration and remittances are socially and culturally complicated matters that involve the entangled mobility of bodies, money, things, and ideas—and, by extension, imaginations. Remittance economies offer insights into the contours of these complications and entanglements. Central to these contours is the issue of exchange. Remittances, despite the etymology of the word, are never mere one-way remissions of money and by definitional extension erasures of debt and obligation. Rather, they are complex exchanges between parties in which encounters between selves and others mediated by money and things conjure up a medley of memories, emotions, imaginaries, and aspirations. Most tellingly, the work of money in a remittance relationship rarely pays off debt and obligation as mere money, functioning as an economic tool, is supposed to do. Instead, it tightly entangles givers and receivers, often complicating and interrogating the foundation of their relationship and, by extension, the people on either side of it.

To the extent that remittances reflect relations of obligation—to family, community, or homeland—their function goes beyond money and seemingly fits well within anthropological concepts of gifting practices. The role of gifts in social life has long been of interest to anthropologists, often traced to Marcel Mauss's classic 1923 *Essai sur le don*, commonly translated as *The Gift* (1967). Mauss enacts a classic anthropological armchair analysis of what appears to be a humanistic universal: the giving and receiving of gifts. Drawing on secondhand accounts of a diverse range of gifting customs from around the world, with a particular focus on the American Pacific Northwest and Trobriand Islands in the South Pacific, he makes a somewhat crude universal argument, which is often the primary takeaway from the work, that gifts must be given, received, and reciprocated everywhere. The symmetry of relationality—I give you a gift, you return it, and we are then in a relationship of recognition and mutual obligation—is highlighted in Mauss's accounts of Melanesian gift practices, drawing on Bronislaw Malinowski's ethnography of Kula circles in which shell necklaces and armbands accompanied more commonplace commodity trade (*gimwali*), contributing to social harmonization among the various Trobriand Islands that in turn facilitated economic cooperation. Mauss emphasizes this narrative of gifting, demonstrating that "to make a gift of something to someone is to make a present of some part of oneself" (1967, 12). He goes on to elevate the selfless humanitarianism of gifting in his conclusion as an ideal inspiration if not model for Europeans to rediscover and emulate in a woeful modern era of extreme capitalist competition, lust, and deceitful self-interest.

Yet the symmetric gift heuristic that many readers take away from *The Gift* overlooks the divergent details of the multiple primary and secondary accounts that Mauss drew upon to assemble his analysis. These include, significantly, the potlatch practices of the North American Kwakiutl, where competitive gifting among rivals supposedly served to establish and reinforce hierarchy and leadership. While Mauss argues that the "three themes of the gift, the obligation to give, the obligation to receive and reciprocate" (1967, 39) are identical in the potlatch, there is nonetheless a focus on credit and honor that characterizes the potlatch differently than the Kula. Parties exchange gifts with ever-increasing stakes until finally the gift can no longer be returned by one of them. The final gifter wins, and assumes leadership of and responsibility for the clan. As Mauss says, "a gift is received with a burden attached . . . to refrain from giving, just as to refrain from accepting, is to lose rank—as is refraining from reciprocating" (1967, 41). Here the focus appears to be on the consequences of asymmetry for power and prestige, rather than the production of harmony through equal exchange.

The multivalent nature of the gift as ascertained and constructed by Mauss is a compelling general framework through which to examine the case of diasporic remittances. This is not necessarily because the crude category of gift can simply be applied to situations of remittances, if we attend only to the gift's functional and logistical work to frame how relations and value are mediated. Mauss himself had "no wish to put forward this study as a model" (1967, 78). Rather, the gift itself, as a loosely idealized heuristic produced by Mauss to gesture the way to a more humanistic future, can in this case be understood as a process but also as an imaginary through which actions of giving and receiving find meaning. Integral to meaning making is the question of the Other, which as David Palumbo-Liu (2012) argues, is a relation as well as a thing. But the production of things—in this case, the gift—obscures details. The diverse ethnographic practices collected and consigned by Mauss to his category of gift demonstrate how the very process of identifying and defining the hopeful action of gifting obscures the messiness of giving across different situations and contexts, from Kula to potlatch. Yet the affective intention of the category has real effects on shaping such a "mess" and the morasses of specificity, inserting diverse practices into a frame that becomes visible and analyzable.[10]

The literature on gifting has fascinated anthropologists in particular, but also scholars in the humanities and social sciences more broadly, because of the many ways the heuristic can help us rethink a range of contemporary problems. Malinowski (1984) was interested in trade and how to cultivate noble etiquette, and Franz Boas (1898) was interested in debt and how to preserve honor. Mauss drew these so-called primitive cases together to interrogate and rethink social relations under capitalism, arguing that "perhaps by studying these obscure aspects of social life we shall succeed in throwing a little light upon the path that our nations must follow, both in their morality and in their economy" (1967, 78). Numerous later scholars have revisited these classics to interrogate a range of contemporary issues, including religion, inalienable value, finance, contracts, gender, and time.[11] As the anthropologist Hirokazu Miyazaki has observed, "the gift has served as an almost infinitely extensible model for anthropology and beyond. Since the work of Malinowski and Mauss, the gift has been explicitly recognized, however, as an elusive analytical category" (2013, 41). The generalized applicability of the gift seems to be boundless, while its elusiveness is precisely why the concept has been so intriguing.[12] In particular, the gift as a heuristic has been mobilized as a horizon toward which new types of social and economic relations and infrastructures become imaginable. In the context of the 2008 financial crisis, for example, Miyazaki has argued that the gift as a category that is both "everywhere and nowhere" (2013, 47) poses an opportunity to restage the issue not as a tedious debate about whether the gift analytically fits individual cases, but rather the fact that it is attractive as a hypothetical framework and process through which diverse interests and agendas find common para-ethnographic ground. In other words, those seeking a way out of the limitations of current epistemologies of knowledge, whether related to theories of anthropology, finance, or economics, may find common ground in using the ubiquitous yet sufficiently generalizable gift concept as an alternative horizon that allows us to think and move beyond the current limits of the imaginable and doable.

Remittances as Flow and Rupture

In such a formulation, the gift works not because it is endowed with specific traits that allow it to function in a prescribed manner with predictable outcomes. Rather, it is conceptually an ideal type as well as a real-life experience in which the disjuncture between what the gift is supposed to do and what it actually achieves produces contradictions that spur imaginaries of alternatives. These contradictions, and the urge to surmount them, drive the perpetuation and repetitive yet ruptured flow of the gifting process. To apprehend the gift disjuncture and its effects, it is worth considering what psychoanalytic perspectives on relationality offer. Central to such perspectives are questions of subject formation motivated by Georg Hegel's analysis of the self and Other in the master-slave dialectic. As Jacques Lacan posited, the intersubjectivity of identity is revealed as humans are ontologically haunted by spectral comparatives: "the *I* with the statue onto which man projects himself, the phantoms that dominate him, and the automaton with which the world of his own making tends to achieve fruition in an ambiguous relation" (2002, 5). Perceptions of lacks or gaps that separate present from idealized real selves are fundamental to understanding human developmental and behavioral motivations and reactions. Maturation of awareness is also externally and comparatively induced, contributing to relationally contingent subjectivities. The supplemental urge to address lacks or gaps that separate present from idealized selves or Others contributes to an evolutionary momentum that is socially and culturally apparent, even if the psychological catalyst is abstract.

Sigmund Freud describes the "uncanny" nature of these encounters, as one confronts a double that appears but is not quite familiar (1999 Vol. 17, 219). One observes Others as well as selves with fascination and fear, drawing attention to the compulsion of comparison. In Freud's analysis of the uncanny, he traces the etymology of the word in German from *heimlich* ("homelike") to *unheimlich* ("unhomelike"), showing how in fact they are one and the same and thus capturing the ambiguity of the word's meaning—and indeed of language itself. The uncanny in this case provides a helpful analytic to contemplate how the perception of slight gradients of difference can be affectively mapped onto the bodies of diasporic Others who may be originally from a shared homeland but who have become un-homelike, altered by distance and time. One becomes fascinated with the similarity yet difference of diasporic subjects, and one involuntarily compares one's subject position and status to theirs. The association may contribute to feelings of unsurmounted lack, resulting in a subconscious repetitive urge to fill the gap that separates and differentially locates a "me" or "us" as opposed to a "her" or "him" or "them."[13]

Relationality is paramount to the work of the gift, where meaning and recognition supposedly flow reciprocally between givers and receivers. However, Jacques Derrida (1992) points out that by definition, the gift is always an impossible category. One cannot simply return a gift, because to do so would strip it of its meaning as a gift, selflessly offered. Yet this practice sits at the heart of its Maussian definition. This basic contradiction has driven a history of gifting inquiry, from Malinowski, who investigated cases of "pure gifts" (1984, 177), to Pierre Bourdieu (1977), who argued that the act of gifting necessarily requires forgetting, thus highlighting the essential role of temporality. But as Derrida correctly points out, if one followed such logic one would then be giving time, which is not one's to give, and hence one would arrive at an aporia or logical disjunction. Mauss's basic logic that gifts must be reciprocated means that they essentially function as payments of debts, which is the work of money to compensate for time lost in loaning value. If the gift worked like money, the loaner-debtor relationship that it mediates would be severed upon repayment, again according to classical economic definitions of money. Yet the process of exchange that is central to gifting entangles and supposedly affirms, not severs, relations. By deconstructing Mauss's category of the gift and revealing its internal contradictions, Derrida argues that Mauss's *The Gift* is more about the word "gift" than about actual practices. But these practices have nonetheless been named as gifting by Mauss, and therefore they have come to be recognized as such despite the contradictions. This, of course, is the work of naming. A linguistic category is produced and, by extension, an artificial expectation of how that category should function. Among other gifting processes, Mauss brought together two very different practices of Kula and potlatch, brushing over their differences and contradictions, particularly in regard to how they facilitated flows of meaning and recognition between exchange participants. The Kula and potlatch became similar and comparable only when he highlighted their generalized commonalities—the associated behavioral obligations to give, receive, and reciprocate. Thus, by extending our case studies and analytics, we incorporate other practices and linguistic designations into the meaning of the word "gift," narrowly turning our attention to its categorical fit within definitional lines rather than its contextual affect beyond them. Ultimately, the category of "gift" fails to function properly because of its own contradictions. As Derrida says, "what are we thinking when we require simultaneously of the gift that it appear in its essence, in what it has to be, in what it is to be, in what it will have had to be . . . ?" (1992, 27) What should we do with this concept of the gift?

For readers less interested in the conceptual and linguistic nuances of whether or not the gift is a functional tool, we might say that of course the motivation for its practice exists, even if only as an ideal. The gift, as a heuristic category, is a bridge upon which we imagine we can momentarily stand and altruistically extend ourselves beyond our subjective and practical limits. It is an aspiration and an apparition that bridges not only the gap between giver and receiver, but also that between reality and ideality. In the case of remittances, the gift as an idealized heuristic also works to bridge the functional distinction of gifting practices from monetary practices. Gifts supposedly bind people together, while money does not; gifts are selfless, while money is selfish. Again, Derrida tells us this is impossible: "a gift that would claim to control money and preserve itself from any simulacrum, will that still be a gift or already a calculation . . . ?" (1992, 70) Thus, the question becomes less if a particular process is a gift, but rather how the idea of the gift works to make connections and shape actions.

In the case of international remittances, the ideal of the gift as a generous act, keeping with its traditional albeit flawed framework, is made possible by the functional connectivity of money, again confining its definition within strict terms. Mauss's case studies primarily draw on gift exchanges in small communities in which givers and receivers were in intimate and familiar proximity. However, again as Bohannan (1955) argued in the case of the Tiv and the British Empire, money acts as an infrastructure that makes long-distance exchange possible.[14] Money connects markets and societies by serving as a mobile, portable, and exchangeable medium. In his reflections on the gift concept in finance, Miyazaki has argued for the extensibility of "arbitrage . . . as a general theory of how to relate seemingly different things" (2013, 45). Drawing on this extended definition of arbitrage in economic anthropology, one might say that remittances clearly arbitrage the traditional definitions of money and gifts by bringing them together as a hybrid unit of analysis. The motivation for offering remittances is embedded in their recognition as gifts, but the infrastructural capacity for them to effectively travel from the giver across distance and then effectively re-materialize to address the specific individual needs of its recipients is based on their functional capacity as money.

In a global economy, the contours of mobility are inescapably defined by money. In its most basic function as a way to transfer value, money proves its efficacy in its ability to flow across political and economic borders with relative ease. Global capitalism is predicated on free flows of money, and neoliberalism (to use the term broadly) works to facilitate this. In a 1993 article that underscores the basic tenets of globalization, John Williamson argues that there is a wide political "Washington consensus" on economic policy measures that promote the free flow of goods, services, and finance across borders. Capital controls and trade barriers are critiqued as naively protectionist and an impediment to local and global economic growth. What is noticeably missing from this consensus, at least among policy makers, is a parallel valuation of mobility for people. Movements of bodies, although also a key component of capitalist productivity and consumption, face much stricter restrictions, primarily due to political considerations. As a result, there are even greater demands for goods, services, and finance to flow across borders with comparatively fewer obstacles to access pools of labor as well as consumers. Misunderstandings of the policy agendas structuring such flows, as witnessed in current political climates from the United Kingdom to the United States, may mistakenly displace popular blame for the consequences of these movements on people's livelihoods. For example, in the case of outsourcing, visible immigrant or foreign bodies in one country may be conflated with workers outside the country to whom jobs in a particular sector may be going. But in reality, opportunities for immigration are limited. Migration occurs on a much more restricted scale, compared to other international flows of capital and commodities. Numbers estimated by the Pew Research Center (Connor 2016) for example, show that despite increases in the absolute numbers of migrants, in the context of global population growth, rates of international migration have stayed fairly consistent over the past few decades, at around 3 percent of the global population.[15] Compare this to steep growth in foreign investment flows reported by the International Monetary Fund (2008), from 6.5 percent of global gross domestic product (GDP) in 1980 to 31.8 percent of global GDP in 2006.[16] Clearly, compared to people, money flows more abundantly and with greater ease in the age of globalization.

Contradictions in Flow

The mobility of money and goods is part and parcel of capitalism, as Marx (1992) noted long ago in *Capital*. Capital circulation extends outward from its source in its quest for accumulation. The disconnect resulting from expanding circulations of capital spatially removed from the production process contributes to a phenomenon of alienation, which is displaced into what Marx called a commodity fetish—in which money and things represent the absent people who no longer produce and exchange them directly. As Marx says, "it is nothing but the definite social relation between men themselves which assumes here, for them, the fantastic form of a relation between things" (ibid., 165). He extends this argument of alienation from commodities to money, noting that "it is precisely this finished form of the world of commodities—the money form—which conceals the social character of private labor and the social relations between the individual workers, by making those relations appear as relations between material objects, instead of revealing them plainly" (ibid., 168). For Marx, the alienating process of abstracting and concealing the social origins of production is the sociocultural work of global capitalism. The lesson of the fetish is that we may find ourselves mysteriously yet irresistibly attracted to the material medium of exchange in part because it offers some reconnection to and recognition of a humanistic sensibility from which we have been systemically removed.

We can consider therefore Marx's argument as a departure point for thinking about the role of mobility in capitalism, and how infrastructural differentials in mobility affect relations through material things (whether commodities, money, or gifts), producing through them imaginaries of social relations and identifications often marked by a sense of lack through comparison. In globalization, transnationalism has been a common trope through which to think about the significance of global flows. Trying to capture and link the multiple mobilities that characterize processes of globalization, transnationalism transcendentally attends to the linkages between the economic and the sociocultural. Transnational flows of money, goods, and services link people, communities, and societies in ways that shape new possibilities and provide new frames for imagining the world—including relationships not only between selves and Others, but also between current and future personhoods. Arjun Appadurai, one of the early anthropologists to articulate the significance of these global flows, argues that the most significant influence of transnationalism is on the imagination. For Appadurai, the imagination has become a "social practice" that acts as "a form of negotiation between sites of agency and globally defined fields of possibility" (1996, 31).

Part of this negotiation arises from the ruptured inequalities and contradictions in mobile flows that characterize globalization. "Washington consensus" prescriptions that prioritize the movement of money and things discount the fact that bodies are increasingly rendered immobile by comparison. Despite all of the contemporary discourse on the significance of migration, central to these discussions is attention to the enormous obstacles that migrants face, especially when crossing international borders. The current debate in the United States surrounding so-called undocumented or illegal immigrants, who live in a constant state of uncertainty without legal recourse, certainly illustrates this. The extraordinarily high fees paid to brokers to take migrants across borders and the raids by border control and immigration enforcement agents against migrants demonstrate this. The ongoing casualties of thousands of migrants crossing the Mediterranean Ocean from North Africa to Europe and the refusal to admit refugees fleeing war in Syria reflect this. And certainly, the long and dangerous exodus of Indochinese refugees from Vietnam, Laos, and Cambodia from 1975 to the mid-1990s (during which, according to many estimates, hundreds of thousands died) reveals the starkly dangerous contradictions in global mobility differentials. Bodies do not flow as freely as money and things do, and some bodies flow with less ease than others.

The transnational turn has often celebrated mobility as a primary feature of the globalization landscape. The anthropologist Aihwa Ong (1999) examined the cross-border lifestyles of Chinese business elites, whose bodies followed the capital flows they managed among transnational ethnic networks across international borders. Identity appears divorced from place in the lives of such subjects, and indeed it is fascinating to see how capital embodies the privileged subjects of this study. In a contrasting research case, however, Ong (2003) looks at a very different Asian American population, whose members are seemingly disembodied and disengaged from global capital flows: Cambodian refugees, who flee from the Khmer Rouge and war-torn Southeast Asia and confront the limits of their mobility capital as they resettle in California. They are politically and economically denied mobility to return to the country they fled, and they certainly experience very little social mobility within the often-marginalized communities they form in the United States. The contrast between these two populations—mobile Chinese elites chasing capital across borders and displaced Cambodian refugees devoid of capital who are stuck within borders—offers insights into transnationalism as a framework of flow but also one of rupture, within which mobility is unevenly distributed. Global differentials in mobility have been explored by other anthropologists such as Julie Chu who, in work similar to the present study, examined the emplaced migratory imaginaries that emerge in out-migrant communities—in Chu's case, Fujian Province in eastern China. Chu draws attention to the "dislocating effects of being stuck in place while others all around were moving to broaden their spatial-temporal horizons" (2010, 12).

Part of the work of the transnational turn in Asia Pacific studies has been to consider the interlinkages of Asian communities across borders (particularly between the United States and Asia), which includes the mobilities and immobilities of people and money as well as the political entanglements, histories, and agendas that produce such links (Espiritu 2006; M. Nguyen 2012; Hoskins and Nguyen 2014). Behind the cultural, political, and economic connections of transnationalism, however, are the infrastructures that make those linkages possible. The details of such infrastructures, although mundane, are nonetheless important as they critically shape the "routes" (Clifford 1997, 3) by which people travel, the channels by which they send and carry things, and how communication across borders is enabled or disabled. Much of this infrastructure is technical, hidden in the details of legal, financial, and even technological frameworks. These range from immigration, visa, and banking regulations to the electronic systems that make cell phones, computers, and ATMs work and connect with each other. Slight shifts in the design or management of those infrastructures, from 2013 U.S. regulatory reforms affecting international remittances to post-2016 U.S. election changes in immigration enforcement attitudes and agendas, shape how and where transnational flows occur.

This book analytically contributes to the field of transnationalism by demonstrating transnational flows and ruptures as processes of both visible and invisible factors that are sociocultural, material, legal, and technical. It looks specifically at how and why bodies in the United States and Vietnam have been shaped by particular political contexts and histories, and how the money and gifts those bodies send and receive as a result are channeled, diverted, or blocked along specific routes. These routes facilitate the practical function of remitting value, but they also shape the affective contours of exchange and therefore are worth investigating ethnographically.

Scope of the Book

For this book, I primarily conducted ethnographic research among remittance-receiving households and communities in Vietnam. I also engaged with the sending side of the remittance equation in the United States, with a focus on California. With international remittances at around $12 billion a year and accounting for 6 percent of its GDP (World Bank 2016), Vietnam is one of the countries in Southeast Asia that receives the largest amount of remittances, just after the Philippines. However, Laos is the largest recipient of remittances in the region in terms of percentage of GDP. The remittance exchanges in Vietnam (like those in Laos and Cambodia) are interesting for a number of reasons. First of all, they provide a case study that can be compared to the experiences of many other countries with significant emigrations and returns, including the Philippines (Parreñas 2001), Peru (Paerregaard 2015), El Salvador (Coutin 2007; Pedersen 2013), Haiti (Glick-Schiller and Fouron 2001), Mexico (Smith 2005), and Somalia (Lindley 2010). But the context of Indochinese migrants is also unique. Having fled a devastated and embargoed war-torn society experimenting with a command socialist economy in the 1970s and 1980s, Vietnamese refugees have only recently begun to return to a country that has been dramatically transformed during their absence, but with which they have always retained communication links and on which they have always exerted influence in their exile through various forms of remittances.

Since the *Đổi Mới* economic reforms, Vietnam has steadily been reintegrated into the global capitalist economy, all but abandoning the command economy from which so many refugees—political and economic—fled. The political symbols of communism nonetheless remain strong, as a one-party state clings to the legacy of revolutionary nationalism to maintain legitimacy and support from its populace as well as the international community. At the same time the nostalgic and uncanny specter of an alternative South Vietnamese modernity preceding and perhaps succeeding socialism, and retained in scattered diasporic fragments, haunts the intimacies and hypotheticals of a national historical narrative increasingly challenged as the state reengages with an often politically averse diaspora (P. Taylor 2001; Duong 2012) and confronts its legacy of unification. The remittance relationship, in its negotiation of this medley of memories and symbols, continually confronts gaps in understanding and transgressing differences, which were always present but have been more clearly revealed as a result of the long historical, political, social, and mnemonic divide experienced by the participants in remittance exchanges. It is in this space of difference that new forms of imagination and agency emerge, with corresponding sociocultural formations and affects.

In the following chapters, I examine the experiential, observational, and interpretive narratives of various participants in Vietnam's transnational migrant- and finance-scapes in an effort to ascertain the effects and affects of mobility and exchange on social and familial relations, temporal and aspirational orientations, and the distribution of the imagination across such contexts.[17] I investigate the broader economy of imaginaries entangled with remittances to reconsider the viability of the gift as we generally understand it, complicated by its necessary entanglement with money. To do so, I draw on two years of ethnographic field research that I conducted while based primarily in Ho Chi Minh City, or as still commonly called by much of the local population, Saigon. Located in the south, Saigon is Vietnam's largest city, and from it a significant proportion of Vietnamese refugees left; additionally, at least one-third of remittances to Vietnam flow through it (Pfau and Giang 2009).[18] I also draw on fieldwork conducted in secondary Vietnamese sites, including Vietnam's south central coast (where I was based in Quy Nhơn) and the region between Saigon and the Mekong Delta (where I took frequent shorter trips).[19] Additional fieldwork was conducted among remittance-sending communities in California, home to the largest Vietnamese communities outside of Vietnam, particularly in Orange County and the South Bay Area. Supplementary archival and policy research was conducted in France and Vietnam. The primary period of research was 2007–2009; on trips between 2013 and 2017, I followed up with some of my original contacts and updated my data.

Remittance Geographies

In this introduction I have provided some introductory background on Vietnamese migration and corresponding remittances. I have also introduced the themes of money, gifts, and flows as they relate to the production and interruption of transnational imaginaries that are central to this book's inquiry. The following chapters explore how variable contexts of remittance receiving and sending can affect the symbolisms and meanings of the particular form that remittances take. The book follows the stories of those who participate in remittance exchanges in three distinctly regional but nonetheless transnational geographies: Ho Chi Minh City and its suburbs (chapter 2), suburban and rural central coastal Vietnam (chapter 3), and suburban California (chapter 4). In addition, the book explores how traditional conceptions of gifting and obligation (chapter 1), as well as the Vietnamese government's policies and attitudes toward the diaspora (chapter 5), contribute to the changing contours and expectations of these flows. In this book I demonstrate ethnographically how remittances act as and appear to be gifts even when they take the form of money, and how they may serve as furtive material actants connecting social actors in search of meaning. On the part of remittance gifters and recipients, as we will see in the stories that unfold, these meanings are frequently elusive and contested.

In the spirit of methodologically representing the complex and open momentum of the ethnographic experience in a reflexive manner in which inquiry is pursued but not necessarily foreclosed (Maurer 2005; Miyazaki 2006; Holmes and Marcus 2010), I also demonstrate in a parallel or lateral analytical vein how various theoretical frameworks can help us apprehend, but not necessarily comprehend, the remittance phenomenon. No foreclosed theoretical framework or application can satisfactorily subject the analysis of these ethnographic materials across diverse individuals, circumstances, and environments to a uniform interpretation, just as remittances (as will be shown) continually fail to supplement the gap in social meaning and recognition as they aspire to do. As the anthropologist Martin Manalansan points out, it is often more productive not to try to "create order out of quagmire" when analyzing ethnographic data, but rather to "gesture to the workings of chaos, mess and morass in ways that deflect simplistic questions of origins, functions and value" (2014, 104). To set aside the analytical demand for understanding is also to recognize and represent the elusive deferral that the subjects of this ethnographic study experience, and resign themselves to, on an everyday basis as they attempt to recover and restore meaning in exchange. This book, then, is a study of processes—of money, gifts, and flows— as they relate to people, things, and meanings across distinctly varied geographies. The chapters that follow are intended to provide the reader with a reflective ethnographic examination of such processes that engages theory to think with, alongside my interlocuters, rather than frame from without. The chapters offer stories that necessarily meander in their journey—along with the money, gifts, givers, and receivers they describe—across different landscapes, imaginaries, and case studies. This narrative approach helps us apprehend and contemplate the effects and affects of migration and remittances as they have taken shape between the United States and Vietnam, and perhaps elsewhere as well.

THE "DANGEROUS" GIFT

In Annamite morality, to accept a present is dangerous.

—Marcel Mauss, *The Gift*

In this chapter I begin by reflecting on the concept of gifting that has been so central to analyses of exchange—particularly in anthropology, but also in the humanities and social sciences more broadly. How can thinking of remittances as gifts in the general Maussian sense help us examine contemporary cases of remittances sent from the Vietnamese diaspora to Vietnamese in Vietnam? The fact that remittances, even when monetary, are also gifts illustrates the limits of money's function of settling accounts and, by extension, eschewing obligations and avoiding personal entanglements. Remittance gifts represent and reveal, but also obscure, the social relations and connections they mediate. To understand this, it is worth first examining the nonmonetary remittance forms that preceded and continue to accompany contemporary financial flows from the diaspora to homeland families.

In the case of Vietnam, remittances have taken many other forms besides money, particularly in the decade and a half after the Vietnam War, when international channels for sending money across borders were not always available. The history of remittance gifting from postwar migrants or refugees illustrates how relations and imaginaries connected to transnational gifting have shifted with and are contingent on the symbolisms, forms, and presentations of the gifting mediums. Due to the lack of financial channels between the United States and Vietnam after 1975 as a result of a generation-long severing of diplomatic and economic relations, a variety of material remittance forms emerged to assist and reconnect kinship networks dispersed after the war. These forms slowly began to be replaced by monetary gifts in the 1990s, but material remittances remain symbolically significant and have never been fully replaced. Since the 1990s material and monetary remittances have increasingly been accompanied by the bodies of the gifters or couriers from within their extended social networks, as diasporic return travel has become normalized. The long-distance nature of Vietnamese refugees' practices of international remittance gifting, which have continued for over a generation, is being compressed with the increased availability of channels for rapid financial transfers. In addition, many formerly exiled Vietnamese are reorienting themselves as transnational subjects and moving back and forth across borders, if only occasionally.[1]

The occasional transnational subject returning to Vietnam may be a somewhat uncanny figure, in the Freudian sense, as encountered by the Vietnamese remittance recipient. The transnational lives in a foreign land, commonly referred to by informants as "over there (ở bên kia)," where new social practices are learned and slowly embodied. Yet these social practices do not only include the foreign; they are hybrid Vietnamese, as often practiced within the collective habitus of diasporic communities. The overseas Vietnamese (Việt Kiều) is commonly described by Vietnamese as simultaneously familiar and unfamiliar, and thus somewhat strange (lạ). Given that remittances are often the medium for bridging the gap that has emerged between dispersed kin, a key question that emerges is how hybrid diasporic practices of gifting as they relate to remittances are received and perceived in Vietnam. This includes assessments of their authenticity or purity, and how they compare to traditional or localized notions of gifting etiquette. The practice of gifting as a Vietnamese cultural concept or custom (phong tục) is commonly invoked by both remittance recipients and senders in explaining the obligations and expectations of remittance exchange.

Remittances as a basket of monetary, material, and social obligations that emotionally and economically tie remittance senders and receivers together are regularly explained by informants as gifts (quà) that are both obligatory and altruistic, and to know and remember this is to be Vietnamese. Money is part of a larger collection of things given and received, in the past and the present, and it is only by conceptually including money in such a grouping that the gift can be recognized and duly reciprocated with hospitality or other material gifts on the part of remittance receivers. Mauss ethnographically recognized as much when he mentioned the gimwali that accompanied gifts; indeed, it was this very pairing that drove the circulation of the Kula (1967). As one remittance recipient described it, "Whenever my sister returns to Vietnam she brings money, of course, but she brings other gifts, too, such as cosmetics or soap. In the past we used to trade these kinds of things at the market, but now we keep them. There are nine siblings, and everyone gets something, even if small. We must also give small gifts to her when she returns to the United States, such as rice paper, green tea, dried shrimp, or squid. Of course, we cannot give money, but we give something that expresses sentiment (*tình cảm*). We are family, this is how we behave as Vietnamese." The behavioral expectation of gifting across multiple mediums, temporalities, and directions in this case is familial but also culturally conceived. It is deemed to be neither selfless nor selfish, but a matter of fact. To understand gifting as a Vietnamese sentimental matter of fact requires some unpacking. To do this, it is worth taking a step back to consider a broader range of local gifting customs than merely the transnational remittance practices that emerged after the Vietnam War. This chapter traces discussions about ideas and practices of gifting across diverse situations in Vietnam and among Vietnamese, with the goal of appreciating the perceived sociocultural context within which remittances may be regarded as gifts.

In Search of the "Gift"

Our first investigation is a curious historical and textual one that begins in Western social and anthropological theory and ethnology, going back to Mauss, but carries us by coincidence to Vietnam. European spectators of non-Western societies have long been interested in the moral codes and functions that governed intracommunity exchanges. Anthropologists in particular have obsessively identified, categorized, and dissected universal codes and categories of gift giving, enthusiastically followed by scholars from across the humanities interested in the intersubjective affects of exchange.[2] Frequently and perhaps mistakenly considered to be the first anthropologist to study the gift, Mauss (1967) relates ethnological stories of gifting practices from a broad spectrum of societies, including Polynesian, Melanesian, and Kwakiutl accounts, drawing primarily on works by Bronislaw Malinowski and Franz Boas that provide the core material for his analysis. But later he uses other sources to consider how traces of gifting in so-called primitive societies survive in other civilizational contexts. In doing so, he mentions in passing Vietnam—the subject of our present study, at the time referred to by its colonial name of Annam.[3] Toward the end of *The Gift*, Mauss highlights the curious fact that "in Annamite morality, to accept a present is dangerous." (ibid., 64). He does not elaborate the remark but attributes it in a footnote to the Finnish anthropologist Edward Westermarck, who "perceived some of its importance" (ibid.).

Like Mauss, Westermarck was an armchair anthropologist and sociologist who drew on the work of other ethnologists reporting from the field.[4] He discusses (1924–1926) the dangers of Annamese gifting in the context of more universal fears and suspicions of strangers and the unknown. Offering an intriguing analytical take on cultural attitudes toward hospitality, Westermarck comments that "it seems likely that the custom of not receiving payment from a guest is largely due to that same dread of strangers which underlies many other rules of hospitality. The acceptance of gifts is frequently considered to be connected with some danger" (ibid., 1:593). Westermarck draws his account of dangerous Annamese gifting—"of the Annamites it is said that for fear of bringing ill-luck into the place the people even decline presents" (ibid., 1:594)—from a German ethnographer, Friedrich Ratzel. In turn Ratzel, infamous for his theories about the role of natural environments and geography in shaping human cultural outlooks and relations, draws on accounts of French ethnographers and traders such as Jean Dupuis, Jules Harmand, and Albert Morice to describe Indochinese society in the late nineteenth century. Further delving into this genealogical maze of secondary sources, we find the grand three-volume work titled *The History of Mankind* (1898) by Ratzel that presented, in the ethnographic fashion of the time, broadly interpretive ethnological insights into various cultures and civilizations around the world. In it, the author offers passing comments on Indochinese customs. The passage on gifts that Westermarck referred to is as follows: "The Annamite, says Morice, lives either on the water or on the mud. The villages are enclosed by palisades or thorn-hedges. Spikes of bamboo hidden in the grass render every approach unsafe; they are placed even round the houses. In the centre of the little place, surrounded by the huts, a small platform is raised on a tree-stump for the night-watchman. Amulets against mischievous spirits hang on trees and poles, and fine threads of cotton, stretched round the roof to keep off spirits, terminate in little sand heaps. For fear of bringing ill-luck into the place the people even decline presents" (ibid., 3:418)." In another passage on Annam, Ratzel discusses Vietnamese relationships to money. Quoting the French trader Dupuis, he notes that Tonkinese (northern Vietnamese) in particular "like making money, but are just as keen about spending as about earning it. The Tonkinese is extravagant, he is a great careless child and fond of jollifications and festivals. No sum is too high for him to pay for showy ceremonies and funerals" (ibid., 3:413).

Further following these ethnographic vignettes to their respective sources (Harmand 1997; Morice 1880; Dupuis 1910), one gets swept away in fantastical ethnological descriptions, tales of daring adventures, and storied colonial and local political dramas. The accounts of explorers, administrators, traders, and missionaries, filled with exuberant descriptions of local geography, political intrigue, and reflections on cultural and social difference, serve as what the anthropologist Jean Michaud has called incidental ethnographies (2007) of Vietnam at an early stage of colonial encounter and highlight what Bradley Davis (2016) has identified as an imperial power vacuum in the Red River Delta, where travelers, explorers, and traders had to appease quasi-governmental authorities and local bandits by disbursing strategic gifts and tribute to gain passage through the region up to Yunnan in China. Men like Dupuis were arms profiteers and had much to gain financially by currying favor with local leaders through gift giving to open channels for their illicit trade. While these ethnographies of early colonial adventurers are admittedly intriguing, what is relevant for the purposes of the present study is that the notion of the gift, like money, has long intrigued anthropologists, ethnologists, and social observers. Indeed the gifting concept has been abstracted from the fabric of countless stories, such as those just related, in various humanistic reflections. The fact that a passing observation on Annamese presents by Dupuis wound its way through at least three scholarly ethnographic studies, eventually showing up in Mauss's *The Gift*, speaks to the analytical valence of the gifting concept. The idea of the gift strongly appealed to Mauss not only because of its seeming universality, but also because it is a human practice that reflects humanity's complex capacities for hospitality and social overcoming of differences through exchanges.

However, the inevitable social limitations of the gift also appear in these localized accounts compiled by Mauss. Gifts mark the circles of social exchange and sharing in which humans participate, but also their spaces of exclusion. Gifts appear almost double-edged in their possibility. One type is the familiar gift, which is given and returned and repeated among intimate community and kinship circles. Another type, the gift from the stranger (or the unknown, as Westermarck has suggested), is feared. Gifts from unknown people and places are surely met with heightened suspicion about their intention, and no doubt the gifts referred to in the ethnographic accounts just related were offered in such a context. French colonial explorers, adventurers, traders, and missionaries (who in many cases preceded or accompanied larger projects of political and military expansion and colonization) engaged in gift exchanges with local authorities, mandarins, warlords, and indigenous communities in pursuit of self-interested strategic agendas.[5] Local Vietnamese governmental and quasi-governmental officials cautiously and sometimes begrudgingly engaged in gift exchanges like these, but with trepidation. Managing gifting relations in such scenarios were likely intended to keep the outsider at a cautious distance. To the extent that they were meant to demonstrate hospitality and extend recognition, it was a tepid performative hospitality and recognition that was intended, as Westermarck suggests, to keep the stranger a stranger, in the hope that he would go away and not return.

Tracing Mauss's description of the "dangerous" Vietnamese gift back to its primary ethnographic source, then, we see that his commentary on it was rather loosely abstracted from the original context. The situation described does not involve traditional intracommunity gift exchange, unlike the major case studies of the Trobriand Islanders and the Kwakiutl that Mauss focuses on. Rather, the ethnographic accounts presented by Ratzel describe the suspicious Annamite reception of gifts coming from foreign places and strangers. Such gifts were laden with ambivalent intentions. In such a scenario the gift and its giver were not familiar or necessarily welcome, and their foreign origins appear to be suspiciously apprehended. Certainly, in retrospect it appears that the hesitation about and suspicion of the perfunctory gift exchanges with the French that preceded colonial intervention in what is now Vietnam were not altogether misplaced on the part of those who had much to lose, given the eventual political outcomes of such relationships.

The historical context of Mauss's Annamese example may appear at first glance to contrast markedly with the contemporary Vietnamese remittance gift scenario. The remittance gift from the overseas Vietnamese, unlike suspicious gift exchanges with radically foreign traders with ambiguous intentions, comes from an intimately familiar and recognizable kinsperson of shared ethnicity, from a place that if not known is at least imaginable as a result of two generations of postwar transnational circulation. Still, fear of the gift's capacity to disrupt settled social worlds is not out of place. Anxieties regarding remittances, even from familiar subjects, have been long-standing. Various Vietnamese governments from premodern and colonial times to the present have monitored the influx of financial and material remittances, gifts, and their accompanying ideas (that is, social remittances) from overseas Vietnamese. For example, many nationalists and anticolonial activists during the colonial period believed that acquiring knowledge and skills abroad was the best hope for eventually overcoming French rule. Ta Thu Thau, a Vietnamese Trotskyite leader in the 1920s, is quoted as saying in an address to a group of students leaving Vietnam for Marseille in 1927: "We students must pick up and conquer the education that we are refused in our country. . . . Do you know my dear friends that at each ship departure, some young Annamites who have neither relatives nor friends aboard abandon their work in order to be present at the pier? They inform themselves of the number of those leaving and their joy rises with the number of emigrants. . . . Those compatriots who thus accompanied us at the departure represent Annam for us, and their hopes are those of the fatherland" (quoted in McConnell 1989, 52).

The young Annamites "at the pier" illustrate that migration not only affects those who go abroad, but also significantly influences the imaginings and social worlds of those who stay behind.[6] Other historical migrants, including the hundred thousand Vietnamese soldiers sent to the Western Front to support the French Empire had significant cultural and social impacts after returning to and reintegrating into Vietnam, as suggested by Kim Loan Hill (2011) for World War I and Tran Khe Nu (1989) and Tobias Rettig (2012) for World War II. This phenomenon has never been ignored by those holding the reins of state power, who have frequently been concerned about the effects of migratory imaginings on social stability at home. During World War I the French government closely monitored the activities, thinking, and even belongings of overseas Vietnamese serving in Europe, as shown by intercepted letters sent to friends and family at home found in overseas archives. Some of the dangerous ideas and materials commented upon by representatives of the French Sûreté include pornographic images and accounts of French prostitutes by Vietnamese soldiers. In a 1917 report, one French official expressed his concern about the effect of the circulation of such images on the prestige of France in the colonies:

> If the spirit of our protégés is generally good, as for their private conduct, insofar as we would desire to hold intact the prestige of the European, there is left much to be desired. Our morality, admittedly, lends itself to their natural lewdness. Prostitution in the big cities offers carnal pleasures that are all the more tantalizing and often more affordable than in the colonies and offer incomparable comforts. The arrivals do not tarry with their praise, as illustrated with great indecency by postcards on which one continues to find nudes in many of the Indochinese battalions, with the sacramental phrase "there isn't anything of beauty, of interest here, except that."[7]

For a colonial subject under French tutelage to travel to the so-called motherland and relate to those at home, via the exposed and embarrassing publicity of a postcard, that there was nothing of interest to be found there but naked prostitutes ("there isn't anything of beauty, of interest here, except that") was a dangerous act of sacrilege that threatened the allure of colonial power.[8] The maintenance and control of power's mystique has been observed in other cases in colonial Southeast Asia, such as Indonesia—where officials even controlled who could wear Western clothes and speak the colonial motherland's language (Siegel 1997). Although British, Spanish, Dutch, Portuguese, and French colonial policies naturally differed, they all sought to favorably manage their subjects' perceptions of the motherland. Such perceptions were deemed important for effective French rule over Indochina and its ideology of *mission civilatrice* by colonial governor-generals such as Pierre Pasquier (Brocheux and Hemery 2009). Maintaining deferential respect for French customs and traditions in the Indochinese colonies was an integral component of the colonial strategy for effective governance. Clearly, official anxieties over dangerous forms of social remittances have been longstanding in Vietnamese society and politics.

After the end of the civil war between the southern Republic of Vietnam and the northern Democratic Republic of Vietnam in 1975 and with official national reunification under the Communist Party in 1976, there were significant state anxieties about the potentially subversive influences of remittance gifts, which symbolized a capitalist prosperity seemingly now denied to southern Vietnamese citizens under the new socialist command economy. The anthropologist Mandy Thomas argued that "the desire of overseas Vietnamese to help their families under a regime they despise is an inherently political act, and for many, the only legitimate form of resistance" (1999, 154). She further noted "as gifts allow individuals to insinuate certain symbolic properties into the lives of the gift recipient, so overseas Vietnamese often wish to place the desire for consumer products within their families in the homeland . . . Here the gifts are viewed as a type of Trojan horse, which could lead to the disruption of the political system in Vietnam" (ibid.).

As with the uncanny personhood of the occasional transnational subject, the gift he or she sends may be uncanny in its dual familiarity and foreignness. The gift as a medium of sociality and sentiment is also a familiar and expected medium of relation building and maintenance within the Vietnamese context, as I will discuss in the next section. A gift from the outside, as we have seen in the account by Mauss (1967), is more suspiciously viewed—a potential Trojan horse. Its recognition sought may be suspended or withheld. The question of the transnational Vietnamese gift and body returning "home" from abroad, with its characteristic mix of the familiar and unfamiliar, is the primary subject of this book. The transnational gift may be familial, but it can also be dangerous, and for this reason deploying the notion of the uncanny offers an appropriate lens to use in considering such a mix of characteristics. To do this, we must further investigate the nuances of Vietnamese gifting behaviors. I turn now to contemporary ethnographic examples, in which key informants reflected on the personal, social, and cultural dynamics of the gifting processes in which they participated.

Circles and Exits

One day Thuy, a key interlocater in Saigon, took me to her porch to show me an ornate potted bonsai-style tree, a common sight at the time of the Tết (lunar new year) holiday, and told me how she had given one like it to her aunt last year. She said she had bought the tree on behalf of her family to return another gift (also a decorative plant, but of a different type) that the aunt had given the year before. She noted that this plant was "nicer and more expensive" than the plant her aunt had given. I asked her if she planned on giving another one next year, and she said yes, of course, and commented that "it would be even nicer than this one." Thuy was young, single, and had a well-paying marketing job in Saigon. Explaining why she gave gifts to her aunt, she told me that since she was "successful and could afford to buy nice things," it was her way of displaying her appreciation and generosity as a member of the family. She remembered the many gifts that relatives had given her when she most needed them growing up, including sticky rice cakes from this aunt; a motorcycle from her father when she went to college in the early 1990s; and even a ten-dollar bill from an overseas relative, which "at that time seemed like a lot of money for me." Now an adult with a professional job, it was her turn to reciprocate and give. She explained that each year her Tết gifts became more expensive, because with the growing economy and her professional promotions, she was able to command an ever-higher salary that she could share with her relatives. Many of them were in the Mekong Delta countryside and had in the past been helped out by her parents, who as city dwellers had more economic opportunities. The parents were now retired, however, and Thuy had inherited the responsibility of displaying generosity, particularly during the holiday period, to extended family members as well as her own parents and siblings who were less economically successful than she was. Although she had wanted to obtain a scholarship to study for a master's of business administration in Germany, she had given up a chance to do so because that would have left these relatives-cum-dependents without a comfortable source of income. She seemed to have acted ungrudgingly, explaining that it was "the Vietnamese way," and that she belonged with her "home and family." Repeating a proverb about the importance of family love and gratitude ("Parents' love for a child is like an overflowing lake [*Cha mẹ thương con như biển hồ lai láng*]"), she explained that one could not simply abandon one's family in search of selfish individual adventure. For Thuy, such cultural family sentiments were important in defining Vietnamese notions of gifting, affirming her ethical compass, and deepening her personal and collective identities and orientations.

Within immediate community and family networks, gifting overtures and performances are regular modes of social interaction. Displays of generous exchange are expected and gauged by the participant's age and capacity to assess the depth of sentiment invested in them. Thuy, as a successful working-age member of the family, was expected to share a generous proportion of her disposable income through gifting to immediate and distant relatives. These gifts were expressed as a reciprocation of prior gifts and an inheritance of familial responsibility, but they were notably measured by perceptions of her capacity and generous intention rather than their distinct economic value. Although her two siblings were also of working age, one worked as a farmer and the other as a shopkeeper, earning meager incomes that were expected to support them, their spouses, and their children. As a single white-collar professional, Thuy took on the responsibility of supporting her retired parents as well as supplementing the income of her siblings. During special holidays such as Tết, she also assumed an ambassadorial role for her branch of the family by purchasing larger gifts for distant relatives intended to symbolize generosity to her kin and belonging to the broader clan. In fact, such gifts were extended not only to family members but also to community organizations, including a Buddhist temple her family was connected to. "I donated $20,000 for the building of this temple," she proudly told me at an annual ceremony she invited me to attend at the site, where freshly painted walls and well-tended gardens were on display for the temple's followers. Family sponsorship of the temple was a source of pride for her parents, and Thuy's income helped them maintain their social standing as patrons of this important community organization and gathering place.

Thuy's belonging in the family and community was predicated on shared histories and sympathies—such as memories of the motorbike and sticky rice cakes her father and aunt had given her growing up, awareness of the difficult financial situations of her siblings, and acknowledging that the monks of the temple had performed rituals to invite auspicious fortune for the family and community over the years. This sense of belonging was also assumed to continue into the indefinite future. Thuy's decision not to leave to pursue a master's degree in Europe in some sense foreclosed the possibility of a *Việt Kiều* life. Although her marketing job took her to many overseas locations on business, she had decided that with her family network in Saigon, that was her home and where she belonged. Gifting relationships as generous rituals of family belonging, therefore, were familiar, conservatory, and necessary cultural practices for Thuy as well as those who participated in the same circles of gift exchanges. For Thuy, the horizon of belonging, concomitant with the ritualized generous exchange of gifts, continued endlessly and prodigally into the indefinite future and firmly rooted her in a community and place.

Phuong, another professional in Saigon whose family lived in Binh Thuan Province, had, like Thuy, an opportunity to leave Vietnam and study in Europe—in her case, England. She had an excellent job in Saigon as a social science researcher and consultant and was well respected in her field. The opportunity to study in England was not connected to her professional training; rather, it was to study English at a small university in a remote rural area. Unlike Thuy, Phuong chose a life overseas. In the weeks before she left, she spoke with me many times about the difficulty she had had in deciding to give up her job and life in Saigon to follow an unfamiliar path abroad. Clearly, however, she hoped that studying English abroad would provide her with as yet unknown opportunities in Europe that would keep her there.

Two weeks before her departure, she invited me to visit her village in Binh Thuan Province. It was shortly before the Tết holiday, and the Saigon East bus station was crowded with people returning to their villages, laden with large bags of goods and holiday gifts. After fighting our way through the crowd to get tickets and seats on the bus, we finally pulled out of the city. The bus was crowded, stuffy, and hot, and it bumped along the dusty highway under construction as it left the city. Turning her gaze away from the window, Phuong stuck up her nose and said: "Vietnam is terrible—so dirty and crowded. The government is bad to let the people live like this. Nothing will ever change in this country. The only hope for change in this lifetime is to leave."

After a six-hour journey during which I was squashed between a rice bag, Phuong, and the dusty window, we arrived in her village, a small municipality largely consisting of generic concrete houses spread along a T intersection of two roads. The difference between Phuong's life in the city, where she made daily efforts to dress nicely in the latest fashion, and that of her family was striking. The original wooden house in the village with a dirt floor was being extended with two blue-tiled rooms in the rear, still unfinished. Under a fluorescent light, we ate a small dinner of rice, fish, vegetables, and eggs. Afterward I took a bath outside by the well, under the stars, while pigs and chickens ran around me. Walking around the town and through the market with Phuong, it became clear that any initial excitement she might have had about coming back to the village had dissipated. "I hate this place. I never want to return here again," she told me. In the market she was recognized by some former high school classmates, now married with children, who asked curiously about her life in the city. She was brief and almost dismissive in her answers, clearly not wanting to engage in conversation and not bothering to talk about her plans to go abroad.

The next day we met Son, a member of the local overseas compatriot (*Kiều Bào*) committee—a meeting that was Phuong's reason for bringing me to the village in the first place. Son offered me snacks and beer as he related the mission of his committee: "Our organization is trusted and prestigious. We help *Việt Kiều* spend money usefully. We have many overseas Vietnamese contacts ourselves. Many of us served in the American army with them and have helped villagers here contact relatives they had not heard from for years.[9] Some families who receive remittances do not know how to use that money successfully. We act as a middle organization between *Việt Kiều* and their relatives: we help them make a plan to manage their money productively and give them advice and encouragement. We also help *Kiều Bào* invest money and do charity work." He told me numerous anecdotes about families separated for years but reconnected as a result of his intervention and kin network research, as well as the ceremonial efforts that went into soliciting *Việt Kiều* contributions for village projects—including gifts and certificates to officially recognize their "love of country (*yêu nước*)" and "homeland (*quê hương*)." The official pitch eventually ended, however, as Son began describing the numerous challenges involved in opening and redirecting transnational gifting flows through the *Kiều Bào* organization: "In fact, there has been little money donated to our projects, despite our efforts. There is still a lot of suspicion." Son explained that some of this suspicion was related to the lack of transparent rules and the intentions of other "middlemen" (courier services, customs officers, or officials in government assistance programs such as the one he was running). "In the past when gifts arrived from overseas," he said, "we had to give gifts to the customs officers to be able to get them . . . and the police—what they really cared about when I started working for this *Kiều Bào* organization was who was getting money." Son suggested that government monitoring of remittance recipient households had an adverse effect on facilitating transnational relations. Remittances were generally being sent via illegal underground channels. He told me that "women [couriers] would show up on bikes and give me money but would ask me not to tell anyone I got money from them. They also would not tell me where they live."

Son's stories of the entangled relationships, corruption, and secrecy involved in facilitating the transmission of gifts from abroad to local inhabitants, and of his role in making sure the wheels were always properly greased so that gifts could be delivered, confirm that remittances have been capitalized upon by rent seekers over the years. Gifts from abroad can be a disruptive force in the community by attracting undesirable attention to recipient households. To receive gifts, one must gift—in this case, present a return gift not to the gifter, but rather to members of local rent-seeking social networks such as custom officers, police, other government officials, and neighbors. Care therefore needs to be taken in receiving and managing the visibility of diasporic gifts. This resonated with what another *Kiều Bào* organization volunteer from Ho Chi Minh City had told me, that many families with overseas relatives "are not friendly to us and sometimes keep their relatives in hotels so they do not have to register with the police." The public gift can become a feared entity laden with dangerous attention, as well as intention.

When we left Phuong's village to return to Saigon, she did not bother to tell her mother that she was leaving the country the next week, or that she would not return for the actual Tết holiday. She did tell her brother of her departure plans, and left her most valuable belongings, including her motorbike, with him. Two months later, the brother called me in Saigon to ask if I had heard from her in the United Kingdom, wondering why she had not sent word from abroad. Phuong's intention was to escape from the Vietnamese community and familial relationships that she felt kept her oppressed and prevented her from becoming who she wanted to be and experiencing personal transformation "in this lifetime." Previously, during an evening motorcycle ride away from the house, I had asked her brother if he expected Phuong to eventually send remittances, and he had confidently responded: "Of course. She is my sister, so why wouldn't she? If you have the opportunity to be in a place where you can earn money, the natural thing to do is to share it with your family back home who are less fortunate. Maybe she'll even bring me over to England one day." Now, the fact that he had not yet heard from his sister or received gifts from her was a disturbing sign that her sense of family obligations were not as secure as he had assumed them to be. Unlike Thuy, Phuong had seemingly made a choice to permanently escape the networked cycles of support and belonging that tied her to Vietnam, her community, and her family. The question of whether she would choose to eventually gift as a symbol of her continued participation in and remembrance of Vietnamese family life and values weighed anxiously on the minds of those she had left behind. Indeed, her family identity as a dutiful daughter and sister depended on it.

The cases of Thuy and Phuong—two women who responded differently to the migratory opportunities they were presented with and their related remittance obligations—demonstrate that there is not necessarily a single predictive model for remittance or migration behavior. Even if there is, there will be a great many exceptions to it. However, these cases do reflect common themes that came up in my discussions with a variety of Vietnamese informants about local notions of gifting as they relate to remittance expectations. First, beyond generalized expectations of contiguous obligation and reciprocity, Vietnamese notions of gift giving are widely encompassing and diachronic. The role of extant memory and sentiment weighs heavily in invoking broad notions of the gift and its overarching importance. Gift givers remember past favors and generous acts, as in the case of Thuy's conscientious remembrance of childhood gifts. Whereas Pierre Bourdieu made the case that gifts must be essentially forgotten and selflessly given anew every time to qualify as gifts—"the counter-gift must be deferred and different" (1977, 11), the temporality and intentionality of Vietnamese gifts illustrates they always take place as part of longer-term circulations in which origins and endings are never clear. This is not to say such practices are merely obligatory returns rather than altruistic overtures. The hope of a future gift is not predicated on a past demand, but nonetheless people remember and value the sentiment that motivated the history of exchange. Forgetting is not an option. Gifts remember (*nhớ*) those that preceded them and also look toward the future by indicating subjective valuations of continued and committed participation in the social relationships they are intended to mediate. It is their mediating and participatory circulation that defines them as gifts, bringing recognition by extension to the networks they cultivate and maintain. Thuy's gifting practices locate her firmly within Vietnam, while Phuong's going abroad and failing to gift in a culturally recognizable manner mark her departure from it.

Second, gifting is networked. Gifting is a symbolically expected mode and medium of participation within a kin or community network, and gifts take many forms, including decorative plants, motorcycles, and money. Gifts can never be repaid but only continued into the future. The continuation and intentionality of gifting indexes one's capacity for sociality and depth of sentiment within a given community. Just as gift networks include, however, they also exclude. Westermarck, as I noted earlier in this chapter, suggested as much in his musings on the limits of gift hospitality that serves to maintain the stranger as an Other. Or, as Jacques Derrida reminds us, hospitality inevitably veils the darker violence of inhospitality that it must necessarily define itself in contrast to, therefore revealing the "the violence of the power of hospitality" (2000, 149). To not give is to signal one's decision to exit the network, a network that one may in fact resent. Phuong's decision to leave Vietnam appeared to be a permanent one: with her departure, she distanced and isolated herself by breaking off communication as well as gifting. If gifts are deemed necessary to hold one's place in a family and community, to cease gifting is to suspend sociality.

Third, gifts are measured by one's capacity to give, rather than the value of the gift itself. The extent to which one gives more than one can afford imbues the gift with the seriousness and selflessness of its intention. One demonstrates that one remembers, and that one desires to remain an integral part of, a social and kinship network by sacrificing (*hy sinh*) to gift. Thuy's gifts to her family far outweigh the past gifts she received in terms of material and objective value, and she admits that it is expensive for her to purchase them. But as a young professional with a decent salary, she feels she must demonstrate that her gifts are not merely token gestures, but rather reflect a personal sacrifice similar to that involved in the smaller gifts given to her in the past—when, despite difficult economic times, family members still made the effort to help her beyond just meeting her basic needs.[10]

Finally, one's ability to give and the types of gifts given mark one's social status but also betray a desire for recognition. Thuy's measured performance of gifting during the Tết holidays reflects a conscious effort to gain recognition for the professional promotions she has had. Her temple donations were also proudly and publicly announced so that others could admire and appreciate her generosity. There may be elements of calculative performance, but the donations are also emotionally anxious and aspirational. For Thuy social recognition was particularly important as her professional advancements often came, as she sometimes complained, at the expense of other traditional Vietnamese symbols of female social success such as marriage and children.

The prodigal cycle of Thuy's family gifting perhaps reflects a mildly potlatch-like exchange process. Mauss, drawing on Boas, described potlatches as gifting competitions characterized by showmanship, in which one seeks to outgift a rival to gain status. In his words, "consumption and destruction of goods really go beyond all bounds. In certain kinds of potlatch one must expend all that one has, keeping nothing back. It is a competition to see who is the richest and also the most madly extravagant. Everything is based upon the principles of antagonism and rivalry . . . it is not even a question of giving and receiving gifts but of destroying so as not to give the slightest hint of desiring your gift to be reciprocated . . . in order to flatten one's rival. In this way one not only promotes oneself, but also one's family, up the social scale" (1967, 37). The description is mildly reminiscent of Dupuis's descriptions of "extravagant" expenditures of wealth in nineteenth-century Vietnam, discussed earlier in this chapter. Yet extravagant displays of gifting not only immediately benefit the giver by promoting oneself and family up the social scale in the short term but also reveal a collectively oriented benevolence in the long term when it comes to accumulating social capital through performances of generosity. Once again tracing Mauss's account of the potlatch back to his source, we find Boas's 1898 report on the northwestern tribes of Canada to the British Association for the Advancement of Science. In the report, Boas defends the potlatch as a system of gift exchange in which participants paid debts to secure their family's future as integral members of the community. In Boas's interpretation, the "first object is to pay his debts. This is done publicly and with much ceremony, as a matter of record" (1898, 55).

The lavish display of gifting and material destruction involved in the potlatch have been widely commented and theorized upon (Bataille 1988; Bracken 1997), with an emphasis on the immediacy of energy expenditure. This aspect of the potlatch analytical framework is certainly an important factor that can help explain consumption behaviors and impulses. Yet Boas also says that the potlatch is also cognizant of the future, and that the participant's "second object is to invest the fruits of his labour so that the greatest benefit will accrue from them for himself as well as his children . . . it is, we might say, their life insurance" (1898, 55). Gifts, then, are not only expressive, reciprocal, obligatory, and seeking of recognition, as discussed. They are also conservatively future-oriented. They attempt to preserve, secure and advance one's status through generous social participation in a community, even if beyond one's immediate means. Through gifting, one conserves a collection of socially affirmed identities in which past relationships play important roles in reminding one of the contingent debts that have contributed to present personhoods. Amid the flux of global migration and remittance economies, when gifters may choose to partake in or depart from multiple communities, where such gifts are directed and the identities they seek to reinforce or promote take on heightened significance. Yet the individual agency to gift, as we will see, is very much in tension with the structural sociocultural obligations and expectations to gift, entangling gifters and receivers in complicated social networks and processes in which the production and preservation of identity is never individuated or isolated.

Chasing Merit

Culture is an elusive and hybrid concept (Geertz 1973; McLeod and Nguyen 2001) and easily critiqued for its essentialist assumptions. As Clifford Geertz noted many years ago, "The term 'culture' has by now acquired a certain aura of ill repute in anthropological circles because of the multiplicity of its references and the studied vagueness with which it has all too often been invoked" (1973, 89). Nonetheless, culture (*văn hóa*) is a notion often invoked by Vietnamese.[11] For many of my informants, how one gifts reveals to what extent one has culture or at least preserves it in the context of emigration. In Mauss's estimation, gifting was a process that was culturally specific (taking the Kula, potlatch, or other forms) but also universal. He called this a general system of "total services" that encompassed culture but also law and the economy, in which "all kinds of institutions are given expression at one and the same time" (1967, 8). For Mauss, it was necessary to explore the diverse ethnological complexity of the concept before discussing the applicability of its abstracted functions. For the Vietnamese informants in my study, gifting was a generally recognized concept that indeed transcended geographic boundaries—whether one was Vietnamese or Vietnamese American, for example—but nonetheless had specific cultural resonances, traces, and origins that remained relevant in valuating exchange and generosity in remitting behaviors. Before returning to a specific discussion of remittances, therefore, it is worth further considering the so-called cultural context of gifting practices in Vietnam. One arena in which notions of culture and gifts are often linked is discussions of religion.

Concepts of gifting, compassion, and hospitality are widely invoked in a range of Vietnamese religious practices. During a temple trip during Tết that I participated in, five busloads of urban Saigonese took an all-day trip through southeastern Vietnam to the coastal town of Vung Tau, stopping at over ten Buddhist temples.[12] In each place, monks and nuns offered gifts of sticky rice cakes wrapped in banana leaves and tea, while the pilgrims would rush through the altars in the temple to pray, light incense, and make monetary offerings to the various deities that had provided them with good fortune in the past year and, they hoped, would deliver more good luck and prosperity in the year to come. The pilgrims varied widely in age and income brackets, but all of them that I observed gave some monetary gift at the temples, whether large or small according to their capacity.

Whereas the definition of gifting to individuals is entangled with and complicated by past debts and obligations, and collective giving through state-run hometown associations (*Hội Kiều Bào*) may be viewed with suspicion, religious organizations in Vietnam have benefited greatly from overseas remittances and are
more trusted than direct government-sponsored conduits for collective and
charitable giving. Throughout Vietnam one finds freshly built and restored
temples and churches—ranging from Buddhist and Catholic to those of local
deities—the fund-raising for which regularly involves active outreach to overseas
communities. Buddhist head monks and nuns often visit religious communities
abroad to raise funds for a temple. For example, Janet Hoskins (2015) has examined how the religious revival of the syncretist Cao Dai religion in Vietnam has
been in part driven by the social, spiritual, and financial energy of Vietnamese
Americans in California. Elderly Vietnamese I interviewed often reported that
donations to local religious groups were a regular use of the remittance gifts they
received from abroad. Many Vietnamese Americans send money to Vietnam for
religious purposes, trusting local relatives to channel the funds to appropriate
church or temple authorities. Anthropologists Helle Rydstrom (2003) and Alexander Soucy (2012) have discussed the complex and contested production of
moral selves within social and religious contexts as they navigate and embody notions of piety and charity. Elderly female populations in particular often have a
unique relationship to religious practices in Buddhism but also other traditions.
As one woman in the central coastal town of Quy Nhơn whom I interviewed explained, "my children in America give me money to do with what I wish. I am
old and do not need a lot of things. I prefer to give money to the temple. It is
good fortune to do so, and the temple community is compassionate in helping
the poor and needy."

Although there has been a significant religious revival in Vietnam, buttressed
by support from overseas remittances, state control over religious organizations
remains tight. Religious donations may be troublesome to the state in their promotion of an independent civil-society sector that may be critical and dismissive
of government oversight policies. In Vietnam there is a long history of political
activism organized by Buddhist, Catholic, Cao Dai, Hoa Hao, Muslim, and Prot-
estant religious groups. In recent years, a number of religious leaders followed by
overseas Vietnamese, such as the Buddhist monk Thich Quang Do, have been
under house arrest or are closely monitored and sometimes harassed by government authorities.

Thích Nhất Hạnh, a monk who was exiled after the Vietnam War and leads
an expatriate Vietnamese Buddhist community in France, returned to Vietnam
for the first time in 2005 and again in 2007. In 2007 at the Vinh Nghiem Pagoda in Saigon, I attended a daring chanting requiem led by Hạnh to pray for

souls of the dead without reference to their past political affiliation. Since 1975 the commemoration of fallen communist soldiers has been sanctioned by the state, as evidenced by well-maintained official military graveyards and memorials across the country. In contrast, deceased members of the rival Army of the Republic of Vietnam have been officially forgotten and literally erased. Yet the past still haunts the present—the postwar razing of former republican state memorials and graveyards, and the countless war dead who remain unaccounted for, has contributed to a widespread cultural phenomenon of wandering, unrequited, and unprayed-for ghosts (H. Kwon 2008). At Hạnh's Saigon requiem, thousands of southern Vietnamese attended the event to write the names of deceased relatives, many of whom had been republican soldiers who died in combat against the communists, on commemorative prayer lists. Incense, candles, and chanting in the temple provided a meditative atmosphere that competed with the buzz of bustling crowds of worshippers dressed in brown and gray trying to get inside and add their family members' names to the rolls. Attendees felt anticipatory excitement but also anxious urgency, as many were unsure whether they would have an opportunity to participate in such an event again. As one worshipper said of the aging monk, "Thích Nhất Hạnh recognizes the suffering we have undergone and understands our needs. The opportunity to see him teach here at the temple, and

FIGURE 4. State war martyrs graveyard.

to remember our losses, is rare." Indeed, although Hạnh was welcomed by thousands of followers in places like Vinh Nghiem on his tour around the country in 2007, with cautious government approval, his Bat Nha monastery in Hue was later cracked down upon in 2009, allegedly with state support (Human Rights Watch 2009), and its monks and nuns were forcibly ousted from the temple grounds.

Both criticized and followed by many Buddhists, Hạnh is often said to bring back to Vietnam a different kind of Buddhism: one that a detractor said has become "more for foreigners than Vietnamese," having lost its religious and cultural roots in Vietnam and become hybridized—with only an uncanny sense of distant recognition for those who follow more traditional sects. Yet the departure and return of Hạnh's Buddhist faith is seen by other worshippers as a return gift to his own country. As one attendee at the Vinh Nghiem requiem explained to me, "Vietnamese Buddhism has lost much of its spirituality and meaning. People go to the temple, but they don't know why. They just wish for good fortune (lộc) but no longer understand Buddhism. Thích Nhất Hạnh has been outside of the country (and away from its political repression) and therefore free to develop his teachings and now can bring true religious meaning back through his preaching and writings. We owe the Venerable Master gratitude for what he has given back to us." The return of Hạnh's style of Buddhism has been accompanied by Hạnh himself, again in 2008 and 2017, despite occasional criticism from some followers that he should not return to Vietnam as long as his colleagues in the Vietnamese clergy remain persecuted. Hạnh has preached that "the most precious gift we can offer others is our presence. When mindfulness embraces those we love, they will bloom like flowers" (1997, 20). Exactly what kinds of flowers will bloom and whether their spread can be controlled is a significant concern for the Vietnamese state, which anxiously monitors the present of "presence" in Hạnh's pilgrimage tours. Indeed, the uproar over the monetary and knowledge gifts that one diasporic monk has returned to Vietnam through his support of a particular Buddhist tradition illustrates that overseas gifts (here, a classic example of social remittances) may be desired for complex reasons yet also deemed potentially dangerous—in this case, by the state from which he had long been exiled but that cautiously invited his return. The controversy also illustrates that gifting affects not only immediate relationships between givers and receivers, but also indirect relations with and among the spectators of such exchanges.

Gifting in Literature

Descriptions of gifting practices pervade Vietnamese legends and literature, another arena that Vietnamese I met frequently invoked to express notions of culture. In this section I discuss how the gift appears either directly or indirectly as an ambivalent organizing theme and metaphor in two classic literary examples— one premodern and one modern, both considered to be canonical literature texts in Vietnam. I begin with the *Tale of Kieu*, a national literary treasure that my informants insisted time and again must be read to "truly understand the Vietnamese."

The Vietnamese literary classic *Tale of Kieu*, from the early nineteenth century, highlights the plight of Kieu, a young woman who forgoes her own happiness to pay off a debt owed by her father. When thugs threaten the lives of her father and brother unless a debt is repaid, she decides to give her body as well as leave her true love as a filial gift to save them. The narrator of the story conveys the personal and moral choice faced by Kieu that betrays the confusing demarcations and entanglements of gifts and money: "By what means could she save her flesh and blood? When evil strikes you bow to circumstance. As you must weigh and choose between your love and filial duty, which will turn the scale? She put aside all vows of love and troth—a child first pays the debts of birth and care. Resolved on what to do, she said: 'Hands off—I'll sell myself and Father I'll redeem'" (Nguyễn Du 1983, 33).

This passage demonstrates the cultural "scale" of value, according to which a gift is measured by its selfless intention and generous spirit. Securing a "bridal gift" of "four hundred and some *liang*" (ibid., 35) to pay off the debt, a marriage contract for Kieu is finalized. The father is freed, but it turns out the so-called bridal gift from the stranger she is supposed to marry—perhaps a gift in the classically dangerous sense discussed when it comes to unfamiliar outsiders—was in fact the purchasing of Kieu for work in a brothel. The money Kieu gives the father to free him from his debts, in contrast, is an intimately generous and familiar gift, insofar as it represents and enforces ongoing sentimental and filial attachments and relations. It remembers and also looks toward the future.

The money to purchase Kieu turns out to not be a gift at all, despite initially appearing to be one. Rather, it works as pure money in the formal definitional sense, operating merely to create an economic contract between parties with no sentimental regard for each other. Once the transaction is completed, Kieu is consigned to her purchased role as an enslaved prostitute. There is no further discussion of gifting that relates to her new identity vis-à-vis her "husband"-cum-pimp in this context—indeed, this character on the other side of the transaction remains charmless and faceless and receives no further description in the story. Eventually escaping from the brothel only to find herself in an even worse situation, for the rest of the story Kieu wanders far from home, experiencing a series of tragedies and forever separated from her childhood innocence. Yet the reader is continually admonished to admire her for the selfless original gift of life she gave to her family, where filial duty trumps or even exemplifies personal happiness. In a sense, Kieu embodies the idealized cultural notion of a traditional Vietnamese gift, the tragedy of her freely chosen fate demonstrating the generous depth and selflessness of her filial sentiments. The money-cum-gift is not merely an external object outside of the participants who exchange it, but it also involves an affective embodied commitment to the relationship that cannot be separated from it. Yet money, which is also an actant in the economic transaction separating her from the family she strived to save—may sabotage and disguise the gift's intention and recognition.

Moving to the more recent late twentieth century, in literature emerging from the Đổi Mới ("renovation") period gifts index shifting social hierarchies and become metaphorical critiques of the socialist transition to a capitalist economy in which every day personal relations appear to be increasingly monetized and unsentimental. By extension, Vietnamese culture (including proper notions and sentiments of gifting) seems to be in decline due to the new political and economic agendas of the state. Nguyễn Huy Thiệp's famous 1988 short story, "The General Retires" (Tướng Về Hưu), offers insights into traditional and transforming meanings of gifts in a description of an ostentatious wedding party: "The wedding in the suburbs was ridiculous and rather vulgar. Three cars. Filtered cigarettes but toward the end of the party replaced with rolled cigarettes. Fifty dinner trays but twelve were left untouched. The groom wore a black suit, red tie. I had to lend him the best tie in my wardrobe. I say borrow, but I knew I wouldn't get it back."[13]

Weddings, in which gifts and displays of generosity are a regular part, are frequently sites of social status performance in Vietnam. In Ho Chi Minh City today, one can reserve a wedding hall, choosing from among standardized packages according to one's budget. Invitations are liberally distributed to neighbors, friends, and acquaintances, with no clear sense of confirmed attendance—thus, the ordering of lots of food. A wedding guest can quickly ascertain by the size of the space, the band, the number and content of the courses served, and so on how much the family has paid to host the celebration.

The wedding in Nguyen's story occurs on the suburban edge of the city, thus spatially indicating a family of lower socioeconomic status. The ambitiously ostentatious yet tacky presentation of gifts to the guests betrays an aspiration for wealth and social standing that is beyond the family's reach. Surplus food has been ordered, with twelve trays left untouched, but the high-quality cigarettes for the guests at the beginning of the evening are revealingly replaced by cheap rolling papers and tobacco by the end. Furthermore, the groom does not even have a proper tie, so the narrator lends him his best. But to lend someone something in Vietnam, he recognizes, often means to give without expectation of return. A loan is a begrudged gift that receives none of the recognition for generosity and altruism usually associated with gifting. While the "vulgar" affair of the wedding is performed as a lavish gift to the community, the tie, given by the narrator, is a private loan and thus not publicly recognized as a gift. Generosity is revealed to be superficial rather than embodied. The public-private disconnect between what the narrator and the wedding audience perceive as gifts emerges as a source of critique. Gifts as strategic economic performers appear to be losing their traditional meaning of indexing generous, sentimental, and selfless intention—even to the point of the embodied sacrifice that we saw in the case of Kieu. The sham of modern, cheap, and selfish gifting emerges as source of resentment for the narrator, resonating with the story's wide renovation-era readership.

Resentment, Recognition, and Danger

Returning to the title of this chapter, then, gifts in Vietnam can be dangerous, not least because they encompass such a broad range of meanings, obligations, and expectations. Nonetheless, they are necessary and symbolically central to Vietnamese rituals of sociality and exchange. Although Mauss's dangerous gift appears to be one from the outside and is thus atypical of Vietnamese gifting practices, further investigation into Vietnamese gifting practices reveals a marked frustration in which one's social identity comes to be marked, shaped, and embodied by gifts, often beyond one's intended meaning. To gift is to participate in a social network that extends beyond one's immediate kinship group and is thus out of one's control. Within those networks are both familiar and trusted insiders and uncanny subjects who strategically pry their way into them and to whom one becomes obliged. As Mauss says of gifting in China, the broader civilizational and institutional culture of which Vietnam has been historically associated (Woodside 1988), "through the [gift] passed on . . . the alliance that has been contracted is no momentary phenomenon, and the contracting parties are deemed to be in a state of perpetual dependence towards one another" (Mauss 1967, 64).

While gifts are public and often token, they index longer-term substantive obligations between givers and receivers, which may draw unwanted attention, require grudging displays of generosity, or be called upon unexpectedly. When I asked Thang, one of my informants in the Mekong Delta province of Ben Tre, how often he receives remittances from relatives, he explained that "if I don't have money, I call to ask for money." It is precisely this attitude that countless Vietnamese remittance senders interviewed in California resent, especially when they are asked for money by more distant relatives who assert kinship ties without concomitant sentiment. The agency of gifting is reversed: givers become obliged, and recipients demand. The gift is no longer a gift, yet it still performs as such.

Remittance givers and receivers generally speak quite openly of the gifts they give and receive. When it comes to loans (those overshadowed begrudging gifts that often follow the token symbolic ones), however, the issue appears as a common source of suppressed antagonism between Vietnamese family members. While gifters receive public recognition and often gratitude, lenders are obscured or even vilified. In the case of Kieu, the daughter's demonstrable agency of voluntary gifting is celebrated. Yet her father also grieved at having to give his daughter away to pay off his debt: "pity the father facing his young child. Looking at her, he bled and died within" (Nguyễn Du 1983, 35). The father's incapacity to pay off his extortive loans and protect his daughter resulted in her having to sell herself, supposedly as a gift but materialized as money. Allowing her to do so is represented in some sense as an affectively begrudged patriarchal gift, as to do so was anguishing and painful for the father. Yet in the end he lost not only his daughter but also face and status as a compromised man who no longer retains the agency to gift. He is both a grudging gifter, in giving up his daughter, and a begrudged recipient, in shamefully accepting the money and relief from extortion that her act provides. He cannot be the hero of the story, for his participation in the gifting process is recognized by everyone to be structurally obliged and necessitated rather than selfless and voluntary—there is no way for him to perform otherwise.

Remittances are often expected and even demanded by family members who stay behind in Vietnam. Routinely taking care of ancestral homes or of sick and elderly relatives means that support money may be obliged from faraway kin who have escaped such in-person family responsibilities. One must give, and to the extent that one displays personal agency and generosity in meeting this obligation, as Kieu did in offering her own life to save her father, gives one credibility among family. Obliged remittance support can be recognized as a generous gift and therefore celebrated as such through the performance of its presentation, but only if carefully enacted. As one informal Vietnamese proverb says, "the way you give gifts is more important than the gift itself (*của cho không bằng cách cho*)." Even more formalized Vietnamese language generally distinguished between the formal verb used for giving (*tặng*) a gift from the more common word for giving (*cho*), emphasizing the importance and etiquette of presentation. It is resonant of Mauss's characterization of the "noble fashion" of Kula gift giving that must proceed in a "disinterested and modest way . . . [D]istinguished carefully from the mere economic exchange of useful goods . . . called gimwali" (1967, 22). In fact, "of an individual who does not proceed in the kula with the necessary greatness of soul, it is said that he is 'conducting it like a gimwali'" (ibid.). Personally presented gifts in Vietnam are routinely refused but persistently pressed by the giver on the receiver until eventually accepted. I have witnessed such performative exchanges by both givers and receivers numerous times, but in the end the money always changes hands, even if conspicuously held for quite a while after the initial prestation in feigned protest. But as one remittance sender quietly grumbled, "it is not a choice, I *must* show generosity . . . then after I've given them everything, they still expect more."

According to another Vietnamese proverb, "mutual giving satisfies the heart (*có qua có lại mới toại lòng nhau*)." The emphasis is on the push and pull of sentimental relations materially represented by gifts that in turn are imbued with the selflessness of selves. Gifting is a social and cultural performance in which one's voluntary and generous intentionality must be emotionally invested and visibly displayed. Monetary remittances must also accompany material ones, so that there is a possibility of reciprocity. By giving money within a basket of other goods and services that does not necessarily have to be financially matched, one has maintained the spirit of the gift. One has only to visit Tan Son Nhat airport in Saigon and see the boxes of goods brought back by overseas Vietnamese to realize that remittances to Vietnam are not only monetary and that material expression matters when it comes to gifts. Nonetheless, to remit halfheartedly or selfishly (below one's capacity)—or, for that matter, to refuse in-kind reciprocity—is to be-

FIGURE 5.   Returning overseas Vietnamese with boxes, Tân Sơn Nhất Airport, Saigon.

tray the spirit of the gift and lose one's credibility and performative status as a gifter and, by extension (as was often emphasized to me in interviews and discussions), one's cultural identity as a Vietnamese.

When one can no longer afford to gift, one loans. Yet loans are often described as veiled requests for gifts. "My relatives ask me to loan them $5,000, so I give them $500 instead. I know that the loan will never be repaid, so I might as well be generous with a gift instead of appearing stingy with a loan that is really a gift anyway," Minh, a Vietnamese American remittance sender in California, told me. The context of the exchange naturally diminishes the reputation and agency of the gifter, who despite gifting may be regarded as stingy for refusing a loan. Of course, in many cases loans are paid back, and remittances are in general a critical source of credit in a country where microfinance options are limited.[14] But the remittance loan is predicated on familial trust and goodwill rather than enforceable legal contracts or collateral that can be confiscated should repayment not be forthcoming. Like the wedding tie in Nguyễn Huy Thiệp's story, one gives never being sure that one will "get it back." A remittance recipient in Saigon who borrowed $40,000 to rebuild and expand his house explained to me that there was no interest or timeline for the loan: "we will pay [it] back when we can." However, a remittance sender in San Jose, California, related the frustrating story of how her family had "lent $50,000 to relatives in Vietnam so that they could build a mini-hotel. The hotel is not well managed or profitable, so there is no chance of them paying the loan back in the near future. But my relatives in Vietnam do not understand that this money is not free. My parents work harder and later hours to earn money, so they can pay off their expenses as well as make payments on the bank loan they took out to support our relatives' business venture. Our Vietnamese relatives don't understand or appreciate the hardship we endure. It makes me very angry."

Gifts may be dangerous, therefore, not only from the outside, but even within intimate family circles, because the obligations and drama they provoke are endless, and the imagined intentions they are designed to signal are never transparent. Remittance gifts come from elsewhere, yet they also attempt to mark one's place within a familiar community. One gifts not only out of compassion, but also strategically and nostalgically to retain a stake in a family or community of origin. Remittance recipient households often see themselves as holding a social and physical place for family members abroad (who remain familiar but nonetheless have been altered in some way by distance and time) and feel justified in using money from them to address the gap. "We rebuilt this house to Western standards with *their* money, so that they can return in the summers to live here comfortably," explained one man in Quy Nhơn. He had upgraded his house with "luxury" amenities such as seated toilets and water heaters using remittance funds, explaining that his overseas relatives could no longer defecate and bathe like Vietnamese in Vietnam.

The transnational family network resides in dispersed locales in which traditional customs and characteristics of Vietnamese gifting—whereby gifts circulate within familiar networks, are diachronically oriented, and gauge realistic measures of capacity and social status—are no longer fully understood. Disconnected imaginaries and suspicions circulate within the same social networks as gifts and people, exacerbating expectations and misunderstandings. Reception of a gift may reconnect one to a past one wishes to forget. Memories, especially in the context of war and refugee displacement, can be troubling and unwelcome. Participating once again in gift relations may also be uncanny in that one may find one's motives suddenly suspect. Return visits by overseas monks offering requiems that conjure up forgotten sorrows are cautiously received and tolerated by the Vietnamese state. But there are many more examples of anxious exchange practices among individuals and families. Surprise gifts or communications by remittance recipients are often read by senders as veiled requests for more money. A wedding or death announcement from Vietnam is necessarily followed by a compulsory remittance transfer from the overseas recipient of the announcement to the family member in Vietnam who sent the notification. A Tết greeting card that arrives in the United States from a forgotten relative guiltily reminds one of abandoned family obligations and the relational recognition the sender has not been granted. The general sense expressed by remittance exchange participants is that remittance "gifts" are obligatory rather than truly voluntary, and there is widespread awareness of the emotional tensions they provoke. "They [the family abroad] are afraid (sợ) of us, because they think we only want money," lamented one of my Vietnamese informants who in the past had occasionally received remittances that are now increasingly rare. Reception of the gift may be accompanied by judgments that one is lazy or dependent and spark defensive reactions. In other cases, remittances are openly demanded as part and parcel of traditional cultural obligations and identity. As one Saigon remittance receiver declared, echoing the attitudes of many others whom I interviewed, "those who do not give [remittances] are no longer Vietnamese." To cease gifting, therefore, may put one at risk of losing one's societally recognized personal and cultural identity.

Insides and Outsides

If remittances in Vietnam appear to be obligatory gifts, in a sense they are akin to what Maurice Godelier has analyzed as "gifts to the gods," emphasizing that not all gifts are reciprocal or voluntary. For Godelier, "in response to the gifts made by the great gods . . . there can be no true counter-gift" (1999, 193), for there can be no gift even approximately equal to that of life. Gifts must be graciously given, and one can only hope for, rather than expect, recognition. Whatever the sense of lack and missed opportunity felt by those who stayed behind in Vietnam, they still confidently claim the authenticity of kinship and even national identity by virtue of the homes and temples they maintain, the family graves and altars they tend, and the soil they live on. Yet the rootedness of such claims, especially in communities where so many current residents have attempted flight, or previously moved from other regions of the country, themselves, are always already tenuous.

The chance nature of refugee flight means that the *Việt Kiều* may be uncanny, not only because they reemerge from an unknown overseas horizon, but also by virtue of the fact that their escape is often attributed to the whims of fate (*số phận*) rather than a rewarded calculation of agency. The gifts former refugees can afford to give as a result of their new lives abroad carry symbolic meanings that are not only from inside a known community of symmetrically aspired exchange but also from an unknown outside—"over there (*ở bên kia*)," a common term used by my informants to describe faraway places where the diaspora resides. It is not merely a geographic and cultural outside, but potentially divine: the vicissitudes of fate that allowed some to leave, some to return, and others to perish remain enigmatic. The resultant transnational community is one that is increasingly displaced, disconnected, and unfamiliar. Gifters aspire to display benevolent agency through remittance giving, but they confront the contradiction that the very capacity to gift was in part bestowed by circumstances of migratory chance, the traumatic stories of which often remain untold or emotionally buried. The sentiment nonetheless remains that wherever fate has taken the *Việt Kiều*, homeland and family are still divine points to which they owe their fortune and identity, to where and whom they can now return, and which they are obligated to acknowledge through gifts.

Thus, whether remittances are duly recognized as voluntary gifts or received as expected tribute is frequently an antagonistic issue for remittance economy participants. It may be for this reason that many overseas Vietnamese—especially those who have been away from the country for a period of time and have already sponsored close family members for emigration, as well as second-generation overseas Vietnamese who do not feel an immediate sense of direct family obligation—often shift over time what they send to Vietnam from substantive remittance support targeted to family members to sporadic holiday familial gifts or collective charitable donations. But for those who retain their family ties and continue to make transnational pilgrimages back to the homeland and home communities, performing remittances as gifts serves as providing token but symbolically compulsory placeholders for absent overseas migrants. At the very minimum, Tết money is an expected and almost required gift for overseas families who maintain close social linkages with home communities. It is unimaginable for an overseas Vietnamese to return to his or her family or community without being preceded or accompanied by gifts. Some do return to the homeland without gifts, but without them one can never comfortably return to one's true "home (*quê hương*)," the ancestral village and community. The tension between the public performance of gifting and the obligations but also avoidances of giving haunt family relationships, maintaining but also straining (and sometimes even severing) kinship networks—as well as the idea and ideal of the gift itself.

SÀI GÒN, OVERLAID BY HỒ CHÍ MINH

Capitalist Desires and Deferrals

Ho Chi Minh City, still commonly referred to as Saigon by local inhabitants, is the largest city in Vietnam and the country's economic center. Although the official population count is around eight million (GSO Vietnam 2016), the actual population is well over ten million, and the city has ambitious plans for metropolitan expansion, as internal economic migrants from around the country have descended on the city to work in the informal sector and send domestic remittances to families in rural areas with fewer economic opportunities.[1] Founded as a Vietnamese city in 1698 in an area formerly controlled by the Khmer, Saigon continued to grow as the center of the prosperous southern Vietnamese frontier region, later becoming the capital of France's only directly administered colony in Indochina.[2] Subjected to three centuries of economic and cultural flows from all parts of the country, region, and world, Saigon has been no stranger to new ideas and bodies. The historian Keith Taylor has discussed the fluid dynamism of Vietnamese geography and identity in the south, which he describes as a region of "openness, vulnerability, possibility . . . [with] little sense of fixity, boundedness, orientation" (1998, 966), toward which the more tradition-bound north, centered around the old capital of Hanoi, often gazed with migratory and transformative desires. The South was a place that for many migrants over centuries of territorial expansion offered "a new version of being Vietnamese distinguished by relative freedom from the Vietnamese past and the authority justified by appeals to that past," where one might "taste the sensory and imaginary powers of unexplored terrain" (Taylor quoted in Reid 1993, 64–65). For many contemporary overseas Vietnamese, themselves originally from (or at least transplanted after

1954 to) this southern region, diasporic communities abroad offer a somewhat similar defamiliarizing break with the past and reimagining of collective and individual identities vis-à-vis the Vietnamese homeland.

From 1954 to 1975, Saigon was the capital of the Republic of Vietnam—the southern part of what is now the unified nation-state of Vietnam, which had been divided by the Geneva Accords of 1954 at the seventeenth parallel. A hard-fought war for Vietnamese independence from France ended in 1954 with the creation of the two competing postcolonial states of the Democratic Republic of (North) Vietnam and the Republic of (South) Vietnam, with Hanoi and Saigon, respectively, replacing the old royal Annamese capital of Hue in central Vietnam. Vietnam was a front in the Cold War, with the Republic of Vietnam, the United States, and other allies ranging from Australia to Thailand and South Korea against the Democratic Republic of Vietnam, the Soviet Union, China, and others in the socialist bloc. As the Vietnam War wore on through the 1960s and 1970s, public support in the United States for its Vietnamese ally began to wane. Following the 1973 Paris Peace Accords, the United States pulled the last of its troops out of Vietnam, leaving South Vietnam to fight North Vietnam alone after a brief cease fire. In 1975 northern troops and National Liberation Front forces victoriously entered the south, as city after city began to fall. Communist forces captured Saigon on April 30, 1975, renaming it Ho Chi Minh City in 1976.[3]

After the war, large segments of the population were relocated to the New Economic Zones, following a general policy to de-urbanize the newly unified socialist nation that was suffering from food shortages, de-Americanize southern Vietnamese citizens corrupted by city capitalism, and develop and "Vietnamize" the population of strategic frontier areas. Saigon's population had fallen to a low of 3.2 million by 1984.[4] Through the 1970s many Saigonese and other southerners, facing persecution and exclusion at the hands of the new Vietnamese government that considered their former loyalties to be traitorous, left the country illegally (đi chui) to seek their luck abroad. The result is a contemporary urban population that is connected to vast extended overseas kinship networks. These networks have been maintained for the past thirty-plus years partially through overseas remittances. At least one-third of international remittances to Vietnam today are estimated to flow through the greater Ho Chi Minh City area (Pfau and Giang 2009), often en route to extended kin further afield.

In this bustling, dynamic, noisy, constantly changing and expanding city, where congested and dusty streets full of motorcycles, cars, and trucks that pour out smoke and contribute to smog competing with an ever-changing skyline of new high-rise commercial and residential buildings, it is not at all difficult to encounter someone who has family members abroad or who receives overseas remittances.[5] I have been visiting Ho Chi Minh City on a regular basis since the mid-1990s, but an extended stay as a Fulbright-Hays fellow based at Vietnam National University Ho Chi Minh City's Department of Anthropology between 2007 and 2009 gave me the opportunity to focus on the primary field research for this study. Between meetings facilitated by the university and local government, introductions through friends and colleagues, and direct inquiries, I was able to identify, interview, and repeatedly visit and participate in the lives of people in over fifty households in Ho Chi Minh City to learn about the remittances they received from abroad and the relationships they maintained with the relatives and friends who send them. Because Ho Chi Minh City is an urban field site, interviews and participant observation occurred across multiple city neighborhoods and sometimes in coffee shops in between them, which reflects the nature of urban ethnography where "ethnographic moments" (Strathern 1988) are everywhere but sometimes ephemeral in the opportunities they provide for reflection. The narrative momentum of this chapter is intended to convey the ethnographic experience of navigating and exploring a diverse cityscape full of diverse stories—at times sought after, but equally often stumbled upon in the midst of the economic and social hustle and bustle of Saigon.

Dematerializing Circulations and Desires

The forms remittances take in Saigon have varied dramatically since 1975, as have the recipients' relationships with the senders. Tuan, a fifty-seven-year-old man who has lived in Saigon's fourth district for over forty years, explained that "in the past subsidy era (*thời bao cấp*) [1975–1986] it was very hard to live, hard to keep contact with family, and hard to receive money. Everything had to be secret. We'd go to the airport and wait overnight for a box. Our relatives in America would send soap, shoes, clothes—things like that, to use or sell. But there were often surprises inside, we'd have to find them. Like a $20 bill rolled up inside the tube of toothpaste. But the authorities knew about such tricks as well—they would insert a spoke into the toothpaste, for example, to find the money, so everything had to be sneakier, and the bribes higher, to get past them." A woman told me that her relatives would sometimes seal money beneath a layer of glue on a postcard sent from overseas, while another related that money would be sewn into the recesses of gifts of clothes and shoes. She commented that "life was so hard then, the money helped us to survive those difficult times." At a time when direct money transfer from the United States was not permitted, remittances from North America were often channeled through relatives in France—where there has been a significant Vietnamese community since the colonial era (Bousquet 1991)—who would send them on to Vietnam.

FIGURE 6.   Ho Chi Minh City, fourth district.

The challenge of limited cross-border financial remittance channels into Viet-nam resulted in many families in the United States and elsewhere in the West resorting to mailing items that could be sold or exchanged on the black market to meet direct subsistence needs. The circulation of such exotic overseas items (from whiskey to watches), intended as convertible material remittances, took on unexpected symbolic and nostalgic meanings, becoming mnemonic signifi-ers of past consumer worlds experienced under the capitalist "old regime (*chế độ cũ*)" now diachronically distant and synchronically inaccessible. The economic sociologist Đang Phong described these symbolic overseas markets and their role in reinscribing imaginations and memories for Saigonese adjusting to new lifeworlds under the communist regime: "*Việt Kiều* [overseas Vietnamese] could help their relatives more easily by sending goods back rather than foreign cur-rency, as there was a market constantly hungry for them, both financially and psychologically. In every street and market place in Saigon as well as other urban centers of the South, the places with the 'brightest prices' were always the shops selling goods sent back from France and the USA" (Đang 2000, 188). The role of these markets in circulating imaginaries of alternative lifeworlds was remarkable. Đang explains that "a system of relations came into being between those who left and those who stayed . . . these relations gave rise to a notion of the West which increasingly grew all out of proportion. The West took on the meaning of a promised land" (ibid.). People selling remittance commodities in the market were described as having a "proud look on their face," acting as "ambassadors for a civilization even higher than the civilization of reality" (ibid.).[6]

In addition to the various material remittance commodities in circulation in the 1970s and 1980s, Đang (1999) discusses a complex medicine market where overseas remittances of Western medicines—rare commodities in Vietnam at the time—were traded for other subsistence items. Remittances of medicines and vitamins from Vietnamese scattered in countries throughout the West, symbolizing the health and security that the gifters empathetically wished for their recipients, circulated in a failing embargoed socialist economy in which much of the Vietnamese population lived close to poverty and sometimes even in starvation. Indeed, medical remittances, which frequently flow in both directions, are a common feature of many migrant labor and remittance gift economies, illustrating the substantive human dimension of care inherent in material gifts (Pribilsky 2008). One woman, telling me about the traditional herb medicines that she sent to her brother in the United States, joked that "*Việt Kiều* give me dollars, I give them leaves!"

Following the lifting of an official remittance tax in 1997, the extension of formal financial distribution channels in 2002, and Vietnam's phased integration with the global capitalist economy that climaxed with its joining the World Trade Organization in January 2007, long-distance remittance deliveries have increasingly moved away from the material and informal courier forms of the past and toward more formal direct financial transfers. Informal distribution networks still remain popular, however. Many *Việt Kiều* regularly carry the maximum allowable amount of U.S. dollars and baggage (if not more) each time they return to Vietnam, for distribution to friends and relatives. As one remittance recipient in Saigon explained simply in an interview, "there are two ways for money to travel to Vietnam—the legal road and the illegal road (*đường*). The first is taxed, the second is not." Like the hidden remittance forms of the past, money is often concealed and or sewn in visitors' clothes, to avoid the prying eyes of customs officials who are feared as bribe seekers. Returnees often also carry remittances for other Vietnamese friends abroad who cannot make the trip.

In my interviews with remittance receivers, it became clear that remittances represent far more than money. They are gifts from kin, friends, and lovers and as such carry a range of memories and nostalgia. An old woman living in Saigon's third district whom I called Grandmother (*Bà*) 7, as she was the sixth child in her family,[7] mysteriously received a hundred-dollar bill hand delivered by a man from California. It turned out that the man was a friend of a former boyfriend, who now lived with his wife, children, and grandchildren in California. When Bà 7 and the former boyfriend were young, they had been in love and promised to be together, but her family disapproved. Later, during the war, the boyfriend was sent off to fight with the army and never returned. At the end of the war he managed to escape Vietnam and settle in the United States, where he eventually met the woman who became his wife. But many years later, he tracked down Bà 7 in Saigon and sent her money via courier with his name but without a note, seemingly to indicate that he remembered her after all these years. Bà 7 took the money but did not reply to the man. As she explained, "he remembers me, and that is enough." In this case the money represented a remembered sentiment and an alternative history that had never panned out. As a gift, it sought to fill a lingering emotional and mnemonic gap. Yet the gap remained. The sender's sentiment was not reciprocated by Bà 7, despite her acceptance of the gift. It is for this reason and in these types of scenarios that the gift repeats, seeking to supplement a felt gap that can never sufficiently be filled. Small symbolic amounts of money continued to trickle in over the time I was acquainted with Bà 7. Time cannot return, but money can, and thus the memory of a once-cherished relationship and its unrealized future between Bà 7 and her former love continued.

Little and Big Money

Some families in Saigon that receive remittances participate in a small-scale capitalist economy through the use of finance capital provided by overseas relatives. They form an emerging yet still marginal entrepreneur middle class that has tepidly engaged in Vietnam's developing capitalist economy through infusions of remittance investments. However, these people lack the political and social capital and connections to expand from small- to middle-, let alone to large-scale enterprises, which is a widespread phenomenon in Vietnam's hybrid late socialist capitalist environment (Gainsborough 2003, 2010). Very few of the remittance recipients I encountered worked for large companies or the government. Instead, many of them ran small family businesses such as coffee shops, pool halls, mini-hotels, or restaurants. Interviewees would mention receiving ten or twenty thousand dollars as a loan from a relative to start a business, with no interest and no fixed repayment date. "We pay back when we can," explained one. While most of these small businesses appeared to garner marginal profits, they often provided a semi-performative appearance of work and entrepreneurship intended to satisfy overseas relatives who were at times grudging in their support. Sitting in one remittance recipient's household when an overseas relative from California called on speakerphone, I listened to the recipient patiently explain the hours and nature of his coffee shop, accounting for how he used the remittance money received. He needed another $400 for business expenses, following the last installment of the same amount. The relative (who ran a billiard supply store in Little Saigon in Westminster, California), repeatedly asked how many hours a day the coffee shop was open. Although the Vietnamese family members told the relative it was open all the time, in fact I saw it, like many other cafés, open only early in the morning, when customers typically stop for coffee before starting their workday. Indeed, the temporal business cycle of Vietnamese cafés was something that the overseas relative, who had not returned to Vietnam for many years, appears to have forgotten in his demand that the coffee shop operate in line with the schedule of American establishments, which perhaps had become his business model—and according to which he agreed to send remittances.

Many families I met were reluctant to acknowledge, and sometimes defensive about, their dependence on remittances. They insisted that the monies received were merely small gifts and rarely admitted complete financial dependence on overseas relatives. "Their lives are hard over there, so we don't ask for money, but sometimes they send gifts to help us with bigger medical, wedding, or death anniversary expenses," explained Loan, an older woman with relatives in Massachusetts. Another said proudly, "I don't need or take money from them, I can live by myself. I am old, I don't need so many things as when I was young, and now I also diet. Before I ate a lot, but now I eat a little food and fruit . . . I don't need their help. They [overseas Vietnamese] often think that Vietnamese always ask for their money. I don't like that way of thinking."

Gifts for Tết, however, are almost always expected, with most respondents telling me that such gifts range from $200 to $300 each year. This was just "little money (*tiền ít*)," in their words. Little money for Tết was commonly explained as spent for the purposes of "fun (*chơi*)" and was not expected to be invested in any serious manner. Most people I spoke with, however, did recognize and acknowledge the added comfort and security provided by remittances, which allowed them to avoid marginal subsistence participation in a local economy with limited formal employment opportunities. As one elderly man who receives monthly stipends from his son in Australia commented, "if it wasn't for the money my son sends, I would probably have to sell lottery tickets or something in the marketplace to survive." Here again we see the lurking presence of a hypothetical imaginary of how things might be—in this case, not only "over there" but also "over here" if not for the support of someone over there.

Sentiment and Empathy

In many cases, remittances have become the normal and expected mode and medium of social relations across international kinship networks. Anh, who has been receiving a few hundred dollars every now and then from overseas relatives she has not seen for many years, said that "in the past this money was important, because times were hard. Now a few hundred dollars is not very much, and I don't need it. But they send the money to show they remember me, because they don't know how else to express sentiment anymore." She explained that sending money was an act of "sending gratitude and feelings (*gửi tri ân, gửi tâm lòng*)." It had been many years since her relatives had returned, and money had become a symbolic substitute for the social relations she remembered having had with them before they left the country.

"Little money," however, has also in some cases come to indicate a deferral of much bigger remittance gifts that are expected when an overseas Vietnamese returns home. Many remittance senders and recipients described to me the bloated financial obligations for a diasporic returnee. "I need $10,000, at least, to visit my relatives in Vietnam," explained one man named Tinh in San Jose, California, who returns to Vietnam infrequently. "It is very hard to save enough money to go. Everyone thinks we are rich and can afford anything . . . they ask for everything and I have to give it to them, even the shirt off my back!" One remittance recipient recalled the fun family road trips in a rented Mercedes van that they would go on to Dalat (a mountain resort area) and Nha Trang (a beach town) each time his uncle returned from America, all paid for by the uncle. Yet just as these expansive shared gifts serve to reunite family kinship networks, they can also isolate relatives from each other. In another case, a woman spoke to me about her relatives who had left in 1975, and from whom she has hardly heard since. According to her, "they're afraid of us—they think we will beg (*xin*) for money. But we don't need or want their money. We are just sad that they don't have sentiment (*tình cảm*) with us anymore."

The obligation to express generosity and "sentiment" upon return through personal presentations of remittance gifts reflects long-standing social expectations in Vietnam. As Thuy, a thirty-five-year-old Saigonite explained to me, "it is better to take all your friends to dinner and drinks and show complete generosity, and then go home and eat rice for a week, than to appear stingy in front of others." It is customary in Vietnam for the inviter to pay for the invitees, with an unspoken expectation that every invitee will eventually become an inviter or else risk exclusion from the group. This can also be seen for example in the Vietnamese rotating credit tradition of *hụi*. In this system, members of a group contribute money to a central fund, with each person in turn borrowing the total for a personal investment and then paying it back the pool. Rotating credit circles are practical community initiatives found in many developing countries, especially in rural areas where access to small loans and credit is extremely limited.[8] The system largely works not because of any collateral provided by the borrower, but because of the social relationships between the group members that would be destroyed should someone not meet his or her repayment responsibilities.

What happens, however, when these close-knit social networks and debt relations become dispersed through migration? One interlocutor in Saigon told me of someone who had left her home in Phnom Penh after the postcolonial division of Indochina into separate countries, in the process absconding with funds from a rotating credit circle that she had been part of there.[9] Although she had moved far away, she also changed her name after arriving in Saigon to ensure that creditors would not follow her. In many cases of international remittances, money has been similarly borrowed by a relative, with the only guarantee of repayment being the relations of familial trust between loaner and receiver. In general the kin relationship seems to promise the intention to repay the money. But in many cases, such loans are interpreted by both sides as gifts to be repaid through favors or hospitality, or during an unforeseen future reversal of fortune. A number of remittance senders related that when they received unrealistic requests for large loans from relatives they never responded by merely saying no, but rather gave smaller financial gifts that did not have to repaid. Other senders lamented about the money borrowed by Vietnamese relatives, the return of which was constantly deferred and renegotiated—straining but rarely breaking the social relations whose maintenance loaners hoped would ensure eventual repayment and continued kinship connection.

Furthermore, the nature of the gift is often unclear. In many cases, remittances are not considered as merely gifts from the diasporic sender, but obligatory expressions of gratitude for favors or care previously or currently given. One man, expressing anger at a nephew who no longer remitted money to him, said that the "half-breed" boy was "*xấu*" (meaning "bad, ungrateful, or ugly") because he had forgotten the many things the uncle had done to take care of him when he was growing up after being abandoned by his mother in Saigon. After the boy had immigrated to the United States under the Amerasian Homecoming Act of 1988, he no longer maintained contact with the family that had raised him in Vietnam. For this informant, the boy's questionable "half-breed" identity as a Vietnamese was confirmed by his failure to honor traditional Vietnamese values of filial obligation by sending remittances.[10] Another woman explained how she had been arrested and sent to jail for eleven months because the local police blamed her for helping a relative flee the country by boat. Now, she no longer had the time to work, because she had to take care of sick elderly relatives. The money that the now–*Việt Kiều* relative sent to her from abroad, therefore, was in her eyes a justified form of repayment for the suffering she had undergone after being left behind and the support she had provided that had allowed him to leave—support that she now gave to others. Many people reflected on the burden of having to take care of older relatives or manage family situations in Vietnam while their siblings were able to experience freedom and new lives overseas. "Vietnamese fam-

FIGURE 7.   Tracing diasporic remittance kinship networks.

ilies are difficult. There are so many people to worry about," said one woman who had a number of Vietnamese relatives abroad. "In America, you only have to care for your parents and children—that's it. Sometimes Vietnamese who leave forget their [extended] family responsibilities." Clearly there were awareness of and anxieties and even jealousies resulting from differing definitions of and cultural attitudes toward extended family support in Vietnam and America, and how they potentially affected remittance obligations as members of the diaspora transitioned to becoming Americans.

Illusions of Intimacy

The cycle of giving and asking is emboldened by trust and an assumed understanding of and empathy with the misfortunes of the Other, in this case one that is seemingly quite intimate and familiar. As I have discussed earlier, questions about and recognitions of the Other, as related to the formation and function of subjectivity, have been central to anthropological inquiry. Yet in the long-distance gifting process and with Vietnam's rapid economic development, the situation of the Other is no longer as static, nor is the result so well understood. A majority of the remittance recipients whom I interviewed explained that regular subsistence remittances generally ended the first time an overseas relative returned to Vietnam.

On seeing that the situation for their relatives in Vietnam was not as bad as they had imagined or been told, and reflecting on their own hard work to raise money to support family members left behind, remittances for many overseas Vietnamese stopped being regular subsistence payments and became instead special gifts bestowed during one's visits home, maintained in between by sporadic holiday remittance gifts or "little money."

At the same time technology has seemingly flattened and reframed the distance between Vietnam and abroad, allowing relatives to maintain regular contact through such channels as Microsoft Messenger, Yahoo Chat, and cheap Internet telephone calls. Internet service and webcams are common features in many remittance-receiving households. One man scrolled, as we talked, through the many e-mail messages on his computer from his brother in Texas, showing me updates on his life abroad that included taking the Test of English as a Foreign Language and applying for work. Other e-mail messages from the brother checked to see if money that he had sent had been received. A woman who used Yahoo Chat to talk with her son in Canada related how exciting it was to see her grandson grow bigger every week through the webcam. Indeed, with changes in technology communication is much easier now than in the past.

Yet while technology can give one the illusion of immediacy and direct communication, the virtual realm also offers many opportunities for misrepresentation. An Internet café I visited in Saigon's first district is full of women who cultivate online relationships with *Việt Kiều* and foreign men abroad. One pays by the hour for access to a computer booth that contains a webcam, earphones, and microphone. Many of the female customers at this café had multiple chat windows with different men overseas open at the same time, with the cameras strategically angled to capture the women's attractive physical features. One woman, who let me observe her multiple chat screens, was carrying on a conversation with a *Việt Kiều* in California who wanted to marry her. She patiently explained to him that to be with her he had to have money! The many accoutrements required for the wedding, such as a "flower wedding car (*xe hoa*)" were expensive. Repeatedly during the chat she asked if he understood and was he really up to the task. Meanwhile, she had a second chat window open with another overseas man with whom she seemed to be just beginning an acquaintance.

There is much room for play in the illusions of identity constructed on the Internet. This is true in both directions. A common criticism made by my interviewees about *Việt Kiều* in Vietnam was that "they come here pretending to be someone that they're not. We actually know that many of them are poor over there." Nonetheless, *Việt Kiều* are often allowed to take responsibility for their performative image of wealth despite changing economic circumstances in Vietnam. During a visit to Saigon, a Vietnamese American man named Duy who re-mits money to his parents and siblings in the Vietnamese countryside remarked that an older brother in Saigon who was quite rich did not contribute anything to the family. When I asked why, Duy said it was "because I have always been the one supporting everyone. Even though times are different now, they still act as though I'm the rich one—because I live in America where money is thought to be 'easy.'" The fact that traditional family expectations of support including that the oldest son should take primary financial responsibility had been upturned by overseas migration was not lost on Duy, yet he seemed resigned to the situation.

Capitalist Teasers

The rapid accumulation of wealth in Saigon during the past generation of Viet-nam's fast-paced economic growth means that remittances, although significantly channeled to the city, represent only one of many financial flows. Some families have taken advantage of the capital infusion to participate in the capitalist econ-omy as entrepreneurs. Others have used the money to send children overseas for education, building an overseas opportunity foothold. The explosion of *Hội Việt Mỹ* English training schools throughout the city is testament to this widespread desire to gain the skills required for an overseas education, especially in the United States. Many students in such schools hope to prepare themselves for future educational and business opportunities abroad. Others, it has been creatively suggested, may study English to try to go beyond the Vietnamese life worlds they feel stuck within. In the short story "!," the 1.5 generation Vietnamese Ameri-can author Linh Đinh reflects that "as the universal language-for-now English represents . . . the rest of the world. English is the world."[11] Đinh suggests that therefore the widespread fetishization of English study and usage in Vietnam "is to insist on another reality" (2004, 17).

For some people, remittances seemingly offer an opportunity to participate in the circulatory flows of the broader capitalist economy that is quickly envel-oping them. The use of remittances to attend English-language schools or invest in small businesses conveys the appearance of participation in Vietnam's new eco-nomic life, especially for families who were marginalized after 1975. However, the insistence on "another reality" is telling. If the aspiration for participating in such alternative realities is overseas migration, remittances appear to also have the effect of reducing rather than increasing participation in Vietnam's new economy by redirecting the recipient's gaze beyond it, especially among the younger generation. In addition, in the case of many older remittance recipients—such as the man who does not have to sell lottery tickets—it may orient one away from the local economy by securing a stable subsistence or retirement income flow that enables one to maintain a lifestyle that resists the city's dizzily encompassing transformations.

Remittances are certainly symbolic markers and were in many cases predecessors to the broader overseas infusions of capital that are rapidly changing Saigon's social and cultural landscape in Vietnam's late socialist era. Wherever one goes in Saigon, discussions of money and its transformative powers abound. Saigonese regularly discuss salaries; bonuses; and prices of new motorcycles, cars, houses, land, and so on during social interactions. With increasing confidence in market-era rules and regulations and concerted policy efforts to "bank" Vietnam's citizens, peoples' relationship to money is slowly transitioning from one of hoarding to one of investing.[12] Banks in Vietnam now offer savings accounts in both Vietnam Đong and U.S. dollars, with the interest rates always higher for the former than the latter—and in recent years often higher than those offered by savings accounts in the United States (Tuổi Trẻ 2008). Yet in general new modes of investing are intended to spread assets widely and relatively secretly. Such secret diversifications of assets are again not dissimilar to the sneaky forms that remittances took in the past, like the previously mentioned money hidden in toothpaste and postcards. Such strategies are intended to obscure assets from not only a rent-seeking state but also from rent-seeking friends and relatives. "I just earned a bonus, but I'm not telling my relatives. Otherwise, they'll ask me for money," remarked one Saigonese woman named Thuy. "Instead, I'm going to invest the money in new land and a house."

Land prices in Vietnam skyrocketed during the early 2000s, in part due to investments of remittances in land. As an agent of CB Richard Ellis Real Estate Services in Ho Chi Minh City explained to me in 2007, "the Việt Kiều are buying up land everywhere: especially in new development areas such as Saigon South or the Danang coastline. They usually do this through a Vietnamese relative."[13] The growing exchangeability of money across different value registers (particularly U.S. dollars, with which real estate is now generally purchased) is widely recognized. One woman, explaining the expansive possibilities of money, told me that "things [material gifts] are inconvenient and useless. Money is better because you can do anything with it." As people's relationship to and understanding of money becomes increasingly accumulative, there is a growing parallel sense that money can beget itself endlessly. However, perceptions on the possibilities of accumulation vary significantly according to the context.

Flows of remittances to Saigon serve as personal samples of a broader accumulative capitalist economy that has been rapidly pervading and transforming the city for the past generation, with economic growth rates in Ho Chi Minh City at times twice the national average. Everyday life in Ho Chi Minh City (as in many other places in Asia that are rapidly becoming more urbanized) seems at first to be characterized by economic displacements of "speed, hysteria, and mass dreams" (Roy 2012). Following *Đổi Mới* economic reforms in 1986, Vietnam embarked on a path of integration with the global capitalist economy. After Vietnam joined the World Trade Organization in January 2007, it signed free trade agreements with the Association of Southeast Asian Nations and the European Union, and a China-led Regional Comprehensive Economic Partnership is on the horizon, which would further entangle Vietnam in global trade and investment flows.[14] Through all of this, Ho Chi Minh City—with its history of and experience with capitalist integration, use of the English language, and consumerist "memories of trade" (Spyer 2000), as well as a large number of people who were politically disenfranchised and excluded from state jobs by the communist government and therefore had little choice but to become small entrepreneurs—has been an attractive investment hub. There was over $10 billion of foreign direct investment annually in the mid-2000s, although that amount was briefly cut in half in 2009 due to the global recession (Lee 2009). Districts of the city such as *Đồng Khởi* (Uprising) Street have regained the capitalist luster they had under previous eras of globalization during the American and French periods.[15] Traditional street vendors and cyclo-bicycle taxis have increasingly disappeared, swept away by the city government as artifacts of an impoverished past with the rationale that they disrupted traffic. Meanwhile, new hotels and high-rise office buildings go up at a relentless pace, following the demolition of the colonial-era buildings that preceded them. Expensive fashion boutiques such as Luis Vuitton and international coffee chains like Starbucks and Café Bene have opened their doors to cater to a new class of wealthy Vietnamese and upmarket foreign tourists and expatriates strolling the leafy streets of downtown Saigon cruised by late-model motorcycles and cars. Such phenomena have led to the common observation that the south lost the military and political war but won the economic peace.

Environments of Accumulative (Im)possibilities

In the popular play "Gratitude (*Tri ân*)" that was performed in Saigon theaters in 2007, a Vietnamese American man sends a gift of silk home to his parents in Vietnam. The silk arrives at the local people's committee, which is supposed to make the delivery. However, various officials and village members come to the committee office and take small pieces of silk for themselves, always justifying their doing so by noting that there is far more than the parents could possibly need. By the time the parents arrive at the office to pick up the cloth, there is only a small piece left. They do not know that much of the cloth was already taken by others and are overjoyed to receive the gift from their son. The catch, however, is that the gift box contains a letter directing them how to use the gift. The son wants his parents to have decent clothes and requests the father to make a pair of pants and the mother to make a nice blouse with the silk that he sent. At the end of the play, the son returns home. He asks his parents to show him the clothes they made. The parents seem embarrassed, but he insists, so they leave to change outfits. When they reemerge on stage, they are wearing long overcoats. Urged by the son to remove the coats, the father is revealed to be wearing only a silk thong and the mother a skimpy silk bra, as these were all they could have tailored with the what had been left of the cloth after everyone else in the village had taken a share. Of course, the scene was greeted with widespread laughter in the audience, and it was certainly a metaphor for the all-too-familiar theme of the complexities and disconnects of gifts from overseas relatives.

Since *Đổi Mới*, Vietnam has progressively entered the global capitalist sphere, in which it finds itself reoriented toward a capitalist core centered on the United States, both a former Cold War enemy and ally—depending on which side of the war you were on. In doing so, Vietnamese exiles and their money have become an affective specter for the nation, a phenomenon that has been observed in other countries with large diasporas such as the Philippines (Rafael 2000). As capitalist subjects and salary earners, diasporic subjects embody for many what Vietnamese can and should become and, in many imaginations, could have become had South Vietnam and its allies won the Vietnamese civil war. Capitalism is both foreign and familiar for southern Vietnamese. A man named Vu whom I met at a coffee shop frequented by unemployed men remarked that "back in the 1960s [South] Vietnam was rich—richer than China or Korea. Now we lose (*thua*) to them." However, capitalism as reintroduced in the 1990s is still seen as crony capitalism. "Sure there's some economic development," Vu said, "but the wealth goes to the rich and doesn't spread to the poor people—who can't even afford to pay for their children to go to school—or to other areas of the country outside of Saigon and Hanoi, where life is still as hard as it was before. You have to have connections to make money, and most people don't have them. Only the big (*bự*) people get rich here. The life of the common people (*dân*) doesn't change."

Another man named Hoang noted the differences in capitalist environments for Vietnamese in Vietnam and abroad: "*Việt Kiều* in America make easy money because the government there is good, providing the people with economic opportunities, offering free education, and taking care of people when they are old. It's easy to earn and save money over there in America and send it back here, where even if you have talent there are no opportunities to make money." Ironically, many of the state services such as health care and pensions that Vietnamese imagined to be freely available to American citizens are those that the Vietnamese communist revolution had promised to its own citizens. In a strange twist, life in the United States becomes the basis to criticize the failure of Vietnamese socialism. Orientations toward and attitudes about money were also affected by context: while it is considered easy to earn money in the United States, it is also said to be easy to spend in Vietnam. One woman who receives remittances from her daughter in Michigan explained that "Vietnamese in Vietnam spend money easily (*thoải mái*) and live more in the present. *Việt Kiều* earn and spend money with a purpose, for a future, to build security."

Remittances from overseas friends and relatives index the idealized possibilities and myths of unfettered capitalism, an environment actively and spectrally worlded (Roy and Ong 2013) into the local imaginary in which money is easy to come by, accumulates, and is oriented toward an achievable future horizon. And yet such world-making and imagining processes draw on legacies of Vietnam's experiences on the periphery of the third world as well as in the socialist bloc. The result is often a fixation on an idealized authentic capitalist first-world there rather than a localized here, extending and deferring expectation and action. To take the metaphor of the silk gift in the above mentioned play, in Vietnam the silk is distributed, dissipates, and disappears, whereas in the United States it is imagined to be indiscriminately available and infinitely renewable, with no shortage or limitation.

A question of comparative scale often directed to me by Vietnamese was how much money one makes at a minimum-wage job in the United States. When one hears that such a job pays around $10 for just one hour, more than a laborer makes for a whole day's work in Vietnam, it becomes easy to imagine the spending and investing power one would have abroad, and the ease of putting a little aside to send back to Vietnam every now and again. In America, even a factory worker can make this kind of hourly wage. In other low-level occupations such as manicurists, one can make up to $200 a day I was told by Vietnamese, a fact that I confirmed after returning to the United States. In fact, market research strategists contracted by international money transfer organizations have targeted nail salon workers in the United States as potential users of their remittance services.[16] Similarly, nonprofit activist groups such as the California-based Viet Unity and the Transnational Institute for Grassroots Research and Action that lobby for migrant rights have identified manicurists as an important client population in focusing organizing and awareness efforts around issues of remittances.[17] Indeed, remittances are often sent by Vietnamese who, like their recipients, are not powerful magnates with extensive political, economic, and social connections.

The sociologist Hung Thai (2014), building on the work of the policy analyst Michele Wucker (2004), suggests that lower-class Vietnamese Americans are more likely to send a significant proportion of their salaries home than richer Vietnamese Americans are, even going into debt in the process to project and maintain status—a phenomenon that Thai terms a "transnational expenditure cascade" (2014, 21). Although the apparent discrepancy between economic capacity and generosity may seem surprising, it is connected to the fact that new immigrants are more likely to have direct family members still living in Vietnam who need support, while many longer term immigrants have already sponsored the chain immigration of close relatives and may be less attached to the homeland. Vietnamese remittance recipients generally indicate awareness of the class struggles and social marginalization faced by many Vietnamese overseas. Sometimes such recognitions were expressed in compassionate solidarity with their overseas kin, but at other times, disparaging of *Việt Kiều* failures to successfully adapt to their new environments. Some informants remarked dismissively for example that Vietnamese abroad are not even fluent in the language of the country they live in, sometimes testing *Việt Kiều* relatives who return from the United States on key English words to check their level of linguistic capital. Yet the perception remains that despite all the low-level positions, language disadvantages, and even discrimination experienced by *Việt Kiều*, they still live in an environment that allows them to earn and invest money, buy houses and cars, receive medical care, educate their children, and send money back to Vietnam.

Living in an environment with such opportunities ("*điều kiện*"), it was widely said, transforms personal character. A woman named Trang in Saigon's fourth district who has family in Canada explained that "in Vietnam people only eat, sleep, hang out—they are dependent. But overseas the environment forces you to work, so you won't be lazy anymore." Overseas capitalist worlds of transformation and opportunity have emerged as a myth that allows many people in Vietnam to imagine an alternative and hypothetical habitus—what they themselves could be if only they too could participate in a truly unfettered capitalist environment in which the opportunity to earn, invest, and accumulate money was accessible to all. Hoping to experience such an environment, many remittance recipients I met apply for six-month family visitation visas in countries where they have relatives, during which time they hope to find jobs in the Vietnamese communities there (such as at family-owned restaurants) to earn under-the-table money ("*tiền thù lao*") to send home.[18] In 2015, about 3 percent of Vietnamese overstayed their visas, presumably because they found such opportunities (U.S. Department of Homeland Security 2016). This population of undocumented Vietnamese workers in the United States has become a source of concern since the 2016 U.S. election. When I discussed the issue with an official in the Vietnam consulate in New York in the spring of 2017, he informed me that consulate staff members were preparing themselves in the event that many Vietnamese might

FIGURE 8.   Waiting for an interview for a visa, U.S. consulate, Ho Chi Minh City.

be forcibly sent back to Vietnam by U.S. Immigration and Customs Enforcement. Indeed, recent 2017 detentions and planned deportations have included significant numbers of Vietnamese (Constante 2017), and Ambassador Osius, the former U.S. ambassador to Vietnam, admitted that his 2017 resignation was due in part to the pressure exerted by the U.S. administration to repatriate over 8,000 undocumented Vietnamese against their wishes (Osius 2018).

Back in Saigon, the chance to participate in Vietnam's changing economic landscape often eludes people who were deported from the United States or are unable to seek economic opportunities there. At first glance, foreign investment flows appear everywhere in Saigon. Yet they often remain beyond the reach of much of the population, who wrap scarves around their faces and wear masks to protect themselves from the rampant street pollution and hot sun on their motorbike trips to find precarious work in the informal economy . . . perhaps in the process passing business executives of multinational corporations riding in their shiny Mercedes Benzes with tinted windows and air-conditioning. Ironically, some of the people in those Mercedes are *Việt Kiều*, sometimes hired by companies to bridge cultural and linguistic gaps and deliver social remittances and capital as they forge new business relationships with varying degrees of success (Carruthers 2008). Remittances appear to many Vietnamese as a small sample of how those living in fully developed capitalist economies benefit from developed modern market infrastructures and the privileges of global circulation. "The Vietnamese government is still corrupt, and therefore our country remains poor," explained a middle-aged man who receives remittances from his daughter in the

United States. "It is a good thing she [the daughter] lives over there. Here [in Vietnam] she would have no job prospects."

The perceived ease of remitting money from abroad to Vietnam suggests to many Saigonese that the development trajectory they are currently riding is far from finished or even promising. In frustration, they await economic reforms that will one day allow them or their children to accumulate money like their over-seas relatives—who, despite possessing little social or cultural capital in their countries of resettlement, appear to have become financially successful abroad and demonstrate this during their return visits. In the meantime, Vietnamese hedge their bets by strategizing how to send more flexible and adaptable younger household members overseas to make their own way in the land of "easy money." The contrast between what Vietnamese in Vietnam are able to achieve and what their counterparts overseas accomplish, regardless of talent, is measured and com-pared in monetary amounts, confirming for those in Vietnam that current Com-munist Party economic reforms and platforms have brought changes to Vietnam but remain far from satisfactory.

Money as Medium, Mediator, and Other

The symbolic and transformative powers of money have been widely recognized and theorized, with a great deal of attention paid in particular to what money is (money is often defined as a unit of account, store of value, means of exchange, and method of payment) and what it does, in particular to sociality. Some social scientists have lamented the prevalence of a generally dismissive consensus among classic analysts of money that "money and the violence of its abstractions erode the sociability subtending human existence, and the very idea of society itself" (Maurer 2006, 19). In contrast, many economic anthropologists have demon-strated that money does not necessarily erode but can instead produce and rec-ord sociality in various forms, arguing that "money does not simply . . . flatten relations and meanings, it can enrich them, multiply them, complexify them" (Maurer 2005b, 103). Allison Truitt argues that money acts as an "infrastructure" (2013, 153) that is not only technical but also offers sociocultural insights into how Vietnam has navigated the radical economic and social transformations ac-companying market reform. The ethnographic evidence in this book confirms the many ways money complicates social meanings and relations and effectively acts as an infrastructure for the reimagining and reconstructing of selves and col-lectives. However, in addition to contributing another case study to the debates about what money does, I note the degree to which users, observers, and analysts of money alike are continually surprised by its diverse manifestations and effects across multiple environments. The subject continues to endlessly intrigue observers. And so, just as the ethnographic stories here and the contexts in which they take place meander, so do theories on money.

Three broad themes that have emerged in social-scientific inquiries into the subject of money are its mystique, exchangeability, and mobility. Georg Simmel argues that "money represents pure interaction in its purest form; it makes comprehensive the most abstract concept; it is an individual thing whose essential significance is to reach beyond individualities" (2004, 129). In reaching "beyond individualities" we see that money plays not merely the role of a social leveler and medium of equivalence, but also that of an unsettling material form as well as a process in and through which the participants of its exchange apprehend ontological possibilities beyond their immediate existence and associated structures of familiar and assigned identities. According to Simmel, money acts as an infrastructure that strives to objectively mediate intersubjectivity: "the technical form of economic transactions produces a realm of values more or less completely detached from the subjective-personal substructure"(ibid., 79). Yet the details Simmel provides betray the institutional limits of infrastructure in terms of formally detaching exchange from the personal, recognizing that "it is above all the exchange of economic values that involves the notion of sacrifice" (ibid., 82).

Simmel suggests that desire for the Other motivates money's exchange, which in turn attempts to mediate and materialize such desire while also masking its origins. Central to this expression of desire is a valuation and awareness of the social significance of sacrifice. Ultimately, despite money's utilitarian function, its deep participation in the process of exchange contributes, if only subconsciously, to the unsettling of social identities and assumptions through relationality, making possible an intriguing but ultimately elusive glimpse into alternative ontologies and potentialities. In the case of remittance economies, material and social gifts—but most often money, as their ultimate expression—act as a medium of exchange between vastly different worlds, attempting to translate between them but continually falling short, as the frustrated accounts of this ethnography illustrate. As Walter Benjamin argues, translation is a process of exchange with liberating and transformative potentials. He observes that "in translation the original rises higher and purer . . . it points the way to this region: the predestined, hitherto inaccessible realm of reconciliation and fulfillment of languages" (1969, 75). The translator is in a unique position to "release in his own language that pure language which is under the spell of another, to liberate the language imprisoned in a work in his re-creation of that work. For the sake of pure language he breaks through decayed barriers of his own language" (ibid., 80). So it is for the gift. By metaphorically attempting translation between exchange parties, it releases each from their own "decayed barriers" of assigned identities unable to achieve desired expression, "pointing the way" to something that may be sensed if not grasped and unleashing an affective energy—"aesthetic emotion" in Mauss's words (1967, 79), that cannot easily be re-domesticated, particularly when it takes the form of money.

Furthermore, the fetish of money is elusive not only in its mystique but also in its mobility. Karl Marx observes that "money constantly removes commodities from the sphere of circulation, and in this way continually moves away from its own starting-point . . . as the medium of circulation, [it] haunts the sphere of circulation and constantly moves around within it" (1992, 213). Money's fetish eludes, yet compels us to chase its illusion of origins, disrupting the settled world we previously inhabited. The global mobility and circulation of money teases the imaginations, desires, and confusions of all who participate with it. The unleashing of new imaginaries through gifting exchange hierarchies across borders is also tied up in money's role in the case of remittances as a gift. Marcel Mauss describes gifting as a "a phenomenon of social structure" that "brings about a remarkable state of nerviness and excitement . . . one fraternizes, yet one remains a stranger" (1967, 38). The gift of money, as the long-distance medium of exchange and interaction across imagined life worlds, is therefore also a central feature and marker of the differences between them.

The concept of "over there" is a horizon both imaginatively intriguing and experientially unfathomable to Vietnamese who have never left their country but who nonetheless interact with a broader world through global media and flows of commodities, finances, and bodies. In the imagined "over there" of ideal capitalist landscapes, money is understood to be invested rather than hoarded, accumulative rather than scarce, and a means toward upward social mobility and transformation. It is something one desires, yet it remains foreign and cannot necessarily be conceptually traced to a tangible source. As Christina Schwenkel (2014) has argued, the current relationship between Vietnam and the West involves a reorientation of alternative globalization spheres. Long embedded in a socialist world extending from Budapest to Pyongyang, the iron curtain limits of which were difficult to transgress, Vietnam has suddenly replaced global socialist visions of modernization with capitalist variants (P. Taylor 2001), leaving notional residues of capitalist Otherness. Vietnam's experiences with development and war show that money, especially from foreign places, has the power to both create and destroy, and that to direct and generate it gives one such power, too. Monetary remittance economies symbolize the possibilities of agency and social transformation through accumulation and assimilation of remittances. Yet they also raise spectral awareness of the fact that contemporary possibilities of accumulation are not equally distributed across political and economic terrains.

Remittances are structurally channeled from unfamiliar foreign and capitalist economies, yet they flow across seemingly familiar networks of sentiment. This peculiar combination has the uncanny effect of confusing social relations with capital. The idea that money is easy to come by in an idealized capitalist environment beyond the reach of Vietnamese in Vietnam heightens their expectations of remittance gifts that flow proportionate with the limitless sentiment that motivates them.[19] The hard lot of the overseas immigrant, while recognized, is understood to be social, not economic. The money that one so easily earns abroad, through even unskilled labor, flows and accumulates "over there" in a way that is not possible in much of Vietnam. This is attributed to the ideal capitalist economy in which overseas Vietnamese live. In contrast, money invested in entrepreneurial activities in Saigon is limited in scale, because its investors are not "big" people, with political and social connections that allow them to turn small investments into big returns. Money may flow to Saigon, benefiting stakeholders in state-owned enterprises embarking on partnerships with foreign investors. Some of the excess may even trickle down and contribute to smaller-scale entrepreneurship, but overall money fails to meet transformative expectations in much of rural Vietnam, where 80 percent of the country's population still resides.

The imaginative transformative magic that money promises can be sampled in Vietnam, but it realizes its fullest potential in the idealized capitalist world abroad from where it comes and where it is always already accumulating and transforming its givers. The individualities of the here and there are confused in the remittance exchange, as receivers imagine not only the world of the giver but also what they might be in such a world. The unleashing of new desires and imaginations through gifting exchange is directly tied up in the monetary form of the gift. The gift of money, as the long-distance medium of exchange and interaction between imagined worlds, is a central feature and marker of the differences between them. Money's mystical accumulative and transformative powers that can beget and develop capitalist subjectivity in some environments; sustain and alter social worlds in other environments; and altogether bypass socially transformative aspirations in still others demonstrate its unpredictable and fetishistic role as a representative of social relations and desires between Vietnamese dispersed across different life worlds. The heightened monetization of social relations via increasing remittance flows in financial form magnifies the spectral awareness of differentiated political-economic landscapes across the exchange spectrum. Far from flattening social relations, it encourages comparisons across them. The city of Saigon, with its complex histories and entanglements of pre- and postwar variants of capitalism and socialism, offers an extraordinary vantage point for observing these processes.

COASTAL FLOWS AND HYPOTHETICAL HORIZONS

Anthropological discussions of imagined worlds in an era of globalization can be compelling but at times elusive endeavors to describe the psychological by-products of heightened transcultural flows that accompany economic interconnectivity. The imagination as a central site of analysis offering insight into the shaping and framing of ontological apprehensions and interrogations of selves, others, collectives, and futures has been explored by a range of philosophers, cultural critics, and social scientists including Gaston Bachelard (1994), Raymond Williams (1983), C. Wright Mills (1959), Jacques Lacan (1966), Benedict Anderson (1998), and—in the context of globalization—Arjun Appadurai (1996), Charles Taylor (2004), and Vincent Crapanzano (2004). The imaginary as a sociocultural force that catalyzes reflexive desires and influences real-world actions has been examined in various contexts, ranging from the origins of tradition (Morris 2000; Anderson 2006) and technological futures (Escobar 1995; Boellstorff 2012) to hope (Miyazaki 2004; Pine 2014) and migration (Axel 2002; Chu 2010; Thompson 2017). In Vietnam, as in many places now integrated into the global economy, newly imagined or reimagined worlds abound, catalyzed by a wide range of mobile sources ranging from media images and foreign investment flows to diasporic returnees. This chapter examines a particular geography and economy that reflect how remittances affect the contours, aesthetics, and material displacements of the imagination as encountered in Vietnam's south central coastal area, with a focus on the coastal city of Quy Nhơn. Extending chapter 2's discussion of remittances and their connections to broader imaginations and geographies of capitalist accumulation, this chapter develops the argument that an important element of the imaginary's catalyst, beyond transcultural flows, is a fundamental contradiction embedded in the premise of mobility as it relates to the neoliberal ethic: the lack of equivalence between flows of finance and commodities and the flow of bodies. The chapter then explores the relationship of such experiential mobility contradictions with horizons of personal and collective dreaming and displacements, and demonstrates how they shape an affective spectrum of aspiration, hope, chance, and frustration.

The most significant flow of remittances in Vietnam, after those to Ho Chi Minh City, is to coastal communities, especially along the south central coast (Pfau and Giang 2009). During the late 1970s and 1980s hundreds of thousands of refugees fled the country in small fishing boats; those with access to such boats were more easily able to leave. The rickety wooden boats, meant for offshore fishing, were commandeered for long journeys over multiple days and weeks to neighboring countries such as the Philippines or Malaysia. Many boats were intercepted by the Vietnamese coast guard (who arrested the passengers), ran short of fuel and supplies, capsized, or were attacked by pirates before reaching their destination. Although the casualty rate was extremely high (according to some estimates, up to half a million people died; see Q. Tran 2012), thousands of Vietnamese took the risky journey on the high seas. Those who made it usually ended up in refugee camps such as Palawan in the Philippines or Bidong in Malaysia, where they would wait months or even years to be processed for resettlement in a third country or in some cases sent back to Vietnam.[1] One result of this fishing-boat exodus is that a multitude of coastal communities in southern Vietnam, particularly along the south central coast, have strong ties to diasporic networks and remittance support. Focusing on the city of Quy Nhơn, I followed remittance connections in the area as well as across a number of south central coastal communities including Vung Tau, Phan Rang, Nha Trang, and Danang, and smaller villages in Bình Định, Binh Thuan, and Phu Yen Provinces. Working in this region was extremely rewarding. Seemingly unceasing ethnographic moments and invitations made me reflect constantly on how significant the postwar movements of bodies, money, and things were to the people who remained in Vietnam. One aspect of the landscape that particularly intrigued me throughout my time there was the heightened spatial and mnemonic relationships that residents seemed to have to a border and horizon that was once porous and transcendent: the sea, and what lay beyond.

Quy Nhơn, the capital of Binh Đinh Province, is located in a coastal region marked by dry, rocky land; fishing villages; sand dunes; and scattered Cham ruins that serve as reminders of the historical southward migration of the Viet people at the expense of the region's former ethnic Cham inhabitants.[2] In 2009 the city's population was around 300,000. Located on a peninsula extending into the Eastern

Sea, Quy Nhơn was not only a fishing community but also a strategic military post during the Vietnam War.[3] A number of residents I met would recall the days when American and South Korean soldiers strolled the streets.[4] Today, the city contains a large number of remittance-recipient neighborhoods along the streets close to the water on either side of town, as well as in the surrounding fishing villages. The material effect of remittances on recipient households in Quy Nhơn (as in other small cities and towns I visited) is more apparent than in Ho Chi Minh City.[5] Recipients' homes are often noticeably newer and fresher looking than their neighbors as overseas money has been invested in their upgrade and expansion. Yet *Nhà Việt Kiều* (remittance households; literally, "houses of *Việt Kiều*") were usually not overly ostentatious. On a few occasions when I saw a particularly large and decorative new house and inquired about it, I was told that the occupants were government officials or managers of state-owned companies, rather than families with overseas relatives. Implicit in such comments were subtle social critiques of state corruption. Nonetheless, modestly upgrading or buying a house is a common use of remittance funds.[6] As my informants noted, these homes purchased with remittances benefited the senders as much as the recipients, serving as homes away from home whenever the *Việt Kiều* family returned to Vietnam.

Through an academic contact at the university where I was based in Ho Chi Minh City I was introduced to members of the Bình Định Province People's Com-

FIGURE 9. A *Nhà Việt Kiều* and its neighbors.

mittee in Quy Nhơn, who invited me to meet members of remittance-recipient households in the area. The local authorities provided an initial sample of fifteen households for me to interview. In most cases, initial formal interviews led to repeated social interactions that covered other topics and contacts, in turn leading to a host of delightfully unexpected insights. Following up on interviews by socializing with my informants usually took me to places outside of their house (where the first meeting was usually held) and away from the government officials who had initially accompanied me. The two areas of town where my informants often chose to meet were cafés by the ocean and those near "the airport (*sân bay*)." This was not actually an airport but the town's only mall—a hangar-like assortment of supermarkets, bars and coffee shops, clothing and book stores, and even a nightclub—that was bordered on both sides by broad boulevards popular with motorbike cruisers. Before 1975 it had been the main airport, which had since moved further north to occupy a former military airstrip. Nonetheless, the space still retained the reference to flight in local parlance. I found it an interesting coincidence that these chosen areas for socializing were also spaces of historical mobility infused with storied memories of departure by boat and plane.[7]

One of the central themes that emerged in my conversations with informants was mobility, as they discussed their experiences with and attitudes toward migration and remittances. The idea of social transformation through bodily and monetary mobility was prevalent, but in this context it was also connected to heightened reflections on how the shifting and variegated channels of mobility available to them made them aware of the role of infrastructure and limitations of agency in navigating those channels. Yet also prevalent in these conversations were reflections on another form of power and causation, which may have lurked below the surface. This was the seemingly mysterious role that chance, and particularly fate (*số phận*), seemed to have played over the years in peoples' lives in Quy Nhơn when it came to immobility.

"Coming to Vietnam Is Easy, Going to America Is Hard"

One day some fishermen from Nhon Ly, a fishing village in the jurisdiction of Quy Nhơn but about ten kilometers from the town center, invited me out on their boat to explore the surrounding area. We loaded up with fishing gear, water, beer, and dried squid to snack on. Thanh, a twenty-nine-year-old fisherman with a wife and child whose older brother went to the United States in the 1970s, started up the engine and guided the boat away from the other colorful blue-and-red wooden boats. As we headed out to the sea and away from the rocky coastline, he extended his hand to the horizon and said, "Keep going that way, and America is there." I asked Thanh if many people had gone there, he said yes, more than half of the families in Nhon Ly had a relative abroad who had fled by boat ("*vượt biển*").[8] He pointed to one of the districts by the sea on the north side of the village behind us and said: "That area over there—almost every household has someone who went by sea. You can see the big houses they build now with the money sent back." When I asked why so many people in that particular area had left, he explained: "Before they were poor, so they would go. Now they are rich. In fact, many of them no longer even need to fish." I asked if the people who had left came back often. Thanh said: "Yes, many of them do, but some never return. But it's easy for them to go back and forth now. For us, we've not yet been anywhere. Coming to Vietnam from America is easy, but going to America from Vietnam is very hard."

Thanh went on to explain how people with boats had been able to flee the country right after the war up until the mid-1980s, since during that time other countries "accepted Vietnamese when they arrived." Groups of people would leave with some family members or friends, and their chances of successfully escaping were about "50-50." One person in the group typically had access to a fishing boat, sometimes just a small one. These escape attempts were highly gendered and generational: I was told that young men were particularly inclined to attempt the journey. It was seen as an escape but also as a kind of adventure and gamble—risky, but with great potential rewards at the end. As Philip Martin (2017) has discussed, the gap between ideals and practices when it comes to Vietnamese masculine cultural scripts shapes the behavioral choices of men navigating changing societal norms, as was certainly the case during South Vietnam's precipitous post-1975 transition to socialism. To brave the sea journey was to perform an idealized notion of traditional masculinity, demonstrating one's willingness to take a chance (even possibly sacrificing oneself) with the intent of paving the way for women, children, and elders to follow via a safer exit channel. Fishing boat refugees would try to make it to the Philippines, Indonesia, or Malaysia and then wait for a country such as the United States, Canada, Australia, or France to sponsor them, where an eagerly anticipated but still unimaginable new life awaited them. After that they could eventually sponsor family members to follow. "But then the door closed (*đóng cửa*)," Thanh said, and the sea route was no longer an option. People were stuck: the dreams of mobility were still alive but no longer as feasible, even for those willing to take a risk.

Reflections on mobility and, by extension, chance pervade substantive remittance economies. There is a strong correlation between reception of remittances and reflections on mobility. Many people I met in Quy Nhơn and elsewhere with relatives abroad were interested in finding a way to go overseas personally or have

COASTAL FLOWS AND HYPOTHETICAL HORIZONS   79

a younger member of the family go. This intention of emigration was notably less immediate among other people I spoke with who did not have overseas kinship networks. In their hopes for migration people spoke not only of economic opportunity but also of escape from stifling norms and expectations and of finding an environment in which they could realize personal potentials. Again, routes and imaginaries of physical and social mobility often diverged along gendered lines, reflecting the emergence of new migratory directions and opportunities since the era of the boat refugees. Ha, a middle-aged woman with an adolescent daughter living with her, explained that "it is difficult being a woman in Vietnam, because everyone judges how you behave. You have to get married early—otherwise you're unmarriageable (*e*). I want my daughter to be educated in a different environment (*môi trường*) so that she can develop and have opportunities." In Ha's opinion, the option to be different was one such opportunity. Pointing to a map of Vietnam, she said that the country was far too small: if one doesn't conform in Vietnamese society, one is teased ("*chế*"). For her, such teasing inhibited the healthy development of distinct articulations of identity. Ha had sent her other daughter to live with Ha's sister in Florida, where she attended high school and was preparing to apply for college. The purpose of overseas education for the daughter was not necessarily to return to Vietnam with new skills and knowledge (gray matter social remittances), but perhaps to remain out of Vietnam permanently by taking advantage of subsequent job opportunities, marriage prospects, or a variety of other chance life circumstances, tied to idealized imaginaries of what an American capitalist environment could offer (Ninh 2011).

Such chance opportunities, stumbled across along the way, were ones that Ha said she could not possibly predict but that surely were attractive, at least compared to life in Quy Nhơn. In the meantime, Ha's family was also planning a move to Saigon. Ha explained that in the city there would be more employment options and education opportunities for the daughter who had remained behind in Vietnam to financially support and physically help her parents, and that perhaps other options for overseas migration would follow.[9] While Ha's daughters' planned routes of migration were different than those of the young men escaping in boats a generation before as described by Thanh, they were similarly rooted in the goal of social transformation through mobility that escaped the perceived limitations of presently emplaced personhoods.

Many of my other informants said that they would willingly give up stable and respected professions in Vietnam to travel to an unknown world of opportunity and risk. "If they [the American government] let me go (*cho phép*), then I'll go!" declared a pharmacist named Hai who had applied for emigration a number of years ago and was still waiting for an official response. Usually when I asked informants what they hoped to do if they moved abroad, they said they didn't know.

Nonetheless, they were always sure that their diasporic contacts would help them find something. "We have relatives and friends there. They'll help me figure everything out once I arrive," said Cuong, a middle-aged small-business owner who had applied for family sponsorship to immigrate to the United States. And according to folk wisdom, any Vietnamese can "do nails [manicure work] and make easy money" in America.[10]

Chance

The spectral unknown overseas world that haunts international remittance communities appears to contribute to a general attitude that migration (and, by extension, much of life) is a matter of chance. This seemed particularly true among the generation of middle-aged men in Quy Nhơn who felt that the opportunity for migratory transformation had passed them by. Many had tried to migrate but had been unsuccessful. Nonetheless, to have tried signaled something to others about who one was. As a man named Nam put it, seemingly assigning agency to character, "some people took a risk to change their life. Some people accepted (chấp nhận) their life." But whether risk taking paid off seemed beyond one's control. Yet one could try again and again. Many of the male remittance recipients I met had unsuccessfully attempted to leave on previous occasions. The boat journey of refugees of course was risky (many people were lost at sea, stranded, or attacked by pirates en route). There were even some stories of people committing cannibalism on board to survive.[11] Nam estimated that "out of every five boats, two would sink." However, many more people were caught by the local police before they had gotten far out to sea, with punitive consequences including prison or a term of hard labor for the offender, relatives, or both. Among my informants in Quy Nhơn many had been caught and returned to Vietnam.

Viet was an older man who taught English at the local university. In the 1960s he had worked with researchers from a midwestern American university who had been conducting agrarian development projects in Vietnam, and in the process he had developed a good command of English. He told me that he had been on sixteen boats that had tried to escape. On each journey he had been invited to travel for free although others had to pay for their passage in gold bars, because he was deemed able to translate for the passengers if a foreign freighter should pick them up at sea.[12] He claimed that there was even a secret acknowledgment of this arrangement with the local police, who let him go with a fine or bribe each time the boat he was on was caught. As I heard in many other stories, there was money to be made at many levels in Vietnam's evolving illicit migration industry in the 1980s. The last time Viet tried to escape, however, was with his wife and daughter. Since that time it seemed that he was seeking to escape permanently with his entire family, when he was caught he was sentenced to two years in prison and hard labor.

Memories of prison were widespread among my informants, and in my interviews there was often a wistful theme of shared failure. Thach, a middle-aged man with whom I sat having coffee and listening to live music one night, spotted one of his friends from the labor prison camp they had both been assigned to after trying to flee by boat. Thach introduced his friend to me, and they recalled their attempted escapes when they were young teenagers. At that time, they had seized any chance they had to leave Vietnam: both men had each tried to escape three times. It was a "youth movement (*phong trào*)," Thach explained, or "something to keep up with (*đua dòi*)" among young men their age. There was a tendency ("*khuynh hướng*") of sorts to try to escape abroad. He acknowledged that part of the reason for this "movement" was that "times were very hard (*khổ*). There wasn't enough to eat for the whole family, so young and healthy sons would try to leave if they were able."

In such reminisces there appeared to be a theme of not only economic motivations for migration, but also a collective youthful and masculine sense of adventure and curiosity that motivated the young boat refugees. Indeed, the narratives appeared almost to recount a rite of passage or a coming of age story for a certain generation, contributing to a sense of communitas (Turner 1969) among men who had shared the experience. While some had successfully escaped, others had been turned back. Lam—a middle-aged man wearing a Tommy Hilfiger shirt and gold watch sent by his brother in California—sat with me one night in a seaside restaurant partaking of a hot pot and Heineken beer. He told me that he had tried to escape thirteen times over the previous thirty years. Finishing off a case of beer with his friends, he looked out at the dark sea, specked by the fluorescent lights of far-off fishing boats. "Other people made it and have new lives," he said, "but I got caught every time. Nothing has changed." Those "other people" haunted Lam's imagination. It was not so much that he had a sense of "them over there" and "us over here," but rather that he felt that "I could have been them over there . . . but I'm still here."

Hypothetical Selves and Transformative Social Horizons

In the stories just related, migration is imagined as a journey for the fulfillment of not only economic opportunity but also particular identities and personhoods that are perceived to be unrealizable in Vietnam. There is a keen awareness of

differentiated yet entangled global social, cultural, political, and economic structures and of how the chance to negotiate them successfully affects future selves. The
horizon of a Vietnamese life overseas offers a comparatively unknown future,
but one seemingly invested with great promise for social transformation. Many
Vietnamese I met spoke earnestly of how a foreign environment could effectively
bring out latent traits in the Vietnamese character, "making one a better person,"
in the words of one informant. Character transformation is most fully displayed
and realized when a migrant returns to Vietnam to visit. The performance and
evidence of character transformation in turn contributes to an emerging transnational social ideal. Generosity, as expressed via gifting overtures by overseas
Vietnamese, was one mode of gauging such latent character evolutions. As a
middle-aged woman named Lan reflected, "the Vietnamese character is generous. But Vietnam is a poor country, so it is difficult to always show generosity.
Overseas Vietnamese are fortunate. They can afford to give [to relatives] without
worrying. Even in the market, they don't have to bargain as much." It is interesting to note in this case how perceptions of generous character behavior within
kinship circles extend beyond the home to include strangers and market transactions, revealing emic challenges to etic formal versus informal socioeconomic
binaries.

Nonetheless, there remains a lingering ambivalence about such character transformations, sometimes reflected in comments about the social and physical
markers of overseas Vietnamese. A young man named Hung noted that his relatives who return to Vietnam are "the same mostly, but a bit different—their skin
is lighter, they're more polite, they get sick easier." Reflections on transformed
bodies as indices of alternative environments were common in the interviews I
conducted. The acquisition of cultural and financial capital and the difference in
overseas living also have a price that was widely acknowledged. Most of my informants believed that life abroad, while endowed with opportunity, is isolated
and difficult—which explains why so many *Việt Kiều* return on a regular basis.
Overseas Vietnamese are often envied for their access to economic opportunity
and the fact that economic transformations have improved their character or even
altered their body. However, they are still commonly seen as separated from their
geographic and sociocultural roots. "Over here life is happy (*sướng*)," exclaimed
a sixty-year-old retired fisherman in Quy Nhơn whose son had escaped by boat
twenty years before and now sends $200 monthly from Brooklyn, New York, to
support his parents. Riding on the back of my motorbike as we went out to eat
and drink (*nhau*) with his family one night, he pointed to the rows of seafood
restaurants along the water filled with groups of mostly men eating, drinking, and
toasting with loud outbursts of "Cheers (*Dô*)"! "The *Việt Kiều* don't drink like
this," he said, "but the Communists (*Việt Cộng*) do. Vietnam may be poor, but

life [here] is good."[13] He went on to tell me that with the money from his son, he no longer had to fish and could now afford to live in the city center, pay for his medical expenses, and treat his friends. He said, "I prefer life here because it is familiar—I have friends nearby and people to talk with. Over there, what would I do? But I do wish I could visit my son to see what his life is like."

Curiosity about diasporic life "over there" was commonplace in Quy Nhơn. The migratory horizon of social transformation and subsequent return is represented by the networks of remittance money across which curious and hopeful imaginaries flow. Remittances index characteristics of mobility and exchangeable value that are increasingly able to overcome the structural limitations of both "here" and "there." In doing so they heighten personal awareness (and in many cases anticipation) of transnational bodily mobility as displayed by *Việt Kiều* and sought after by many Vietnamese for whom remittances increase their desire to travel to and see their source. Remittances become a material manifestation of migratory aspirations, and as such are desired for far more than just what they practically afford.

"Money is best," explained an older man named Na, answering a question about whether he preferred money or material gifts from his overseas relatives, "because with it you can do anything." This sense of money as enabling limitless social transformation reflects new capitalist perceptions of class mobility that remain ambiguous in Vietnam's late-socialist societal structure, as discussed in the previous chapter. There is a large and growing disparity between rich and poor in Vietnam, where a strong middle class (whose members typically embody economic and social mobility) has yet to find a securely defined place. On the one hand, there is the multitude of small, family-owned businesses participating in a burgeoning market economy.[14] On the other hand, there are large enterprises, formerly or still owned by the state, partnering with foreign investors on deals in which inside connections and privilege are required for successful accumulation of assets. As the political scientist Martin Gainsborough has pointed out, despite the appearances of reform and state retreat from economic management, there remains much "continuity, in the form of existing power structures, elite control of the economy, and particular forms of rule" (2010, 4). Despite rapid growth, firmly establishing medium-size enterprises and a solid middle-income sector remains a challenge in Vietnam. Without political connections, access to capital and lines of credit remain limited, although this is starting to change.[15] Remittance recipients often belong to the still relatively small and emerging Vietnamese middle class, whose members may be escaping dire poverty through the help of overseas relatives but do not have the social and political capital and connections to take further advantage of Vietnam's so-called market economy with a socialist orientation.[16] Many remittance-recipient families I encountered owned small businesses such as cafés and billiard halls or worked household farms or gardens (*làm vườn*) that turned only a marginal profit. It was worthless, according to many of them, to invest in anything more significant without established government connections that they did not have. The political disenfranchisement of families that had supported the former southern regime was directly connected to both refugee flight and economic marginalization in Vietnam's new economy, which remittances served to ameliorate and highlight.

Although the power of capitalist transformation is quite visible in core economic centers like Saigon, as well as imagined in overseas nodes of diasporic resettlement such as Little Saigons in California, in Quy Nhơn there were timid "build it and they will come" hopes for future modern utopian living through large-scale capital investment in new industry and tourism projects. Across the newly built Thi Nai bridge from the city is the Nhơn Hội industrial zone, a fishing village now zoned for not only factories and refineries but also beach resorts, residential districts, and shopping centers. An official from the Binh Đinh tourism authority explained that "the manufacturing industry and tourism sector in the province are still small. Hotel occupancy rates are only 40 percent, for example, and the road system is not very developed. But that is all changing. Come back in fifty years, and Quy Nhơn will be totally transformed." An, an older man with daughters in Australia and other relatives in America and Europe, eagerly took me out on his motorbike one windy day to look at the new road to the Nhơn Hội district, lined with billboards painted with images of suburban office complexes, homes, and cars, while another map divided the area into industrial and residential districts. Yet besides the billboards, there was only a single long bridge leading to an empty industrial park. For the most part in 2009, Nhơn Hội's future as a node for capitalist flow and circulation remained hypothetical. A lonely, mostly empty supermarket and billiard hall on a wide and dusty road still under construction were all that existed so far of this future capitalist pleasure and production utopia. Indeed, I found little change on a return visit in 2017. As foreign investment waned in the post-2008 global economic downturn, and with fluctuating global markets in certain sectors such as crude oil since then, Vietnam lacked the capital base to complete such industrial and tourism projects (see, for example, Lý 2016).

Large-scale capitalist transformation still remains outside the purview of waiting-to-be middle-class Quy Nhơn residents, for whom paltry remittance flows from core neoliberal utopias overseas are only a hint of what could be but can never be fully grasped within what they critically see as the limitations of Vietnam's still-undeveloped system of capitalism under late socialism. The realization of Quy Nhơn's developmental dreams remains dependent on infusions of corporate capital from as-yet-unknown foreign investors. In the meantime, desires for continued social and class mobility, particularly as dreamed of by or assigned to the younger generation, are displaced onto an idealized overseas capitalist landscape. In such a utopian economy, as in the Saigon imaginary of the capitalist West discussed in the last chapter, dynamic upward class mobility is imagined to be accessible to all. The proof is manifested by the bodies of uncanny diasporic kin who return from the West, seemingly economically and socially transformed.

Agency and Money

Remittance recipients reflect their aspirations for mobile and transformative neoliberal subjectivities in their stated desires not only to spend money, but also to earn it and send it to others. I constantly heard references to how much one earns in a day in America versus how much things cost in Vietnam. The power of money earned there but spent here haunts the imagination of many remittance recipients, who if they had the chance would prefer to be on the generating side of the money relationship. "I want to go to America so *I* can send money back," said Quynh, an unemployed remittance recipient who related her dreams of being a house cleaner in the United States. As another man named Sang told me: "Talent in America is rewarded—you can achieve success and make money. In Vietnam it doesn't matter whether one is talented. There is no opportunity to use it [talent]."

This desired transformation through work, performatively demonstrated by remittance giving, emulates the momentum and agency of money as a mediator of exchange relations. Successful migrants are perceived as possessing heightened agency, as represented in the money they direct and sometimes follow across the route of original departure. They display their power and talent to control and direct the monetary gift and its representation. This includes the channels through which money is transferred. As discussed previously, the preferred way to send remittances is through personal courier networks, and it has become a general expectation that a returnee to Vietnam will carry gifts and money for family and friends, thus personalizing the financial gift exchange and embuing it with trust. If personal networks are unavailable, many remitters still prefer private services providing home delivery to the anonymity of formal banks or money-transfer companies. Remittances are usually accompanied by a short note from the sender indicating his or her remembrance of the recipient and followed by a phone call or e-mail to confirm the arrival of the gift. This capacity of money to travel, return, represent the agency of the sender, and mediate relations with the receiver demonstrates the highly transformative, mobile, and imaginative dynamics of remittance economies.

In post-renovation Vietnam, where remittances now easily take monetary form and arrive from all parts of the globe overnight at one's doorstep, the expanded flows and efficiency of inbound remittance channels contrast with the inefficiency of and seemingly unlikely chance of success in un-transparent and bureaucratic emigration channels as encountered by remittance recipients and would-be migrants. On a return trip to Saigon from Quy Nhơn one month, I ran into Minh, one of my informants from Quy Nhơn who regularly receives remittances from relatives in California. Minh was waiting at the airport to take the same flight to Saigon that I was on, where he would accompany his nephew for a visa interview at the U.S. consulate. Minh winced as he remarked how "hard" and unpredictable these visa application performances were. No amount of information on the content of such interviews collected from others who had gone through the process seemed to reveal a pattern that one could effectively prepare for. "Why do they [the consular officers] ask so many unrelated questions, when all we want to do is visit America, and why are they different for each person?" he wondered.[17]

Large crowds gather daily across the street from the U.S. consulate in Saigon—mostly family members awaiting the outcome of the interview of someone inside. The interview has become legendary as a mysterious event that defies understanding or advance preparation. Sidewalk vendors sell food and drinks to those waiting for friends and relatives undergoing the process, and there is a general sense of anticipatory spectatorship. The interview is the final step in the emigration process at which applications are denied or forwarded for processing. Many informants showed me the various forms and papers they had filled out for emigration, at times exhausting every possible visa type (including spousal, student, and family reunification), as well as documentary evidence of their transnational relationships (such as letters, family photos, and remittance receipts). They have prepared themselves and their documents in a manner reminiscent of what Julie Chu calls "file selves" (2010, 103) in the context of aspiring Chinese migrants preparing for the visa interview at the U.S. consulate. Yet there was a widespread sense of frustration that no matter how much one prepares, and even if one has all the right documents in hand, passing the visa interview is unpredictably dependent on the whim of the officer and the mood of the moment. All of one's careful preparations and aspirations could come together or fall apart in the space of just a few minutes. Again, the theme of chance emerges centrally in this process: one cannot anticipate the event or its outcome. The interview then becomes a liminal spectacle to all who patiently wait on the plastic stools across the street from the consulate, observing and vicariously imagining the ontological possibilities that are on the verge of realization or failure for the anxiously aspiring migrant inside (see Figure 8 in chapter 2).

Gambling with Chance

The tension between desire for the transformative agency of mobility and encounters with mysterious migratory obstacles that prevent the realization of that desire are becoming increasingly displaced into a supernatural and divine culture of chance also supported and represented by remittances. In Quy Nhơn, freshly painted and restored temples to the whale god can be found in various districts.[18] The whale god is a traditional local deity worshipped by south central coastal fishermen. It is said to help provide a bountiful catch and good weather to keep fishermen safe at sea. Stories of the whale god go back hundreds of years. An account by the court chronicler Trinh Hoai Duc describes the whale god cult in the early nineteenth century:

> The spirit of the Temple of the General of the Southern Seas is that of a whale . . . When fishermen lower their nets to catch fish, they usually call out to this spirit, and then it chases throngs of fish into their nets . . . When ships are endangered by waves and winds, this fish [the whale] is often seen coming to support the ship until the waters are calm again. If a ship founders, and water pours into it, this fish will ferry the passengers to the shore; the protection of the Whale Spirit is thus very clear. Only our southern country . . . has a supernatural spirit of this type; in other seas they do not have anything like this. This is because in the southern regions, the mountains and seas produce sacred vapors, which secretly provide assistance to our people. (quoted in Dutton, Werner, and Whitmore 2012, 325)

The whale is said to support a sinking boat in a storm by perching it on its back, risking its own life and sometimes getting beached in the process. The phenomenon of beached whales is attributed to the whale's physical proximity to and sacrifice on behalf of humans. The term used for the whale god's temple is in fact closer to mausoleum (*lăng*).[19] Ông Nam Hải mausoleum-temples are common throughout the south central coastal area. For example, in the Van Thuy Tu whale god temple in Phan Thiet, enormous bones from beached whales going back hundreds of years are stored in honor of the selfless sacrifice they made for fishermen. Many people in fishing communities, including fish sellers, pay tribute to this deity in what the Vietnamese anthropologist Mạc Đường calls a popular regional cultural belief not quite in the categorical realm of religion.[20] In more recent years, many refugees who left Vietnam on fishing boats and successfully made the dangerous sea voyage also send money back to support the cult of the whale god. They often explain this as an expression of the gratitude they feel for its divine assistance in their times of greatest hardship.[21] As one temple keeper explained, "the boat journey was very dangerous but they survived. Now they give thanks for their success through their offerings." On Xuan Dieu Street in Quy Nhơn, a newly restored whale god temple carries a plaque honoring the temple's main benefactor—"a Vietnamese immigrant in America" who gave $26,000 to help rebuild the temple, catalyzing a host of smaller donations from both *Việt Kiều* and local residents that ranged from U.S. and Australian dollars to donations of cement.

Each spring, various coastal communities open the mausoleum-temple [*lăng*] of Ông Nam Hải to the public to celebrate the deity (Lễ Hội Ông Nam Hải—Festival of the South Sea God). The festival is like a carnival, with food stalls, merry-go-rounds, and children playing everywhere. Hát bội, a traditional Vietnamese opera, marks the event. Members of the community squat in the courtyard to watch the opera, while the male elders of the fishing communities, sitting on the platform of the temple behind the stage, take turns going to the front to pound the drums in time with the upbeat tempo of the play. While playing the drums, they attach money to the drumsticks, frequently tossing them to the performers to express their appreciation. On stage the money is removed, and the drumsticks are then tossed back to the players.

Some of the most active drum players and hence benefactors receive their money from *Việt Kiều* relatives, and it is common for the festival organizers to collect money, usually about $50–$70 per person, from overseas former fishermen to support the temple. "The *Việt Kiều* have more money, so they can help support maintaining the temple and funding the festival, which does not receive any government assistance. The local people donate their time to perform and organize," explained one of the festival committee organizers. Here money is equated with time, both seen as personalized gifts to the community collective and therefore establishing some equivalency among the donors regardless of their formal financial capacity. Nonetheless, the performative connection between money and drumming affords greater visibility for those with financial means. The festival culminates in the drum-playing elders in traditional outfits (*áo dài*) joining the Hát Bội performers who are dressed as traditional deities—including Ông Địa (Mr. Earth) and King Tran Hung Dao—to pay obeisance (*cúng*) to the gods at the altar.

Yet the whale god does not serve everyone. While successful *Việt Kiều* give thanks for their safe sea journeys through remittances, in other homes, portraits of those lost at sea stare blankly out on ancestral altars. Some families try to identify appropriate death anniversary (*đám gio*) dates for them based on approximate dates of departure and probable time of decease, but for the most part such lost migrants are forgotten in terms of traditional cultural rites—with the circumstances of their death outside normative structures of remembering. "My father

FIGURE 10. Putting money on a drumstick at a whale god festival, Quy Nhơn.

left us behind in 1981 to take his chances on a boat. He was never heard from again. There is no death ceremony. He is forgotten in our family because we do not know what happened to him," one woman told me.

The whale god in many ways might be understood to signify chance, a life gamble that some win and others lose. Faith in, and indeed addiction to, the vicissitudes of chance appears to live on in contemporary Quy Nhơn. Remittance-receiving households ("*nhà Việt Kiều*") are often criticized by neighbors for their card playing, gambling, and drinking. On a walk I took with a resident of Quy Nhơn named Huong in a neighborhood near the water, where many of the nicely renovated homes belonged to such households, she pointed out to me the various families lounging in their pajamas in the open living rooms, drinking and playing cards: "See, look at these people. They don't want to work or do anything. They are just parasites (*bám*) living off their overseas money." Not only did the members of these households appear to be dependent, but they were also conspicuous in their gambling proclivities, further highlighting their comparative advantage in privilege through consumption. Huong went on to criticize their haughty ("*kiêu ngạo*") overseas relatives who helped them to arrange fake marriages ("*kết hôn gia*") with *Việt Kiều* for even more remittance dependence, remarking dismissively that should any of them ever stop receiving money, they would have no idea how to make a living. Here we see that despite the new gendered opportunities that were emerging in the new global economy—such as international marriage discussed previously—access to such migration channels were also often dependent on a transnational network of contacts that Huong, who came from a family without overseas relatives, did not have.

There are many similar neighborhoods in cities, towns, and villages along the central coast. One such area in Danang, also located near the water over which many refugees escaped, is even called "Dollar Village (*Xóm Đô*)" because of the large numbers of residents who live off overseas dollars. Visiting the village of Xuan Hai in Phu Yen Province, whose skyline is dotted by a number of tall, multistory houses newly rebuilt with remittance money, I came across makeshift tents scattered along the beach that provided shade from the hot afternoon sun. The tents were filled with groups of boys, girls, men, and women playing cards, a popular pastime after a night of catching (in the case of men) and cleaning (women) fish. One day when I was drinking beer with such a group of young men at their invitation, they learned in the course of conversation that I was Vietnamese American. As soon as they discovered this, they demanded that I buy the next round of ten beers and squid snacks to continue the party. When I asked why, they jokingly but somewhat aggressively related a local saying: "*Việt Kiều* who return to Vietnam have to treat; if they don't, they're not *Việt Kiều*." This scenario resonates with the notions of gifts connected to Vietnamese identity discussed in chapter 1, where the monetary gift serves as an index of relational intention, not merely blood and ethnic kinship ties.[22] This is what allows overseas Vietnamese to be re-included in the social life of the community. I complied and the party went on, but for me it was no longer in the congenial spirit of hospitality that I had been familiar with receiving during my time in Vietnam. Indeed, at that moment, I could feel some of the irritation related to obligated and thankless gifting that many *Việt Kiều* shared with me.

From another perspective, such modes of play and gambling that critically stereotype *nhà Việt Kiều* neighborhoods are perhaps fairly representative of the liminal social world of waiting, chance, and escapism in which many remittance receivers, with their deferred migratory and transformative aspirations, exist. One resident of the Xóm Đô neighborhood in Danang, where many families had overseas relatives, said that he had been waiting for seven years for approval of his application to emigrate to the United States. In the meantime, he has a small tailoring job that keeps him occupied and provides some steady income. Although his income is supplemented by remittances, the job keeps up his appearance as an employed man for his overseas relatives, as well as local government officials and neighbors. As one resident of the fishing village of Nhơn Lý explained to me, "those with *Việt Kiều* remittances often stop fishing, because it is a hard life—

you have to work all night, and the work is heavy and dangerous. Instead they do small jobs around town. It is an easier lifestyle, and they can afford to do so because their income is supplemented by their overseas relatives." Such jobs that provide daily routines and allow one to stay close to home include selling general merchandise from one's house or food or drinks at the local market. Like other common occupations among remittance recipients, including running cafés and pool halls, such businesses turn only a marginal profit but were attractive in their combination of work, leisure, and flexibility near home.

I met a married couple in their late twenties who lived with the wife's mother. The couple regularly received remittances from relatives in the United States and Europe. They lived in a large pink house with a host of modern appliances such as large televisions and washing machines, and they received on average $2,000 per month from overseas. Nonetheless, they both continued to hold routine jobs: the husband as a motorcycle repairman, and the wife as a hair stylist at a beauty salon. As the husband explained, "if we didn't work, our [overseas] relatives would be mad and say we are lazy." The jobs allowed them to maintain a routine and work identity to avoid criticisms of remittance dependency. Such households betray the complexity of tracing migration and remittance flows, whereby families in Vietnam are frequently connected to multiple diasporic households spread across different geographies of resettlement. Indeed, tracing remittance kinship charts across Vietnam as well as multiple diasporic resettlement locales was part of my interviews, and revealed that despite the U.S.-Vietnam connection focused on in this book, remittances are rarely a dyadic affair (see Figure 7 in chapter 2).

Hierarchies of Mobility

In the anthropologist Marcel Mauss's description of the gift, the "*hau*" (or spirit of the gift's giver) is carried and represented by the thing given, always seeking to return to the source (1967, 11). This notion of "*hau*" might be seen as similar to the agency of the giver and is reflected by the characteristics of the money that he or she sends the recipient. If gifts, according to Mauss, must be given, received, and reciprocated, a central question in this inquiry is whether and how there is reciprocity in the case of international remittances. In some cases the answer appears to be no: there are those who say "we are poor, we have nothing we can give them." Indeed, remittance gifts are often seen as an expected expression of sentiment or gratitude in the absence of personal interaction, allowing the *Việt Kiều* to continue to participate in the community they lost through migration. But in reconsidering the gifting question, most Vietnamese remittance receivers did eventually acknowledge the in-kind gifts and hospitality they offered, the pre-migration support they had provided, or the treats they often tried to send when a visiting relative or friend of a relative returned abroad.

Yet the international remittance gift is difficult to reciprocate because the form of the return gift does not have the mobility of money. The desire of remittance recipients to counter-gift is often not fulfilled because of the return gift's inability to travel on the same terms as the money received. Return gifts are commonly in the form of locally produced semiperishable items such as rice paper, green tea, and dried shrimp, endowed with sensory memories of home. Sending these gifts requires personal networks willing to carry such items back to the remittance senders. Requests to take return gifts are often refused, as it is not easy to carry food items on international flights, some of the items may even be too smelly. "Sometimes my relatives don't want the dried squid (*mực khô*) I give them, because they say they can't take it on the airplane," complained Lan, a resident of Quy Nhơn with relatives in California. Unlike the senders, who have a variety of personal courier networks, private and black-market remittance services, and formal financial services at their disposal (tapping into the global infrastructure designed to facilitate monetary transfers), remittance recipients often remain dependent on the acquiescence of members of mobile social networks in which they are only partial participants to carry material return gifts back to the original gifter. The twenty-four-hour delivery time of the Vietnam-bound remittance contrasts with the waiting and requests for social favors required by the countergifter—whose obligation to return, if felt and acted upon, is hampered and defamiliarized by the structural and practical obstacles to mobility represented in the types of gifts he or she can afford to return. Only money (in particular, money from the outside, such as American dollars) seems to flow freely. As the anthropologist Allison Truitt has noted, dollars carry an affective symbolic resonance in Vietnam: "US dollars signal the possibility of communication beyond Vietnam's territorial borders, a monetary passport that allows one to escape state-imposed restrictions that govern [the] domestic economy" (2013, 81). Foreign money then becomes master in this unequal dialectic of representative exchange, its characteristics affectively taking the place of the absent sender.

Maussian-inspired gifting theory usually emphasizes the Durkheimian solidarity and symmetry of the gift, particularly as observed in Mauss's secondary Melanesian accounts: gifts must be given, received, and returned, and they facilitate a degree of harmony and cooperation among the disparate parties involved in the exchange. Yet in the Vietnamese case we also see shadows of power, agency, and failure that are more akin to Mauss's northwestern American potlatch descriptions, drawing on the work of Franz Boas, than to the more commonplace gifting references to South Pacific Kula circles documented by Bronislaw Malinowski.

In the potlatch, one gifts to outperform a rival, leading to seemingly exuberant performances of destruction and waste as the gifters compete to exert dominance through exchange. Mauss's interpretive emphasis in describing the gifting practices of potlatch still aspire to symmetry, however, in that one supposedly feels shamed when outgifted. The gift is a medium and extension of one's embarrassment, exiled from the body with the expectation that the return will be honor. But in the potlatch one not only seeks to outgift but often also destroys the gift received. The destructive motivation to overcome shame, and the ever anxious yet tenuous holds on power by potlatch victors who must expend all of their resources to maintain power, offers suggestive ethnographic insights into a theory of the gift that exceeds Mauss's categorical domestication of the phenomenon.

Georges Bataille focuses on potlatch rivalry to suggest an alternative motivation for gifting: the necessary expenditure of excess energy. The rivalry of the potlatch is not predicated on symmetry but rather on destructive consumption, in which energy is not conserved for reciprocated returns but lavishly dissipated outward. In Bataille's words, it is "the return of life's immensity to the truth of exuberance" (1989, 76). Here, we catch a glimpse of an outbound energy in which circulation does not desire to return home but seeks permanent escape, much like the migrant who successfully leaves Vietnam. The monetary gift such migrants return is an embodied trace of a diffusive energy in which escape, rather than return, is the primary momentum. When discussing relations to money with remittance recipients, I was often told that "money wanders everywhere, one cannot control it (*tiền là phù du*)."[23] It is perhaps this exuberant and wandering momentum that many remittance recipients viscerally desire and seek and that despite all of the known risks, drove young men to board boats in the 1980s and head out to sea toward the eastern horizon. One may wish to migrate to escape the parameters of one's assigned—or, in the case of former South Vietnamese soldiers or officials—diminished identity in postrevolutionary life, with the possibility of ultimately arriving in an overseas environment where one might consume lavishly and even selfishly (or perhaps self-fully). This is seen as better than being told how to invest deliberately and responsibly by a distant remittance sender who has economically earmarked his or her gift. As we have seen, even in transnational remittance relationships one generally desires to give rather than receive, reflecting a need for not only rank and prestige but also the self-satisfaction that comes with bestowing, controlling, and directing value. One does not want to be eternally consigned to the infantilizing role of the dependent and necessarily grateful recipient. This was the case in the situation of Quynh, the woman who dreamed of being a house cleaner in America so that she could send money back to Vietnam. Control and even destruction of the gift (including the hierarchical relations it imposes upon the recipient) rather than its reciprocity appears to be the goal. Ultimately the urge is one of decoupling the monetary and gifting aspects of remittances, liberating money so that it can freely circulate in the Marxian sense rather than be obliged to return home in the Maussian one.

Therefore, the gifting process itself highlights the circulatory mobility of money and juxtaposes it against the relative chance of and difficulties in bodily mobility. With the emergence of long-distance diasporic gifting networks, the space between giver and receiver represented by invisible boundaries that money can pass but bodies cannot becomes a productive site of emergent imaginaries. The increasing prevalence of telephone and Internet communication technologies, especially in households with overseas relations where the technological hardware for communication is often a gift from abroad, means that overseas migrants can regularly perform for their kinsfolk the personal transformations they have undergone overseas—enabled by money earned and spent on education, fashion, material items, and even spouses.[24] In contrast, parallel performances of *Việt Kiều* remittances to relatives are comparatively modest amounts intended for an ambiguously emplaced Vietnamese middle-class subsistence. Such remittances are small and sporadic, and in the post-2008 economic downturn even briefly declined. This drew awareness to the international scope of the financial crisis and Vietnam's interdependence within the global economy. Furthermore, remittances intended for immediate family members are almost always expected to be shared with neighbors and friends, in order to maintain and build social capital. As one man put it, "if you get $100, then you take everyone out to *nhau* for four days." The result is the common adage that "money is bottomless; there is never enough (*tiền là vô tận, biết bao nhiêu cho đủ*)," cited by both remittance senders and receivers.[25] Remittance money sustains life, but among Vietnamese remittance receivers money is not widely perceived to be accumulative. Money in Vietnam therefore appears to be constantly inadequate to satisfactorily transform life, due to practical limits of quantity as well as structural economic and political factors.

Coastal Affordances

Money suggests the possible eventuality of controlling not only its reception and consumption but also its generation. Remittance exchange disrupts social norms and expectations, increasing awareness of the limitations and margins of one's environment and the possibilities that lie beyond as represented by transformed yet still familiar overseas kin. The limited local economic development remittances catalyze heightens what Arjun Appadurai has termed "the capacity to aspire" (2013, 179), shifting structures of expectation. The realizations of such aspirations, however, are often imagined to lie overseas rather than locally.

Local "cultures of migration" (Cohen and Sirkeci 2011) are entangled in webs of knowledge and experiential memory related to accessing migratory channels, and they influence the motivations and choices of friends and neighbors as many of the stories in this chapter illustrate. The broader migratory cultures that permeate communities where migrant departure and return is widespread have been observed in other regions with significant histories of emigration, from Fujian, China, to Puebla, Mexico (Chu 2010; Smith 2005). The momentum of migratory mobility that follows new opportunities discovered along the way, contributing to people's confidence that something will work out over the horizon, has also been examined in other cases, such as that of Filipina migrants (Parreñas 2001) moving across transnational fields of ethnic labor opportunities. Communities from which migrants depart and to which they eventually return tend to become permeated by migration experiences and desires. In many cases a rural community's economy may be transformed in a single generation from locally situated and generally self-sufficient to largely urban or internationally oriented and dependent through migration and remittances. Indeed, resisting participation in developing migratory cultures is to risk in situ (Feldman, Geisler, and Silberling 2003) displacement within one's own community, perhaps avoidant of physical and economic risks but also separated from potential sources of external income that fuel new local economic activities that shape consumption patterns, recognitions, and identities.

The migratory culture of central coastal Vietnam has a particular aesthetic that is spatially highlighted. In my field notes I frequently dwelled on what I called the gaze that characterized the kind of hanging out that frequently took place at Quy Nhơn's many oceanside cafés, where I conversed with men in the cool interior shade while we gazed listlessly toward a bright doorway beyond which stretched the blue sea. Coastal communities sit at the edge of the constructed nation-state within sight of an oceanic horizon. Endowed with memories and histories of migratory yearnings and journeys, the omnipresent view of the sea continues to spark the imaginaries of residents, producing what Lauren Berlant (2011) might call "cruel optimism."[26] Each morning and evening they routinely stroll along the ocean's margins or sit staring out across it, contemplating the hypothetical possibilities of what lies beyond. The visual perception psychologist James Gibson (1979) describes affordances as explicit or implicit environmental factors that shape the possibilities deemed available to an actor at a given moment. In the case of the Vietnamese coast, with its extensive histories of refugee boat exoduses, the landscape has also become endowed with latent and submerged mnemonic qualities that shape orientations to mobile possibilities and pasts.

Littoral environments are defined as the physical space where the land meets the sea, a key feature of Quy Nhơn's landscape. In increasing awareness of broader

ecological relations and larger scales, such physical horizons often seem to catalyze reflections on so-called personal horizons. In *The Lure of the Sea* (1994), the
historian Alain Corbin traces shifting European attitudes toward the sea and the
production of the beach as a socially interactive and reflective space in the late
eighteenth and early nineteenth centuries. He argues that this emotional relationship to the sea, which we may assume feels like a universal and timeless human
response to the natural landscape, is in fact a particular product of modernity. It
was subliminally caught up with overseas explorations and expansions that accompanied the Enlightenment, the vicarious unsettling that comes from others'
having crossed to the other side. For Corbin, "seeing" the horizon changes in this
period from being a theological limitation to an aspirational reassessment of the
possibilities of self and collective, leading in his words to a "revolution of the imagination" (ibid.).

The contemporary coastal landscape in Vietnam as experienced by its residents
is, therefore, one that may represent more than mere geographical beauty that
inspires quiet self-reflection. It also indexes an intrinsic revolutionary history related to chances to emigrate and attempts to escape. In Appadurai's framework
of aspiration, imaginaries of what lie beyond the sea cultivated what he might call
"a navigational capacity" (2013, 179), increasing a visceral sense of agency over
one's affairs that allows one to look toward the future rather than simply seeing
and accepting whatever may come. For over a decade in the relatively recent past,
the ocean was a horizon representing a visible channel that many people desperately tried to use to flee. In this collective history of Vietnam's boat exodus, a
period that lasted through most of the 1980s, and its subsequent closure after the
1989 international Comprehensive Plan of Action, the meaning of and associations with the horizon have changed. Looking (*nhìn*) at the horizon, as so many
coastal residents still do as they squat and chat with their neighbors at the start or
end of each day, is no longer a gaze toward the unknown. Nowadays thousands
of overseas Vietnamese and their gifts regularly return from beyond the horizon
to tell their tales about the other side. In the process, the horizon became endowed
with nostalgic memories and longings for a once-imagined future that never arrived for those left behind.

The horizon beckons, yet it remains mysterious and dangerous. Some people
reached the other side, but others who attempted to do so never returned or
sent word home. Perhaps they were lost, or perhaps they forgot those they had
left behind. For those stuck on the Vietnamese side of the ocean, it has become a
particular kind of what the anthropologist Vincent Crapanzano might call an
"imaginative horizon" characterized by "dialectic between openness and closure"
(2004, 2). It is a landscape that heightens hypothetical reflections on what spectators of it might be if they too had crossed during momentary opportunities of

openness, but it also indexes the limits of those possibilities. Such are the reflections of people like Lam who sit drinking and staring at a sea that he has repeatedly been unable to cross, or the drum players at the whale god festival who commemorate a "fish" that helped some people reach the other side while forsaking others.

For those who stand on the edges of Vietnam's coast, the horizon remains but no longer invites one to imaginatively look across it. It is no longer a horizon open to flight, escape and self-transformation on the other side. It is a landscape that may continue to stir the imagination, but to act on one's imagination has become more difficult. The horizon no longer provides the agency and future possibilities it did in the past, particularly for a generation who grew up in the 1980s aspiring to leave but who are now resigned to the local lives they have settled into. Imaginaries in their modern agential form, unfurling at the cusp, meet the limits of their intention and aspiration.

FIGURE 11. Boats and the horizon.

The mobile imaginary therefore disrupts and complicates utilitarian economic development as well as anthropological interpretive frameworks of gifting that emphasize symmetry through exchange. In the shadow of every story of productive investments by families happily reunited by remittance gifts lies another story of exuberant consumption, risky gambles, frustrated hopes, betrayed loyalties, hierarchical power relations, disappointed memories, and unrequited desires and recognitions. The gift becomes a mirror and embodiment of what should be and could be but rarely is. Remittance recipients still aspire to expanding agency through migration, gazing upon horizons of social possibility across the sea. But those horizons are now seemingly beyond reach, and once hopeful aspirations shift to reflections on the vicissitudes of chance. The relational exchange between selves and diasporic Others devolves into a meditation on self, but one that remains always already haunted by the uncanny specter of an Other—transported by fate and transformed by money from elsewhere—that one might have been and might still become.

This meditation on the seemingly failed imaginaries of circulation is also about a re-imagination and transformation of the self and the space it occupies. The Vietnamese experience of gift exchange with the diaspora does not merely produce an abstract imaginary of another life beyond borders that remains fixed on the static fate of immobility. It also leads to dynamic transformations in immediate personal and collective social identifications and relations to spatial landscapes. Where physical mobility is denied, imaginative mobility is seized. Vietnamese remittance receivers imaginatively traverse and inhabit the "over there" across the sea—asserting creative agencies as they reassess personal potentials, rearrange ritual forms, reimagine deities, reengage with the spiritual, reorient family and community relations, and re-envision lives for younger relatives in the hope for vicarious social transformation. The resultant hypotheticals of the self index the emergence of ever more liminal subjectivities that can never be re-domesticated, contributing to creative ontological reorientations and reinventions. Contemporary sociocultural transformations in Quy Nhơn and other south central coastal communities are significantly shaped by the diverse imaginaries that are catalyzed, accompanied, and embodied by transnational gift exchanges from across the sea, including the variegated channels of mobility they highlight and foreclose.

THE BEAUTIFUL, TIRED COUNTRY

As my car travels south through the Bay Area to San Jose, the temperature rises steadily and the geography gets increasingly arid. Red-tiled suburban buildings dot the brown desert-like landscape under a clear blue sky, with competing signs for gas stations and fast-food drive-through restaurants. For the last part of my primary fieldwork for this book, I based myself in California, in the United States—or as the Vietnamese call it, Cali in *Mỹ* (or America, the Chinese name for which means the "beautiful country").[1]

For many Vietnamese refugees, the United States was the preferred destination for final resettlement. Residents in refugee camps through Southeast Asia commonly requested migration to America instead of other countries that were accepting Vietnamese for resettlement. In California, Camp Pendleton in Orange County was one of the arrival points where high-profile political refugees, often associated with the former republican regime of South Vietnam, first went after leaving days before the surrender to North Vietnam and the National Liberation Front. A small community of Vietnamese formed in the area, with the cities of Westminster and Garden Grove eventually having a sizable enough Vietnamese population that the area came to be known as Little Saigon, and the business district was officially designated as such by California's governor in 1988. California's strong economy, cultural diversity, established Asian American populations, and warm climate made the state a preferred relocation site for many Vietnamese, and as the community grew, it offered the benefits of tightly knit ethnic neighborhoods in which Vietnamese language and customs were normative. Despite official resettlement policies in the United States that attempted to counteract the "clustering" tendency of refugees by dispersing Indochinese to different and often remote parts of the country (Pedraza and Rumbaut 1996), an eventual process of voluntary secondary migration by Vietnamese who had settled in other states led to California's becoming the headquarters of Vietnamese abroad, with the state containing 39 percent of the 2.1 million Vietnamese in the United States (Zong and Batalova 2016).

While the Vietnamese community in southern California grew rapidly, the Bay Area became a secondary site of Vietnamese resettlement. In the South Bay, the city of San Jose and the surrounding area now ranks as the second largest Vietnamese community in the United States after Orange County, and there have been controversial efforts to call this slightly newer community Little Saigon, too.[2] While Little Saigon in Orange County is generally home to Vietnamese who arrived in the United States earlier and are more financially secure, in San Jose a population of more recent immigrants, many of whom are working class with strong transnational connections, produces significant remittances. As discussed previously in the book, recent immigrants have been found to remit more of their income to home countries. This is in part because of their closer emotional and nostalgic ties, but it is also because they are more likely to have immediate family members still in their home country, whereas earlier immigrants often have already sponsored close relatives for emigration and family reunification.

I have long been familiar with the vitality of the Vietnamese communities of California, having lived in southern California for three years and having often visited the Little Saigon area in Orange County. In 2008, basing myself in the Bay Area, I spent time in both Orange County and San Jose to conduct interviews with Vietnamese American remittance givers. The types of communities they lived in were vastly different from the bustling and more closely knit neighborhoods I had become used to in Vietnam. Often located in sprawling suburban residential areas, the California communities centered on shopping centers in which Vietnamese goods ranging from food to music were widely available, or at temples and churches where community members congregated for religious services and gatherings. However, the residences were often stereotypical suburban California homes made of stucco and set in cul-de-sacs. My interviews, carefully timed around busy work schedules, took me to many such houses, as well as sometimes to lively Vietnamese restaurants or coffee shops in the shopping centers. I interviewed approximately thirty Vietnamese American (or what in Vietnam would be called overseas Vietnamese) individuals and families during the summer of 2008.[3]

Fatigues and Frustrations

A striking sense of remittance fatigue emerged in many of my interviews in California. As I have discussed, remittance giving patterns tend to follow an arc starting with dedicated family assistance and sponsorship of close family members, followed by a social shift toward focusing on life in the United States, and then an economic shift toward second-generation earners who become primary family supporters. Second-generation Vietnamese, who grew up in the United States and are more likely to focus on nuclear family relations, generally provide financial support within families out of a sense of cultural obligation and upbringing. In keeping with traditional patterns of extended kinship support, it is often the older generation whose members redistribute the remittances from the younger earners to family members in more extended kin networks, many of whom remain in Vietnam.

Xuan, a young Vietnamese American woman who grew up in San Jose, earmarks part of her monthly salary from a local civil service job to give to her parents.[4] Her parents, she said, "use the money for everyday needs but also send some of it back to Vietnam. They go back once every two years, so it is important for them to keep in touch with family there." Xuan said that she was sometimes frustrated by the fact that her earnings supported not only her parents but also distant relatives in Vietnam, who did not have to work as a result of the remittances she sent them indirectly. Yet she also reflected that her relationship to those relatives was different than her parents' relationship to them: "To me, I see my money being given to a distant uncle or aunt who I barely know. But to my parents, they are sending the money to a brother or sister. I guess if my brothers and sisters needed money from me, I would not hesitate to give it." However, for Xuan remittances also complicated her marriage to a Caucasian American: "My husband grew up here, and there is no tradition of helping parents in his family. He often asks me why I give money to my parents, when we are financially struggling ourselves. Over time, he has come to accept that this is part of my Vietnamese upbringing, even though I am an American like him, but of a different background. I do worry that if I ever stopped working, it would be difficult to ask him to give money to my family."

Remittances not only cause cross-cultural misunderstandings but also can increase tensions or promote the proliferation of secrets within Vietnamese American families. In one home I visited, the husband was an unemployed engineer, and the wife worked as a nursing home aide. Her income helped support remittance gifts to her and her husband's families in Vietnam. However, their daughter later told me that the mother felt that since she brought home the income, it was her own business (*chuyện riêng*) to decide what happened to it and therefore right to support her family more than his. So she would often go to the nearby Le Gởi Tiền Lẹ remittance service office after each payday to send a little extra money to her family, never telling her husband. It was better to keep it secret, the daughter explained, because as long as the father did not know it would not matter. But if he knew, they might fight about it. Insecurities about his inability to find stable work and serve as the family provider were exacerbated by the remittance-sending patterns that had developed in the family. This is consistent with research finding that Southeast Asian men often had difficulty in their diminished postwar status as refugees stripped of former positions of political and community authority, with women stepping in to play an important household role as income earners after resettlement in the United States (Ong 2003). In another family, the father sent money to relatives whom the mother felt had been inhospitable to her when she was in Vietnam. She resented this so much that she refused to accompany the father on his return trips to visit his family. As I have noted in previous chapters, remittance support from abroad maintains a kinship connection for diasporic family members and a home in Vietnam to return to. In cases of extended kin networks, who is worth maintaining relations with, and whose home one wants to return to, is an important and sometimes contentious factor when families make decisions about remittance gifts.

Generational Engagements

Generational differences in remittance-giving patterns are notable. Many older generation interviewees prioritized remittance giving to family members in Vietnam and frequently returned every few years to visit them. The second-generation Vietnamese Americans I met in California seemed less likely to remit money directly or travel on their own to visit family in Vietnam. Many of them I spoke with found the family trips tiring. "The weather [in Vietnam] was hot, it was dirty, my father kept telling me what to do and how to behave, and I didn't remember anyone even though everyone remembered me," recalled Duy, a twenty-five-year-old from the Bay Area who wearily recalled a month-long trip to Vietnam with his family. Like many others, he related stories about the classic Vietnamese returnee "family road trip" in a rented van full of extended relatives, traveling from the beach resorts of Nha Trang to the highlands of Dalat to see the sights. "I couldn't wait to get back [to America] be on my own again, and not have to spend every minute with family," Duy said. Unlike his parents, he felt no obligation to give to Vietnam, and even a journey to the homeland did not produce a sense of emotional connection that might translate into a gifting relationship. In contrast, Tuyet, a middle-aged woman, told me about her regret that her children had grown up without the chance to go to Vietnam: "Fifteen years ago it was more difficult to go. We were still afraid of returning. Our children grew up in America never knowing their own culture and language. Now we go back and try to show it to them, but it is too late. They are too Americanized and not interested." For many first-generation Vietnamese Americans, Vietnam still holds a place in their memory as a homeland (*quê hương*) or place of roots (*gốc*). Many of them left involuntarily as political or economic refugees and dreamed for years of returning one day, despite having worked so hard and suffered so much to leave. But for the second generation, while Vietnam holds a strong place in the imagination as a source of their ethnic and cultural origins, American—or even Vietnamese American or Asian American—culture is much more familiar to them than the society they find upon "returning" to Vietnam.[5]

Karin Aguilar-San Juan (2009) has argued that diasporic Vietnamese communities should be viewed as no less Vietnamese than communities in Vietnam. According to her, the former represent a different mode and generation of place making and cultural production that does not prioritize the authenticity of space. The social vibrancy of California's Vietnamese communities does indeed demonstrate that ethnic cultural production continues despite geographic distance from Vietnam. Many of the members of the older generation whom I interviewed identified themselves strongly as Vietnamese and criticized the current regime in Vietnam for inhibiting cultural expression and tradition. Some of them felt that it is actually in exile, rather than in Vietnam, where Vietnamese culture is preserved and maintained. One of my informants in his late sixties said: "The com-

FIGURE 12. Phước Lộc Thọ Asian Garden Mall, Little Saigon, California.

munists have destroyed Vietnamese culture. It is shameful!" Occasionally there are fierce debates among the community when cultural shows (including singers, art exhibits, and traditional water puppets) sponsored by the Vietnamese state tour the United States, which often lead to calls for boycotts and protests among segments of the Vietnamese American community.[6]

For the first generation of Vietnamese refugees and immigrants in America, however, bodily and financial return to Vietnam can symbolically represent a completion of the circulatory journey of escape from Vietnam, social and economic transformation abroad, and finally reconnection to homeland and family. Đinh, a taxi driver in San Francisco whose father died in a Vietnamese reeducation camp in 1976, escaped from Vietnam with his wife and children by boat in that same year. They spent three days and nights at sea before finally arriving at Renai Island, in Indonesia. In the refugee camp there, Đinh applied for resettlement in the West. He was accepted for emigration to Holland, but he chose to stay in the camp longer in the hope of being able to immigrate to America. "My father, when he was alive, loved and respected America. I grew up thinking it was a wonderful place, so I wanted to bring my family there," he explained. Eventually his family was transferred to Battang in the Philippines, where they spent six months before ultimately moving to Southern California after a brief time in Hawaii. After working in a factory and getting his feet on the ground financially, he moved to San Francisco, leasing a taxi that he drove to support his two daughters—one in college and one in high school.

Đinh explained to me that he remits a thousand dollars (more, when he can afford it) every month to his mother and extended family on the island of Phu Quy, off the southeastern coast of Vietnam. He also sends money for the various family death anniversaries (đám gio), usually $100 to each brother and sister and $10 for each of their children. On top of these remittance gifts he pays a 3.5 percent transaction fee to the local Vietnamese remittance service he uses—a fee that is higher than usual because of the geographical isolation of the island. Đinh said that his mother is happier living on Phu Quy than she would be in the busy city of San Francisco. It is his filial obligation, he insisted, to do everything he can to help her live out her life in Vietnam in comfort. He is able to stay in regular communication with her due to vastly improved technologies. While previously they could correspond only by regular mail, now he is able to call her six times a month, using a $10 calling card that gives him two hundred minutes to talk. His sister and cousins, who also remain in Vietnam, take care of his mother's daily needs, and the money he sends helps support them, too. Sending money, he says, also helps him remember the daily life of his village and the island. Đinh described it as a small and peaceful place where everyone knows everybody else. "Really, I know 99 percent of the people in Phu Quy!" he told me. Indeed, according to him, because so many people on the island had fishing boats, almost everyone there had family members who had escaped by boat after 1975. Each year there is a Phu Quy reunion in San Francisco, where a large group of Vietnamese originally from the island reside. They eat special seafood dishes from the island and share news about what is happening back home. Because many now return regularly and the Phu Quy population is small, it is easy keep up with affairs back home at such annual social gatherings. This is a common theme among many diasporic subcommunities, where members of the same village (*làng*) have found each other abroad and initiated community-organizing activities based on their shared geographic origins.

A sixty-four-year-old woman named Lan explained to me how dear to her heart are the remittances that she sends back to support her ninety-two-year-old mother in Hue. The money she sends goes to pay for her mother's health care but has a sentimental purpose as well:

> My mother is sad—two of her children have died already. When I call her on the telephone she can't hear, so instead I send her money. Sending her a little money brings her so much happiness. Each time I send some money, just a hundred dollars every few months, I can imagine her carefully putting the money away in her breast pocket. With it she can go to the market to buy some bananas or sweet sticky rice, which she loves so much and used to feed me as a child. For the most part, she does not spend much, but just enjoys having and holding the money. It makes her feel secure, remembering her daughter in America who has not forgotten her.

Lan also sends money to her younger sister to buy other foods for her mother, the process of which she imaginatively detailed: "In the morning my sister will take the money and go to the market to buy *bún bò* [beef soup] or *cháo* [rice porridge] for a small healthy lunch. Then in the afternoon, around 2:00 or 3:00 p.m., she will make *bánh canh* [a thick tapioca noodle soup] another of my mother's favorite dishes." For Lan, remittances to her mother evoked sensory memories of the past and imaginaries of the present. Remittances to her sister also replaced the labor and care she would provide for her mother if Lan were in Vietnam and helped alleviate her guilt about not being there. Our discussion of her support to family members back in Vietnam opened up a stream of memories, and Lan and I talked late into the night about her past days in Vietnam and the food, youth, romance, and adventure she remembered from her life before migrating to the United States. She brought out family photographs and mementos to support the memories she related. These days, she said, the journey back to Vietnam was difficult for her. Nonetheless she tried to return every three years or so, and she intended to make another journey there soon. Her husband had passed away and her house was empty, with her now-adult children geographically scattered. For Lan the vibrancy and immediacy of life was not in California but in Vietnam, where her siblings, mother, and memories resided.

Transnational Orientations

For many of the more elderly members of the first generation of Vietnamese Americans, returning to Vietnam has become a viable retirement option. The low cost of living in Vietnam, coupled with the availability of family members in both the United States and Vietnam to take care of empty homes and various logistical details, makes a transnational lifestyle accessible and cost-effective. In San Jose I became acquainted with Joanna, an investment adviser who specializes in helping Vietnamese Americans design retirement plans that allow them to live almost full time in Vietnam. She advises them on how to invest their life savings in stock portfolios. If the interest they earn added to their social security payments can come to at least $1,500 per month, they can live very comfortably in Vietnam. Meanwhile they have the satisfaction of helping out family members: their children are able to take over their property in the United States, and they are able to buy or rebuild homes that they can then share with their extended family in Vietnam. Joanna is Vietnamese and comes from a family whose members arrived in the United States in the early 1980s as refugees. Some of them had returned to Vietnam and invested money they had earned in start-up businesses there. For example, Joanna had a sister in Saigon who ran an American-style restaurant and real estate investment venture. The sister, whose restaurant I had occasionally patronized while living in Saigon, had used business investments in Vietnam to help other family members but had been disappointed that many of them seemed to take advantage of her assistance. Businesses often failed whenever she was not around to manage them herself. However, Joanna explained to me that for her family, reconnecting with Vietnam was more than just a business venture. Rather, it was an almost spiritual matter that helped her feel complete in life.

One day Joanna invited me to a Buddhist temple in the desert south of San Jose. She wanted to show me the spiritual strength of the Vietnamese American community and their cultural connectedness to Vietnam. When we arrived at the former ranch house turned into a temple, we found scores of Hondas, Toyotas, and Lexuses parked around the grounds.[7] Inside the temple, about a hundred people sat or squatted on the cool tile floor with fans whirring above, listening to the head monk give a talk on compassion. Afterward, a light vegetarian meal was served by volunteers in gray robes, and we then strolled around the grounds. Joanna stopped at many of the stone markers in the gardens to explain the meaning of the short poems engraved on them. Destiny was a unifying theme in the poems that Joanna seemed to strongly connect with. "It was meant to be that my family came to America, became successful in business, and then could return to Vietnam," she explained. Her father had paved the way for a transnational family lifestyle and business, first returning to Vietnam in the 1990s to open a French restaurant in downtown Saigon. Going back to Vietnam revitalized his spirit, she explained, which had been broken by the end of the war and the hard life of refugees in America. Two of her sisters had followed their father, but one had since returned to the United States. Joanna's niece, whom she introduced to me, was on the staff of a local college and planned to visit Vietnam for the first time in the following year. The formation of their transnational family network meant that business capital traveled in two directions, helping out family on both sides of the Pacific. Initially capital from America was invested in Vietnam, but the profits from the business ventures in Saigon were sent back to the United States. In these businesses they were able to employ and therefore help out members of their extended family network. For Joanna and her family, the ability to go back and forth rather than being in one place or the other had brought success. The fruits of that success, she emphasized, should be generously shared with the wider community, particularly through religious charity. Such generosity, according to Joanna, follows the teachings of the Buddha, which is why she had become closely involved with the community at this temple.

In both California and Vietnam I met a number of transnational individuals who, like Joanna's family, maintain lives and residences on both sides of the Pacific. A Vietnamese man named Hai who lived in San Jose, but whom I initially met in Quy Nhơn, explained to me his rationale for transnational living: "The U.S. is a good place to make money, but life in Vietnam is happier. I have a green card, I can go back and forth, to and from America. I stay in San Jose six months with my daughter, but my life is in Vietnam. My daughter—her life is in San Jose. There are more opportunities for her in the U.S. because she is young. But we can live in both places and be a family." Hai is typical of the many transnationals able to take advantage of improved economic, legal, and travel opportunities to establish a life that spans homes and identities across geographies and generations, in the process building up significant "network capital."[8] Each year Hai would visit his daughter in California and relatives in Texas and Toronto. Yet he was always content to return to Vietnam and his modest house by the ocean. Hai said that America made Vietnamese into better Vietnamese: the "environment" in the United States, in his view, provided opportunities and resources that facilitated character development. Education, careers, resources—all helped one move beyond a survival mode and cultivate admirable etiquette and a generous character. Such etiquette and character, however, are always rooted in culture, and he was quick to add that one must always retain links to the homeland (*quê hương*) and "stay Vietnamese."

The Vietnamese American transnational subject has been structurally facilitated by significant policy changes in both the United States and Vietnam in the past decade and a half. In the next chapter I will discuss the specifics of policies encouraging and facilitating transnational movement. Overall, however, in the past decade return visits from overseas Vietnamese have increased significantly, and half a million individuals such as Hai and Joanna now return annually to visit their homeland (Gribble and Tran 2016). The reestablishment of kinship and social networks has facilitated family reunifications and transnational marriages, whereby relations living abroad sponsor family members in Vietnam or help arrange marriages to facilitate immigration, as was the case with Hai's daughter.

For some, transnational life provides an ideal lifestyle and identity. It offers liberation or at least a temporary escape from the structural social and economic barriers in Vietnam that are often blamed on a corrupt, failed socialist government. In addition, it offers a respite from the discrimination and isolation widely acknowledged as endemic in the experiences of Vietnamese in the United States who have neither the time nor the resources to return to the homeland. The opportunities for Hai's family to move back and forth—to take elements of two different worlds and combine them into a single transnational life—not only gives Hai personal satisfaction but also offers a chance for his children to "become better Vietnamese" outside Vietnam while retaining connections to it.

It is worth noting that Hai's transnational social aspirations are part of a networked collective identity in which he imagines his daughter's future life. Hai came to America with the help of friends and family members who had left Vietnam before him and sponsored his immigration. Hai extended similar help to his daughter, by helping arrange her marriage to a Vietnamese American. In a sense Hai is reminiscent of Aihwa Ong's "flexible citizens" (1999), characterized by global mobility, capital, agency, and heterogeneous belonging. Hai is forging a transnational and transgenerational identity in which collective and comparative familial transformation across generations and communities is a gauge of success. He may not desire to live permanently in the United States, but he wants his daughter to do so. The ability to move back and forth between the United States and Vietnam provides the security and satisfaction that allow Hai and his family to feel they have made themselves the best Vietnamese they can be across multiple cultural and geographic worlds. The social evolution of such transnational characters on two sides of the Pacific is followed with keen interest by Vietnamese and Vietnamese Americans alike.

A key question is what effect such networked transnationalism has on remittance flows. In many of the interviews I conducted, I learned that regular sending of long-distance remittances intended to subsidize family household incomes tended to taper off as the bodily returns of diasporic family members became more commonplace. In a sense, the remittance gifts that preceded their return and represented their absence during long periods of exile, when travel between Vietnam and the United States was more difficult, are replaced by the physical performance of traditional family roles. Since the 1990s the political environment in Vietnam has dramatically shifted to make overseas relatives' returns—and, by extension, their transnational identities—easier to manage. However, this does not mean that gifts, financial or otherwise, end. Rather, in most cases financial gifts become increasingly sporadic and symbolic, as discussed in the previous chapters. Gifting for Tết, for example, rarely ceases, and most Vietnamese American families I interviewed reported regularly sending token amounts of at least a few hundred dollars.

At the same time, gifting becomes highly concentrated during physical returns to Vietnam. When overseas Vietnamese visit family members in Vietnam, they typically bring significant financial but also material gifts, which are tightly interwoven with the maintenance of status and credibility. Most families I interviewed said that when they returned to Vietnam, they typically carried $3,000–$10,000 in cash. According to a man in his early forties named Phong, "returning to Vietnam for us is much more expensive than the plane ticket. We have to bring money for every relative and friend, close or distant. Everywhere you go, and every family member you see, means money out of the pocket. It is like a waterfall of money from us every day that we are there, until eventually the vacation ends and we go home broke: back to work to earn the money all over again." My Vietnamese American informants also shared their challenges finding appropriate material gifts to take with them on their return visits. Selecting desirable material gifts to supplement the monetary ones is not always easy. The types of preferred material items from America described by my informants ranged from clothes to beauty products. Particular emphasis was placed on their authenticity, quality, and manufacture in America, supply-chain characteristics that are not at all easy to ensure when shopping for goods today. Suffice to say, one cannot carry a textile product bought in the United States but labeled "made in Vietnam" back to Vietnam as a gift. The preparations for trips to Vietnam are clearly exhausting, as is the return to America—after which one must immediately go back to work to make up for all of the resources expended through gifting.

Preserving family relations therefore means maintaining the gift that mediates them. For many people, gifting patterns established over the years of exile have become normalized. It has become habitual to distribute money to Vietnamese relatives even when they no longer need it. "Money is our way of showing love," explained Thuan, a Vietnamese American from San Mateo, California. But with increased family return visits, there is also heightened awareness of the logistical details and realities of daily life in Vietnam, and how different they are from the past. While Vietnam is still a developing country, it is significantly better off economically than it was in the late 1970s and 1980s, when it was rated as one of the poorest countries in the world (World Bank Vietnam). Many Vietnamese Americans who regularly return to Vietnam feel that the situation of family members there is no longer as dire as it once was, and that indeed many relatives have sufficient opportunities in the new economy. Furthermore, many Vietnamese Americans with whom I spoke, some of whom work long hours at blue-collar jobs in the United States, have begun to feel that the remittances they pay from their hard-earned wages are no longer helping family members, but rather are contributing to laziness and reducing their family's incentives to find work or develop viable business opportunities in Vietnam. Regular remittance subsidies for relatives' household expenses tend to taper off after one or two return visits by overseas Vietnamese family members, replaced by significant gifts (including money) on the occasion of another return visit or sporadically and symbolically sent in honor of special occasions such as Tết, a wedding, funeral, or death anniversary.

While some members of the Vietnamese diaspora, such as Joanna and Hai, have thrived on the new transnational identities they have forged as travel back to Vietnam has become easier, others, such as Phong, find the concentrated family gifting that requires thousands of dollars for each return visit to be prohibitive. Another man I interviewed explained that "although things are relatively cheap in Vietnam, going there is so expensive because we have to give money to all the family members. You must be generous, even if you don't have money. I went once eight years ago and gave away ten thousand dollars, which took me a long time to save. Now I cannot afford to go again for a while, because it requires too much money and I have many other expenses [in America] to worry about now." Many overseas Vietnamese express exhaustion at the endless expectations from family members of receiving remittances from them, which even when fulfilled, the efforts to do so seem to go largely unappreciated. A turn toward charitable giving among Vietnamese American communities has been one attempt to redeem the desired meaning of the gift from endless cycles of frustrated obligation, as I will discuss ahead. In general, there appears to be a widespread desire to restore the sociality of the gift in a transnational exchange environment where the reciprocity and recognition that the gift is intended to achieve seem not to materialize.

Recuperating Agency

Yen Le Espiritu (2006) and Mimi Nguyen (2012) have critiqued dominant policy, media, and sociological narratives related to Vietnamese Americans. The representations these authors discuss often portray refugees as victims receiving the benevolence of U.S. sponsorship, rendered helpless and with little agency over their own affairs. Such narratives ignore U.S. responsibility for the refugees' plight to begin with. After all, the United States intervened in and expanded the war in Vietnam. In much of the sociological scholarship on Vietnamese refugees produced during the 1980s and 1990s, the dominant question was how to assimilate and empower Vietnamese who had recently arrived in the United States and were deemed to be traumatized, needy, and unable to reconstruct their lives in an unfamiliar land without assistance. This contributed to an epistemological framing of immigrants' financial capabilities and assistance programs geographically oriented toward kinship responsibilities in line with American nuclear family sociocultural norms. In other words, cultural considerations of extended family support obligations that branched transnationally back to family in Vietnam were not part of how U.S. social assistance programs conceived of their Vietnamese clients' needs. Supporting and cultivating a healthy nuclear household was the goal of many U.S. aid agencies dealing with Southeast Asian refugees, which often involved particular forms of neoliberal subject making and training—as Aihwa Ong observed in the case of Cambodians in California (2003).

However, this book has highlighted the extended nature of Vietnamese sociocultural expectations of kinship support and also elucidated a theme of aspiration and performance of agency through remittance giving. Gifting back to Vietnam concretely demonstrates that one has attained financial and social success in one's country of resettlement. Money indicates status and represents the social transformation of the giver, as it is accompanied by stories and images of the physical and material transformations undergone overseas. The ability to take back one's life abroad after leaving everything behind in Vietnam begins with the assertion of one's commodity purchasing power. To then send money home so that relatives and friends there can purchase needed items reflects an intentional gift that also seeks to bestow agency upon the receivers. The anticommunist political views of many overseas Vietnamese appear as not only an expression of regret for a lost political cause, but also a critique of a failed state socialist project and the accompanying structural environment in which individual agency and work appear to go unrewarded. "We Vietnamese are hardworking people, but the communists have made everyone lazy," explained one middle-aged Vietnamese man in San Jose who decried the feelings of entitlement and dependency that, according to him, many of his Vietnamese relatives have.

Sending financial gifts is certainly an example of the performance of agency through giving, but so is sending the material gifts that often accompany them (though the latter are less significant than in the past). Among the many forms of material gifts described by remittance senders, one item that stands out is medicine—particularly vitamins, aspirin, and oils. Joanna, the Vietnamese American retirement adviser with transnational family business ties, told me, "each time I return to Vietnam I carry all sorts of things to give away: individual gifts for family members, letters from family members in the U.S. for family members in Vietnam, a few thousand dollars in cash, as well as vitamins and đậu xanh (eucalyptus oil)." Later she mentioned that some of the gifts from Vietnamese relatives that she brought back with her to the United States were also medicines—antibiotics or other medicines that were either expensive in the United States or required prescriptions there, but also eucalyptus oil. The two-way flow of medicines struck me as curious. Joanna explained:

> in Vietnam conditions are bad, a lot of people are poor and sick. In the past we sent medicines to family because it was so hard to get them in Vietnam, and even if they didn't need them they could easily sell the medicines in the market for cash. Now there are many medicines available in Vietnam, and they are quite cheap, which is why we also take them home with us. But their quality is not guaranteed, and they are not always authentic, especially Western medicines. If I bring multivitamins or Tylenol from America, my friends and family trust that these medicines will improve their health. Bringing health back to Vietnam is one small thing I can do with these vitamins. I often give a small bottle or two to people who have been kind to me, and they are always happy to receive them. They also like to give me đậu xanh when I return home, although I sometimes bring that to them from the U.S. as well. It is easy to find both here and there.

While clearly people preferred certain items, like vitamins, to come from the United States, there was no particular importance attached to the origin of eucalyptus oil, and it freely flowed in both directions. This oil is a symbolically compassionate gift that recognizes the suffering of the receivers and evokes their social and physical transformation. It is used for a variety of aches, pains, and other ailments and is seemingly universally valued by Vietnamese for its recuperative qualities. While the oil is of Asian origin and is a standard gift from Vietnamese to returning overseas relatives, the fact that it is a gift often sent from America to Vietnam underscores the fact that both gifters and receivers consider bodily and familial health important and are concerned about it. Of course, the exchange of medicine reveals a complex system of cross-border valuation of quality, cost, and purity, but because medicine is a gift that can be reciprocated, it also reflects a particular performance of compassionate agency through healing and transformation on the part of the givers on both sides of the relationship, who recognize each other as Vietnamese cultural subjects who appreciate its unique traditional healing powers. Medicines help restore energy to the body. Having restored health to themselves after difficult refugee journeys, labor conditions, and cultural adaptations, overseas Vietnamese can turn to helping others. The returning of medicines to families in Vietnam illustrates a widespread desire to help relatives left behind and debilitated by poverty begin to recover and take control of transforming their lives. Similarly, gifts of medicines by Vietnamese to returning overseas Vietnamese acknowledge the suffering of relatives in the United States and the fact that not everything there is easy: it is a way of saying "we know their life is hard." Even if Vietnamese perceive money as easier to come by overseas, they also know that money does not go as far there due to differentials in costs of living. Providing cheaper, affordable Vietnamese antibiotics as well as traditional eucalyptus oil as gifts to relatives returning to their home abroad is also a way of trying to help relatives overcome physical and financial hardship and achieve personal transformation.

Such exchanges also reflect the normalization of kinship relations across time and space and the reestablishment of more traditional relationships. The "time-space" compression (Harvey 1989, 260) said to characterize the contemporary globalized world affects extended family networks in Vietnam, particularly as changing political conditions have facilitated more cross-border travel and gift exchange. Whereas the medicinal gifts of the 1980s were often sent by members of the Vietnamese diaspora who feared what life might be like for relatives left behind, nowadays the types of gifts that are exchanged, while still carrying the residue of such motivations, are largely determined according to perceived needs and financial capacity, gauged on return visits to Vietnam. Medicines, which are a general household need, are purchased and exchanged among family members based on differential market access. As explained above, whereas family members in Vietnam have access to medicines that are cheaper, family members abroad can purchase medicines whose quality is ensured.[9]

Eucalyptus oil, widely available both in Vietnam and abroad, is significantly featured in two-ways flows for the simple reason that it is enjoyed and desired by recipients wherever they are located, and it can be easily and affordably acquired by people on both sides of the remittance relationship. Giving eucalyptus oil levels the gifting field, providing a momentary restoration of symmetry in the otherwise highly unequal dynamics of transnational gifting exchanges and illustrating that monetary gifts are almost always included in a collection of various material items that must all be taken into consideration when understanding how and why Vietnamese view remittances as gifts. The widespread two-way exchange of such a gift also reflects the fact that in many ways, the reestablishment of extended kinship relationships after years of separation—facilitated by changes in diplomatic and economic policies, the reduced cost of travel, new communication technologies, and eased or waived visa requirements—has become possible despite the spatial dispersion of family networks. As Peggy Levitt (2001) describes it, the "village" may have become transnational, but the relationships that define it continue across distance. In short, Vietnam has reengaged with the globalized capitalist world, and the Vietnamese diaspora, once mostly isolated in exile, is able to participate again on a regular basis in transnational family affairs, as is the case with diasporic populations of many other countries.

Remittance Politics

What, then, is significant about the situation of Vietnamese Americans in the United States who now return on a regular basis to Vietnam? Vietnam, once a cold war enemy of the countries where many Vietnamese refugees resettled, has normalized diplomatic and trade relations with those governments and in the process reestablished social and cultural relationships with its global diasporic population at the state level. The strongly anticommunist sentiments of many overseas Vietnamese in the United States appear to perhaps be weakening with time.[10] Return travel to Vietnam is no longer difficult, and even the establishment of transnational business relationships with Vietnam has become widely accepted, along with philanthropic engagement in the country. A popular chain of Vietnamese sandwich shops found in U.S. Vietnamese communities was mentioned by many of my informants in California as an example of Vietnamese American companies that now have significant business dealings in Vietnam. EB-5 visas that allow Vietnamese to move money out of Vietnam into the United States—often invested in Vietnamese American businesses—in return for green cards are popular, and their number is growing.[11] One Vietnamese American entrepreneur explained how she was planning to expand her local coffee shop to five U.S. cities as a franchise, with the help of EB-5 investor funds and connections. A Vietnamese American radio-show host, reflecting on the evolution of his audience over the past generation, explained that advertising for fund-raisers for charitable causes in Vietnam is now commonplace. In the 1980s and early 1990s, such transnational business practices and even humanitarian dealings were difficult given the U.S. embargo on Vietnam, and according to many of my informants, when they did happen were extremely controversial in the Vietnamese American community, sparking boycotts and even threats of violence. A 1994 *New York Times* story highlighted one such incident, in which the office of Vuong Tran, a travel agent promoting trips to Vietnam, was firebombed (Mydans 1994). Even private ethnic Vietnamese remittance companies were at times viewed with suspicion and accused of having links to and support from the Vietnamese government to conduct transnational business operations.

By the 2000s the idea of Vietnamese Americans conducting business in Vietnam had become largely accepted. The Vietnamese American Chamber of Commerce in Orange County supports and provides training for companies seeking to conduct business in Vietnam and also helps facilitate investments from Vietnam in Vietnamese American business ventures. One member of the chamber even organized a weekly Vietnamese-language class for young Vietnamese American professionals in Little Saigon, in part so they could learn appropriate business vocabularies to facilitate transnational investment opportunities. Anticommunist rhetoric to some extent remains an important symbolic community identity mechanism,[12] but it now rarely leads to sustained political action. The idea that the communist regime in Vietnam will soon fall is, as many of my informants soberly noted, an unrealistic dream.

In her 1997 memoir *Monkey Bridge*, Lan Cao poetically reflects on growing up in the early 1980s and the generational gap she experienced between her and her mother's orientations to Vietnam as she approached college age. She recalls that "it was near the end of April and my mother and I were both occupying a common space, the space that exists during an exact moment in time before ice melts or water freezes. We were both in the space where all things linger, only to turn unpredictably with the exquisite swiftness of a hard flower. We all enter this space when we wait—for motionless shadows to shift with a moment's notice, and hopes to become possibilities. I was waiting for an answer from Mount Holyoke, and my mother, along with the rest of Little Saigon, was waiting for a change in the political fortunes of Vietnam's Communist Party" (1997, 202). While many first-generation Vietnamese Americans at one point hoped that Vietnam's communist regime would be short-lived, the reestablishment of U.S.-Vietnam diplomatic and economic relations in the 1990s legitimized the current regime as, for better or worse, the representative of Vietnam in the world community. However, the former South Vietnamese yellow flag with its three red stripes still proudly flies over Vietnamese American shopping centers across the United States. Sometimes called the "Vietnamese heritage and freedom flag," it continues to be fiercely defended by a number of politically active Vietnamese American community groups as representing the Vietnamese nation, leading to campaigns in Vietnamese American communities from Virginia to New Orleans to Seattle to pass resolutions to this effect. Yet it is also viewed as an emotional symbol of the history of the Vietnamese diaspora, rather than a direct contestation of the current

Vietnamese regime's existence. For example, the city of Westminster, California (one of the two municipalities that Little Saigon straddles), passed resolution 3750 in 2003 to promote the symbolic display of the flag in place of the current flag of Vietnam. While the language of the resolution conceded that "the flag of the one party regime currently holding power in occupied Vietnam may be the flag of a government," (Westminster City Council 2003, 1) it argued that "it is not the flag of a Nation" (ibid.). Members of Vietnamese American communities continue to be active in protesting human rights abuses in Vietnam, often expressing legitimate humanitarian concerns, but these serve as more of a check on the current government than an attempt to overthrow it.

Nonetheless, anticommunist political activism continues to flare up in unexpected places. In the summer of 2008, many Vietnamese Americans in San Jose were upset about the proposed designation of the Vietnamese business area—a series of strip malls on Story Road—as the Saigon Business District. Madison Nguyen, a Vietnamese American city council member, had championed the designation as a way of showcasing the extensive Vietnamese business community in the area. The name originally proposed for the area was Little Saigon, which was already the well-known name of the Vietnamese American area in Orange County. However, the anticommunist activism that the name Little Saigon had come to represent over the years led some people who wished to move away from the politicized symbolism of that name to prefer another one, so "Saigon Business District" was suggested. The decision of the city council to go ahead with the alternative name enraged a significant segment of the Vietnamese American community who felt that they had not been properly consulted. In 2008 a movement to recall Nguyen (which was defeated in 2009) was being organized, and many stores in the Vietnamese shopping centers around San Jose had signs in the window signaling their opposition to the name Saigon Business District. As one woman explained her anger to me, "Madison has connections to the communists in Vietnam, and now she listens to them more than she does to us. When we were asked what we wanted the name to be, we told her 'Little Saigon.' So why then did she go and change it?" The larger issue in the controversy seemed to be an aggrieved sense of Vietnamese marginalization in American society, further aggravated when a Vietnamese American public official voted into office by the Vietnamese American community ignored the community's voice. Indeed, a great deal of Vietnamese American political activism appears to be in reaction to such perceived exclusion and to articulate a plea for the Vietnamese American community to be more visible, heard, and respected.[13]

Gazes and Vantage Points

Years of diasporic exile in the United States have produced a generation of Vietnamese Americans who have come of age in a multicultural and racialized society that encourages and necessitates identifications with ethnic heritage and roots.[14] For some, this search for identity turns their gaze toward what Ronald Takaki termed the strange "different shore" of Asia (1989). As many teenagers and people in their twenties start to connect with a Vietnamese homeland they never knew, remittance giving has also become an important mechanism for facilitating a transnational identity as a Vietnamese American and an overseas Vietnamese.[15] While many Vietnamese Americans of the first and 1.5 generations have significant memories of Vietnam, as well as cultural and linguistic capabilities related to their background, members of the younger generation are seeking new ways to connect with their Vietnamese heritage. A number of U.S.-based Vietnamese groups have emerged in the past decade that bring together younger Vietnamese Americans to address issues within the community both locally and transnationally.

Vietnamese student associations in college are starting points for the formation of many such groups. Campus chapters of student associations help organize younger Vietnamese Americans, focusing on activism, identity, and heritage, hold fund-raising or awareness campaigns related to issues that affect Vietnamese both in the United States and Vietnam, and send students to Vietnam. One outcome of a 2005 conference of the Union of North American Vietnamese Student Associations called Vietnamese Interacting as One was a collective philanthropy project, in which Vietnamese student associations could nominate nonprofit organizations working on issues relevant to the Vietnamese community and help raise funds for their projects (UNAVSA). Some college graduates have taken advantage of summer volunteer opportunities offered by a range of Vietnamese American NGOs, as well as initiatives such as the former Viet Fellows program (supported by the Ford Foundation and managed by Asian Americans/Pacific Islanders in Philanthropy), which sent Vietnamese Americans under the age of thirty to Vietnam for short-term volunteer assignments. Jodie Pham, a former fellow, explained that the program offered "the chance to connect to our roots and understand the intense resources needed in Vietnam. There is something that can be done and a young Vietnamese American, like myself, can be a part of that" (Viet Fellows 2011).

A common fund-raising strategy among diasporic philanthropy organizations is the development of giving circles that bring together young professionals who are potential donors to address issues of sociality and identity. Asian Americans/Pacific Islanders in Philanthropy, a nonprofit organization based in the Bay Area that ran the Viet Fellows program and was active in promoting the giving circle model during a 5-year campaign from 2011–2015, describes the tradition of giving circles that includes the Vietnamese tradition of *hụi*. "Communities around the world have long and deep traditions of supporting individuals, families, organizations, neighborhoods and communities. *Zakāt* is the Islamic practice of charitable giving based on communal responsibility for the poor. *Giri* is the Japanese sense of obligation to support those who are less fortunate. It's a *huei* in Chinese, *tong-tine* in Cambodian, *hui* in Vietnamese, *geh* in Korean—any way you name it, it's a Giving Circle, where everyday people like you come together in living rooms, church basements or even the local bar to pool money together and then use it to empower others" (AAPIP). Happy hours, dinners, and other social events are common forums for attracting and building such giving networks, and help institutionalize social pressure for collective giving. At one such giving event that I attended in the South Bay, potential donors were invited to attend a catered Vietnamese dinner at a private home, during which representatives of a Vietnamese American NGO gave a presentation about their organization's work and then fielded questions and responded to suggestions about its operations. Although money was not collected at the dinner, the guests went home with literature about the organization that included instructions on how to donate to the project via its website.

There is increasing consensus among organizers of collective or charitable remittance initiatives that building a sustainable base of donors among younger diasporic Vietnamese means connecting the humanitarian issues at stake to notions of identity and even branding strategies in fund-raising. As two leaders in their twenties of one group promoting Vietnamese American philanthropic activity in Vietnam explained to me over beer and pizza in San Francisco in 2008, "the first step [in developing a donor base] is making Vietnam cool and trendy among a younger generation that has turned away from it. In the way K-Pop has caught the attention of Korean Americans, we need to make Vietnamese social and cultural issues a part of Vietnamese American identity that people are excited about and want to be a part of."

What is apparent in the shift toward collective and second-generation giving is that the orientation and vantage point of the gift is changing. Whereas the crux of the traditional kin-to-kin remittance gift is the exchange between the overseas Vietnamese giver and the Vietnamese receiver, in these scenarios the Vietnamese receiver subject becomes ever more distant. As immediate family members are sponsored over time for family reunification emigration, the remittance relationship with extended kin becomes more sporadic and symbolic of securing for the giver a sense of status in a community of origin and return. In collective remittance scenarios where money is raised for charitable causes, the recipient of such gifts may become generic, stereotyped, and nameless: a Vietnamese orphan, a Vietnamese handicapped person, a Vietnamese victim of trafficking, and so on. The direct relationship between the giver and the receiver begins to recede, and the sociality of giving shifts to relations among the givers. The social dynamics of interaction among circles of givers who come together to raise money for a cause arguably has more to do with localized identity productions and relationships than long-distance kin obligations.

In collective remittance scenarios, there is also a noticeable process of reimagining and reinventing Vietnam as a place of nostalgic origins and connecting communities that share an ethnicity if not a geography. Homeland-bound remittances flows not only maintain identity, as the political scientist Adil Najam (2006) has argued, but they also serve to sustain the illusion of producing a coherent diasporic and transnational cultural identity that masks divisions and marginalizations. For the Vietnamese refugee community, in which support for the communist regime in Vietnam is rare, this has traditionally meant focusing community celebrations on cultural and geographic aspects of the nation, rather than on the state. Yet if the blame for structural poverty is generally placed on the Vietnamese communist party by members of the overseas diaspora, collective giving to alleviate poverty issues must in some sense address the politics of the state rather than merely the abstraction of the nation. This is not easy to do, and many diasporic charity organizations working in Vietnam have faced resistance to their work in Vietnamese American communities, especially if they do not operate in a politically sensitive manner. While such organizations must work with the People's Aid Coordinating Committee (the Vietnamese government's aid management branch) in their projects, the political necessity and reality of collaboration is downplayed in fund-raising and promotion overseas. Yet the rise of collective giving illustrates that there is increased interest among members of the diaspora in reconnecting with a physical place of origin and people who share their ethnic heritage but are separated by history and space—including constructing such connections and emotional linkages for the second generation.

The number of charitable giving initiatives in the diaspora is growing, motivated by development models such as Mexico's hometown associations (Orozco 2000 and 2013). Charity and development philanthropy is a unique disaggregated form of collective gift giving that falls within the broader category of remittances. Nonetheless, while remittances have long connected members of the diaspora to their places of origin, the integrity of their intentions sometimes remains ambivalently perceived by individuals receiving them. While providing important financial support to help address basic needs, the ability of remittances to be recognized properly as gifts is frequently dismissed by Vietnamese Americans. Too often, in their eyes, remittances seem to be obligatory, expected, and unappreciated.

Reflecting this frustration, one Vietnamese American man involved in transnational charitable activities told me that he had stopped sending direct family remittances years ago: "I used to send my family money, but they waste it all on useless things, become lazy, and only expect more. They did not help me out so much when I was a child over there, so I don't feel that I should be obliged to send money back. But I do love my homeland, Vietnam. It is the place where I was born and the culture that makes me who I am. I still send money therefore to Vietnam, just not to my family. There are many people who need more help than my family does, so my focus is now to assist them." When I asked how this has affected his family relationships, he said: "I don't visit my family often anymore. They do not understand why I give to and help other people but not them. They only think about themselves but not the greater good. There are so many poor people in Vietnam—compared to them, my family is doing okay. Besides it is good for them to work and not just receive money without effort."

Money thus appears as an embodiment of a work whose intention is to be altruistic. When monetary remittance gifts are expected and demanded rather than graciously and appreciatively received, and particularly when remittances make it possible for the recipients to stop working, the benevolent intention of the gift falls short, and the recognition it seeks is not forthcoming. For many diasporic remittance subjects, work becomes a defining characteristic of the transformed identity that they have adopted overseas. We have seen in previous discussions of willing professional underemployment by migrants in the service industry that what the work is matters less than what it earns. Work is a mode of being that time and again has been viewed as a luxury of living in the West. In this mode of work-cum-money, work (not as an occupation, but as a mode of embodied action) is entangled with American neoliberal ideals that promote the social power of economic self-transformation. As the anthropologists Jong Bum Kwon and Carrie Lane argue, "work produces value—material, moral, symbolic and social—and constitutes ways of life and forms of individual and collective identity as well as exclusion" (2016, 7). Remittance senders direct gifts with the intention of helping their families, but when they perceive that the gifts they send prevent family members from producing new value and inhabiting the imagined neoliberal work mode of self-transformation, the intention behind the aid relationship is frustrated.

Repeating the adage that "it is better to teach a man to fish than to give a fish," one volunteer with a Vietnamese American humanitarian organization in California explained that the goal of his philanthropic giving was to help Vietnamese help themselves. The types of programs that are widely supported through overseas Vietnamese charitable giving, including by a confederation of organizations that have come together in the Vietnamese American Non-Governmental Organization Network, are ones that emphasize the embodiment of work in the lives of gift recipients (Vietnamese American Non-Governmental Organization Network n.d.; see also Truong, Small, and Vuong 2008). Various diasporic aid organizations provide scholarships, job training, microcredit, and other services aimed at promoting economic development, social justice, and empowerment. We see in these programs a generalized desire to give a pure gift that does not need to be returned. While recognition is widely sought through such humanitarian giving, it is not appreciation alone that acts as a return gift for the giver, but also a hope that the intentions of the gift to lift people out of poverty and promote self-empowerment individually as well as collectively will be realized. Constructing a gift that can be directed, controlled, and appreciated and that can transform others is a key intention behind the humanitarian and philanthropic giving by many donors in the Vietnamese diaspora.

While the promotion of self-transformation through aid-driven capacity building is an important dimension of charitable giving, as discussed another significant aspect is that charitable community organizing expands the gift exchange away from the dyadic giver-receiver relationship toward multivalent relationships with other givers. Whereas the individual family remittance relationship is generally focused on the kinship between the sender and receiver, in cases of collective remittance giving the focus on the receiver recedes as the gaze of the giving community becomes more prominent. Whether the target of charitable aid may be an unemployed job trainee or a senior citizen lacking health services in Vietnam, he or she becomes an increasingly distant recipient without name or voice who nonetheless is assumed to be the needy and grateful subject of diasporic benevolence, validating the sense of generosity and goodwill by which donor organizations and their members define themselves.

In the meantime, diasporic organizations collaborate as well as compete to provide services to Vietnam and seek publicity and further support for their work, often through fund-raising events. At such events donors' identities, altruism, and even politics are performed, gauged, and monitored by others in the community and the circles of givers. The spectacle and performance of giving before others within diasporic communities not only offers personal fulfillment but can also serve to advance agendas of political and social leadership and prestige. At one fund-raising event that I attended in Orange County, the focus of the evening appeared to be as much on the emcees, singers, local politicians, and businesspeople who were introduced on stage as it was on the cause of the event (raising money for scholarships for youth in Vietnam). Of course, such phenomena are not unique to Vietnamese philanthropic community practices. Nonetheless, it is important to consider what other functions charitable giving serves. In this case, it certainly seems that it plays a key role in bringing together and organizing scattered diasporic communities around certain benevolent tropes. In doing so such practices offer alternative ethnic group relationships and collective identifications within and in contrast to the larger societies in which such organizers and donors live. These shared local needs and desires must also be recognized as motivating factors for organizing collectively around international humanitarian issues in faraway Vietnam.

Normalizing Transnationalism

Once again, all of these patterns point to an overall normalization of transnational relations between the Vietnamese homeland" and the diaspora. Whereas in the past the imaginaries of different lives beyond borders were heightened, sometimes floating in the realm of fantasy or horror, depending on one's vantage point, today Vietnamese family networks have a more grounded and sober view of what life is like for family members both in Vietnam and abroad. Many members of the second generation cohort of Vietnamese Americans are seeking to ground their diasporic Vietnamese identities in experiences, either vicarious or direct, through new engagements with a Vietnamese so-called homeland they never knew but that nonetheless has been important in the background of their identity formations and interrogations. The reestablishment of gifting relationships as regularized two-way flows between specific family members regardless of geographic location, as well as between overseas Vietnamese and the nation more generally, illustrates the widespread normalization and, in some cases, the reinvention of homeland-diaspora relations. In such gifting relationships, demonstrations of agency, identity, and sociality are important performative factors and are increasingly enacted not only by Vietnamese overseas, but also by Vietnamese in Vietnam who want to symbolically reciprocate the gifts and assistance their overseas counterparts have generously given for many years.

Yet while Vietnamese overseas have been invited back to participate in homeland affairs with the blessing of the state, the actual policies under which they are able to return betrays the fact that structural political factors also play an important role in constructing and governing citizen subjects beyond the family and heritage connections that motivate their returns. The *Việt Kiều* returning to Vietnam has become the subject of extended policy calculations in Vietnam and a familiar stereotype in popular culture. How the Vietnamese state manages and categorizes the increasingly engaged and returning members of the diaspora, and to what extent such state policies, incentives, and categories are accepted by those members, is the issue I turn to in chapter 5.

CROSSING THE BRIDGE . . . HOME?

As the previous chapter has illustrated, the Vietnamese American diaspora is becoming increasingly transnational in its orientation, in contrast to its largely exilic status from the 1970s to early 1990s. In this chapter I focus on contemporary Vietnamese American returnees who are living and working on a regular and semi-permanent basis in Vietnam, as I consider the aspirations and challenges of state policies that seek to influence the return motivations and experiences of members of the diaspora. Many first-generation Vietnamese Americans who left as refugees have cautiously welcomed the reestablishment of cross-Pacific kinship connections, although political suspicions of the current regime often linger. Many second-generation Vietnamese Americans have also forged an attachment to the Vietnamese homeland although they were born elsewhere, but their connections often emphasize spatial and not necessarily familial proximity.

A large young professional *Việt Kiều* population in Ho Chi Minh City live expatriate urban lifestyles in a somewhat familiar cultural and linguistic context, having returned to the "homeland." Although there may be a sense of curiosity about Vietnamese culture and society that influence their return engagements, many express feeling distant from and even avoid addressing extended family social expectations and obligations while in Vietnam.[1] A twenty-nine-year-old Vietnamese American named David from the California Bay Area, working for a bank in Saigon, described what he called the city's "VK bubble." He explained, "living in Saigon is ideal because there are many other *Việt Kiều* like me, who live on a bridge between cultures. We never felt that we fit in growing up in America, but then coming back to Vietnam we realize we don't really fit here either. Our relatives judge us and ask too many probing questions. Yet living among each other [in Saigon], we have a support community that recognizes and understands each other." Many *Việt Kiều* come to Vietnam in search of economic opportunity and professional mobility. The anthropologist Ashley Carruthers (2008) observed that in the 2000s many overseas Vietnamese professionals were recruited to Vietnam by companies to bridge a perceived business and cultural gap between their foreign representatives and local people. His finding however, was that the young *Việt Kiều* professionals were not always successful in their bridging capacities and had to find other ways of being at home in an assumed homeland. In many cases, those other ways involve finding alternative professional niches such as in startup businesses, an area where many *Việt Kiều* have achieved some success. Such career trajectories are often quite different from the original occupation or professional vision that brought them to Vietnam in the first place. Nonetheless, a number eventually discover Saigon to be a place that they can eventually call home, even if only temporarily.

Facilitating Return

Kim, a *Việt Kiều* from the state of Washington, whose family had fled the communist regime by boat after 1975, traveled back and forth regularly between the United States and Ho Chi Minh City, where she worked for a prominent international medical NGO. Her professional motivations for return are shared by many second-generation Vietnamese Americans in Vietnam, and they shed light on the infrastructural role played by the Vietnamese state in managing diasporic return mobility. Kim was a senior project manager, and although her salary was modest by American standards, it allowed her to live in a prime condominium overlooking the Ho Chi Minh City skyline and one of the few major parks left in this rapidly urbanizing city. Her American passport had a "five-year visa exemption" specially granted by the Vietnamese government to overseas Vietnamese returnees, which enables them to move freely in and out of the country. Having this visa allowed her to network locally and find her current job, although eventually she was required to apply for official working papers. The visa exemption program had been implemented in 2007 to promote returns to the homeland and encourage investment from overseas Vietnamese settled in Western countries

Increased return migration coincided with a time when foreign investment flows to Vietnam were increasing, and there was a demand for professionals who would be able to culturally and linguistically navigate this new emerging market, as Carruthers has discussed. In such an environment, entrepreneurial opportunities for middlemen abounded. Catherine, a *Việt Kiều* in her thirties from California, had given up her salaried cubicle job in suburban Orange County in 2005 to begin a textile production and import business that benefited from lower labor costs in Vietnam and by 2007, newly reduced tariffs on Vietnamese textile imports as a result of Vietnam's joining the World Trade Organization. Using her connections and capital, she was able to liaise across transnational networks of producers, suppliers, and distributors to have clothing made in Vietnam and bring it to the U.S. market, drawing on labor pools of ethnic Vietnamese on both sides of the Pacific. Like Kim, Catherine's work required her to have a mobile lifestyle that took her back and forth between the United States and Vietnam on a monthly basis. Both women enjoyed the benefits of the state-encouraged mobility that made their jobs possible, and they are examples of the type of overseas Vietnamese often celebrated in the state media as returning to their cultural roots while economically contributing to the homeland.

Đức is a middle-aged man who was born and raised in Saigon but moved to California as a teenager after 1975. Depending on whom he talks to, he has been variously called "*Người Việt Hải Ngoại*" (overseas Vietnamese), "*Người Việt Nam ở nước ngoài*" (Vietnamese in a foreign country), "*Người Mỹ gốc Việt*" (American with Vietnamese roots), and "*Kiều Bào*" (overseas compatriot).[2] Yet the popular designation for Đức, used on an everyday basis by his friends, acquaintances, colleagues, and himself while living in Saigon, is "*Việt Kiều*." After spending much of his adult life in California, Đức decided to return to Vietnam in the late 1990s. At the time he was a software engineer employed in Silicon Valley. As return migration to Vietnam became easier with fewer state restrictions, as well as less controversial among the California Vietnamese community that had lingering anticommunist reservations about permanent resettlement or business investment ventures in Vietnam, Đức started to think about becoming an entrepreneur back in what he still considers to be his home country. He had developed knowledge about the software industry during his years in the United States, relatively little start-up capital was needed in Vietnam, and there was a significant emerging pool of talent among the younger generation of Vietnamese. With contacts back in the United States to distribute the products, Đức decided to launch a software company in Vietnam, hiring engineers at a fraction of the cost of their American equivalents to design software for the U.S. market. Working with a Vietnamese American partner, Đức oversaw a young and eager staff and occasionally hired Vietnamese American and American talent to interface with some of the U.S. investors, marketers, and distributors. "Having an American accent on the telephone makes international business dealings much easier," Đức noted, highlighting an important linguistic dimension of identity orientation and recognition.

Although initially Đức maintained a transnational lifestyle, eventually the idea of a permanent return to Vietnam became attractive. The Vietnamese government had passed a series of measures and adopted policies to incentivize overseas Vietnamese resettlement in Vietnam and was offering workshops in major cities to help overseas Vietnamese navigate these laws and policies, recognizing the potential of long-term and comparatively stable diasporic economic investments. While Đức still had a home base in California through the members of his extended family who remained there, he started to reconnect with his family network in Vietnam. Đức identified himself as *Việt Kiều*, saying that "some Vietnamese in the U.S. think it has negative connotations, but I don't think so. *Việt Kiều* look to the future, rather than the past, and aren't afraid to return to Vietnam and make a life here. We have a lot of knowledge and skills that are needed in Vietnam. Here in Saigon, *Việt Kiều* has become a positive word, not a negative one."

Life in Vietnam was also in many ways a social and material upgrade from the one Đức had had in America. He had been a middle-class suburban bachelor in the United States, but in Vietnam he found an attractive Vietnamese woman to marry and moved into an apartment in one of the upscale neighborhoods of Saigon's third district. Đức was quite active in Ho Chi Minh City's expatriate and *Việt Kiều* community, volunteering to support candidates in U.S. presidential campaigns, coordinating fund-raising events for and sitting on the boards of various charitable groups in Vietnam, and organizing social events. A number of his high-school classmates from Saigon, many of whom had also left Vietnam after 1975, had reconnected or returned over the years to conduct business in Ho Chi Minh City, and he participated in an alumni group from the school that included members from both California and Saigon that frequently organized reunions and networking opportunities.

Although Đức had not yet taken advantage of the overseas Vietnamese land law that allowed returning *Việt Kiều* to buy land, as the law remained "too ambiguous" in his view, he had made some real estate investments through extended relatives. In the early and mid-2000s land values in Vietnam were rising so rapidly that if one had capital to invest, there were quick financial returns to be had. He was one of the first to sign up for the five-year visa waiver for overseas Vietnamese in 2008 and was planning to apply for Vietnamese dual citizenship. Doing so would facilitate his business interests by allowing him to ease reporting requirements and maintain more control of his company as a local owner.

Prosperous in business and generous to those less fortunate than himself, Đức believed that his return to Vietnam was one of the best life decisions he had made for personal, cultural, and financial reasons. Vietnam felt familiar to him, and while he had previously tried to help his relatives in Vietnam through making occasional remittance contributions out of his hard-earned salary, now he could afford to help them generously and even give them jobs. There was always more money to be made in the emerging Vietnamese economy. "One only needs to look in the right places and have the right connections," Đức explained. As a Vietnamese American with start-up capital, it seemed easy to make money in Vietnam, he said, but at the same time nothing was very predictable or transparent.[3] "You never know when the government is going to suddenly step in and try to take your money." But if should that happen, he continued, "I still have my American passport and can go back to America." When I asked where home was, he said: "Vietnam is home, because it is where I was born. But it is easier to feel at home when I have the security to leave it." For Đức, home was geographically rooted and familiar but also contingent on the security of financial and physical mobility that gave him the agency to name Vietnam as "home." Yet the felt agency over the naming of "home" also provoked anxieties about belonging and identity that I observed among many overseas Vietnamese living in Vietnam.

Linh is a Vietnamese American woman based in San Jose, California, but working with a Vietnamese American NGO in Vietnam. Shortly after my arrival in Saigon in 2007 to begin fieldwork, I found myself traveling on a bus with Linh to the Mekong Delta to volunteer with her organization, which provides scholarships, job training, and support. She chatted eagerly, full of passion and zeal for her project of providing educational and employment opportunities as a means to prevent human trafficking, and indignant about the insufficient efforts of the government and larger organizations to address the issue. Her organization had a critical advantage, she said. With its staff of both Vietnamese and overseas Vietnamese, it could combine local knowledge with Vietnamese American connections to resources and awareness campaigns to stage more effective interventions. The primary program that her organization ran was the provision of scholarships to keep girls from dropping out of school. The lack of local employment opportunities frequently meant that such girls were tempted by the allure of work and remittances across the nearby Cambodian border, where a thriving sex industry awaited in Phnom Penh—in many cases the ultimate destination of girls who were recruited for what they were told would be work as domestic servants.

Shadowing Linh on her visits to government officials, local partners, field staff members, and clients, I was amazed at how this woman, who had a husband and child in San Jose, found the energy to fly back and forth between the United States and Vietnam on a regular basis, largely unpaid, to manage the program. Linh was constantly on the phone and on the move, and her "giving" to this humanitarian cause in her country of origin, which she had left as a teenager, involved not only financial but considerable personal expenditure. She differentiated this kind of giving—both financial and social—from personal remittance giving, which she said was more obligatory and filial but often did not go to as good a cause. Humanitarian giving to broader development causes, she said, could do much more to bring Vietnam out of poverty in the long run than individually targeted remittances could, and her goal was to encourage the Vietnamese American community to engage more with this type of collective charitable giving in the future.

Motivating Return Engagements

Many *Việt Kiều* in Saigon, like Vietnamese Americans in the United States, are active in raising funds for charitable causes in Vietnam, such as for the organization that Linh worked for. One organization that was energetic during the time I was conducting fieldwork in Saigon in the late 2000s was called *Việt Mới* ("New Vietnamese"). *Việt Mới* was a term that was defined by the group's organizer as reflective of a generation of Vietnamese who grew up overseas but were now returning to live and work during what he called a transition between the old and new Vietnam. In 2008 *Việt Mới* regularly organized fund-raising events in Saigon, complete with music and fashion shows, to demonstrate solidarity with a country and heritage its members (who come from countries such as Australia and the United States) sought to engage with. Although many participants that I spoke with shared that they were not supporting their extended family members in Vietnam through direct remittance support, they still were donating to charitable causes in a homeland they felt emotionally attached to, but on what they felt was more of their own terms. This is reflective of a broader shift over generations in many immigrant situations from family to collective remittance giving, illustrating that financial gifts also increasingly serve as "identity maintaining mechanisms" (Najam 2006, 127), or even identity constructing mechanisms, rather than mere demonstrations of familial obligation in extended kinship scenarios.

Personal and collective identity was a motivating issue that repeatedly emerged in my interviews with Vietnamese Americans of the second and 1.5 generation living in Vietnam. The social, political, geographic, and economic differentials between Vietnam and the United States force many Vietnamese Americans to reflect on the circumstances of their identity and the critical role of chance in shaping it. A Vietnamese American woman in her thirties named Margaret, who was born in Vietnam but raised in the United States, travels regularly between the two countries for business. Margaret had a personal project for which she took a series of photos on the streets of Vietnam. She would find women who were approximately her age, usually working menial jobs such as selling goods on the street. She would approach these women and strike up a conversation, learning their life stories and how they had come to be in their current situation. In turn, Margaret would share her own family's story of fleeing from Vietnam as refugees.

At the end of each conversation, she would ask to take a photo of herself with the woman. She had over forty such photos. For her, these photos of herself and another Vietnamese woman of similar age represented a hypothetical identity for her, or what Cathy Schlund-Vials has termed "imagining otherwise" (2014, 321) when diasporic subjects confront the vicissitudes of migratory origins and arrivals. "If history had turned out differently," Margaret mused, "I could be any of these women." Engaging with and learning about a cultural place of origin that nonetheless had a significant air of mystery was a defining experience and an entry point to engage with Vietnam for many of the younger Vietnamese Americans I spoke with. Direct kinship connections, however, were relatively marginal to their longer term personal, cultural, and economic motivations to live in Vietnam.

Managing Mobility

All of these stories reflect the increased international circulation and return of bodies that have accompanied financial flows as Vietnam integrates itself into the global economy. In the past decade the Vietnamese state has promoted the idea of homeland return and has reimagined its external overseas diaspora as now internal to the nation, creating a variety of institutions, policies, and structural incentives to promote and reflect this new relationship. In 2004, the Vietnamese Politburo passed Resolution 36-NQ/TW, which symbolically welcomed returnees to the homeland (*quê hương*) and promised protection of all Vietnamese overseas, regardless of their location or occupation. Resolution 36 and its related policies reiterate that "overseas Vietnamese are an inseparable part of the community of Vietnamese nationalities" and encourage them to return and contribute to the homeland.[4] Such initiatives reveal how the "state sees" (Scott 1998) and correspondingly valuates, manages, and manipulates mobility in the interest of national development. As the sociologist Beverly Skeggs notes, "mobility and control over mobility both reflect and reinforce power" (2004, 49). The emotionally laden notion of homeland return is strategically deployed and economically calculated by the Vietnamese state when engaging with members of its diaspora. Nonetheless, there remains a significant gap between state discourses on rationales for return migration, and personal experiences of and motivations for it.

The people just discussed all fall into the state-defined category of "Vietnamese in foreign countries," the oversight of which has been delegated to the Committee for Overseas Vietnamese Affairs, which is modeled after similar initiatives in other countries with large overseas populations. However, the vernacular term for overseas Vietnamese is *Việt Kiều*, and it often connotes the perception that these people who return to Vietnam enjoy a privileged lifestyle of interstate mobility, the very mobility that many local Vietnamese aspire to. Although the term *Kiều* (from the Chinese word root *qiao*, meaning sojourning overseas) is often rejected by resettled Vietnamese immigrants abroad because of negative historical associations and the connotation of temporary status in countries they have moved to, I found that for reasons similar to Đức's explanation, it was generally embraced by those returnees or transnationals who have chosen to return to Vietnam from the West for long-term employment or resettlement. The word is also a homonym for bridge (*kiều*), identically spelled in romanized *quốc ngữ* although the words are not necessarily directly etymologically related.[5] But for *Việt Kiều*, transnational mobility does reflect a bridge-like identity, in that the return bridge is two-way: they retain U.S. passports, meaning the possibility of crossing back to the other side is never foreclosed. *Việt Kiều* are frequently referred to by journalists, politicians, and businesses as "bridges" between the West and Vietnam. Vietnamese government reporting on a 2016 Overseas Vietnamese conference in Ho Chi Minh City encouraging investment from the diaspora, for example, stated that "Overseas Vietnamese people are an inseparable part of the Vietnamese nation and a *bridge* (emphasis added) linking Vietnam with other countries around the world" (Voice of Vietnam 2016).

For *Việt Kiều* the state order of mobility is experienced as one that constantly encourages overseas Vietnamese to return by tactfully reminding them of where the bridge and homeland intersect, constructing the latter as a place of nostalgic but inevitable return. Welcoming returning overseas Vietnamese to Saigon's Tân Sơn Nhất Airport during Tết in 2008, for example, was a large banner over the immigration counter saying "The homeland welcomes our overseas compatriots returning to celebrate the New Year (*Quê Hương Chào Mừng Kiều Bào Về Đón Tết*)." Here, the choice of the designation *Kiều Bào*, an official term roughly translated as "overseas compatriots," underscores the state's efforts to strategically promote homeland return in the interest of national development and global integration. The Sino-Vietnamese word root of *bào* means womb. The official usage of the term *Kiều Bào* therefore suggests an agenda of constructing diasporic subjectivities intimately linked with the womb, nation, or homeland. Overseas Vietnamese subjecthood is metaphorically constructed as a bridge always pulling them back (returning) to their primordial origins, even in a globalized era of widespread mobility and emigration.

Despite these linguistic constructions and state-promoted welcome agendas, return is still recognized as an agential choice by those *Việt Kiều* living overseas, outside the purview of the Vietnamese state. Most, after all, are no longer (or never were) citizens of the Socialist Republic of Vietnam. Many of those who return, often holding residual or sometimes inherited anticommunist sentiments not un common in Vietnamese American refugee communities, do so in spite of, rather than because of, the state. Nonetheless, through efforts to encourage and welcome overseas Vietnamese returning home, the Vietnamese government has sought recognition and relevance among this significant group of diasporic returnees, whose homeward returns and transnational subjectivities more often have personal and economic, rather than political and nationalistic, motivations.

As this book has discussed, a fundamental contradiction in the neoliberal ethic is the lack of equivalence between flows of money and goods and the flow of people: mobility of finance is privileged over the mobility of labor.[6] Citizens as well as governments are beholden to a broader global political economy in which mobility is both desired and managed: where money flows, bodies and states attempt to follow, with varying degrees of success. The experiential dimensions of such differential hierarchies of mobility are displaced into an ontological framework in which mobility itself is paramount. "Motility" (Kauffman et al. 2004, 745), or mobility capital—the ability to access global mobile channels and networks, plays a significant role in shaping diasporic subjectivities. The vexed notion of homeland return, as deployed by the state and experienced by returning overseas Vietnamese, offers some insight into how broader structures and specters of global migration are not only structurally governed but also ontologically navigated. In the process we see how money and bodies become conceptually linked, contributing to a heightened imaginary between Vietnam, and the United States in particular, due to its large permanently resettled Vietnamese diaspora that fuels migratory aspirations in Vietnam. The compelling tangibility of this embodied imaginary linking Saigon to Little Saigons differs markedly from other global capitalist nodes from which investment capital may flow but do not have similar critical masses of resettled immigrants that aspiring migrants can imagine becoming.[7]

In the past decade the Vietnamese government has implemented numerous structural policies to encourage various forms of economic and bodily return. In contrast to 1991, when the Ministry of Finance imposed a detailed tax regimen on goods brought into the country by returning *Việt Kiều*, in 1997 the 5 percent tax on overseas remittances was lifted. In 2002, the government expanded the range of financial institutions permitted to deliver foreign currencies remitted by overseas Vietnamese. In 2005, a network of Vietnamese American NGOs was formed in coordination with the Vietnamese government's People's Aid Coordinating Committee, facilitating the flow of humanitarian funds from the Vietnamese diaspora to local aid and development projects. In 2007, Vietnam joined the World Trade Organization, attracting new international investment and increasing its exports. Alongside economic reforms, Vietnam also began instituting a wave of new policies designed to encourage Vietnamese in Western countries to return to Vietnam for tourism and investment. This included legislation in 2001, 2006, and 2010 allowing overseas Vietnamese to own property in Vietnam. A symbolic milestone, as discussed, was the Politburo's Resolution 36 of 2004 affirming that overseas Vietnamese were an integral part of the nation. The creation of "Overseas Compatriot Organizations (*Hội Kiều Bào*)" intended to encourage state linkages with overseas Vietnamese communities followed. In 2007, Prime Ministerial Decision 135 allowed five-year visa waivers for overseas Vietnamese, which have been quite popular among members of the diaspora. Less taken up by overseas Vietnamese is the offer of dual citizenship in the amended 2008 Vietnamese Nationality Law.[8] The government also passed ambitious measures in 2007 to develop and expand its export labor program, with a goal of sending 100,000 workers abroad annually—a number that has now been surpassed. By 2014 there were 500,000 Vietnamese contract laborers working overseas (Miller 2015) and sending valuable remittances back. In November 2009, the government sponsored a conference on the global Vietnamese diaspora in Hanoi, which was attended by 1,500 people (including 900 representatives of overseas Vietnamese), to discuss four main themes: building an overseas Vietnamese community, attracting the return of overseas Vietnamese intellectuals, preserving Vietnamese cultural identity and tradition overseas, and attracting overseas Vietnamese businesses to Vietnam. There have been many other similar conferences on general and specific themes related to diasporic contributions to the homeland, such as a 2016 conference in Ho Chi Minh City focusing on the role of overseas Vietnamese in promoting technology and building a knowledge-led economy. Returning Vietnamese diasporic bodies, capital, and knowledge to the homeland is certainly a goal of the state, but it is clearly conditional on the value inherent or at least assumed in their intersection.

Patriots or Puppets?

It is helpful to reflect on the overall spectrum and chronology of migrant and remittance mobility in Vietnam. Its history, extending through the 1970s to the present, illustrates both the power and anxiety of the state in managing diasporic mobility and return. Recent policies encouraging diasporic physical, financial, and social engagement with the homeland starkly contrast with earlier state attitudes toward the overseas Vietnamese population. Following the end of the Vietnam War and the communist reunification of the country in 1975, the Vietnamese government encouraged Vietnamese expatriates abroad to return to the homeland for the purposes of national reconstruction. Many South Vietnamese students studying in the West were urged to return, and those who did were celebrated as patriots—in the tradition of Ho Chi Minh, who spent thirty years overseas before coming home to lead the revolution. *Kiều Bào và Quê Hương* (Ủy Ban Nhà Nước Về người Việt Nam ở Nước Ngoài 2006), a publication of the Vietnamese government's Committee on Overseas Vietnamese, is a 966-page account of various overseas Vietnamese patriots who loved their country (*yêu nước*) and contributed to the homeland, including stories of those who returned from abroad after 1975. After the Vietnam War, overseas Vietnamese who chose to stay abroad, as well as those in Vietnam who chose to flee as refugees, were severely criticized. In an early 1979 decree on *Việt Kiều*, the motivations for international mobility were critiqued as antinationalist and unpatriotic. Vietnamese who left the country as refugees were described as former "puppets (*ngụy*)" who abandoned their homeland and the national reconstruction effort. The state suspected hostile motives for remittances from overseas Vietnamese that in some cases funded antigovernment efforts. In 1998, the War Remnants Museum in Ho Chi Minh City hosted an exhibition that depicted treacherous overseas Vietnamese terrorist groups whose members, having abandoned their homeland and living in exile, raised funds abroad for the purpose of undermining and sabotaging the Vietnamese nation.

Until the 1990s most former refugees overseas were kept outside the Cold War's iron and bamboo curtains. There were no diplomatic relations in the 1980s between the United States, where the majority of refugees had settled, and Vietnam. Remittances sent from abroad largely took the form of goods that could be exchanged on the Vietnamese black market due to prohibitions on financial channels. For Vietnamese exiles abroad, the possibility of return seemed unlikely unless there was a counterrevolution and regime change in Vietnam. By the early 1990s the Cold War was ending. With Soviet assistance gone, Vietnam became more amenable—indeed, it had little choice—to economic and political reform and reintegration into the capitalist world. After renovation (*Đổi Mới*), the Vietnamese government hoped that opening up the economy to tourism and investment would bring much-needed capital to Vietnam. In 1995 the United States and Vietnam reestablished diplomatic relations, and in 2000 trade relations were normalized through the U.S.-Vietnam Bilateral Trade Agreement. Following these changes, the return of refugees from Western countries expanded from a trickle to a steady stream. While there were only 8,000 overseas Vietnamese returnees in 1987, in 1992 there were 87,000, by 2002 over 380,000 overseas Vietnamese were returning annually—and by 2015 over half a million.[9] A significant *Việt Kiều* return economy emerged, and the Vietnamese government quickly came to appreciate the growing economic power of *Việt Kiều* through remittances, spending, and investment. No longer as suspicious of them, the state began to welcome *Việt Kiều* and their money to the homeland.

Chasing Circulation

The anthropologist Liisa Malkki (1995) notes a tendency in migration studies to naturalize sedentariness and exceptionalize movement, despite empirical observations that suggest the opposite is the case. The interest of the Vietnamese state in monitoring and managing the mobility of ethnic Vietnamese across the globe betrays this tendency to equate identity with resedentarized bodies. As was the case with environmental policy discourses in Vietnam analyzed by Pamela McElwee (2016), when it comes to contemporary migration discourses the Vietnamese state is intervening in social planning and producing policies that are ostensibly justified by rendering visible an issue that thus becomes governable. In this case the nation-state—itself a relatively recent construct (Anderson 1998)—is naturalized as home. The nation-state must therefore account for its migrant citizens, and those citizens are deemed accountable to it. The notion of "returning" becomes possible only when the accompanying concept of "home" is secured. Of course, this is vastly complicated in an entangled and interdependent but also highly unequal global world. Aihwa Ong (1999) has examined the convergence of capitalist and state interests in producing an overarching regime of neoliberal governance, and the corresponding subject formation of global citizens embodied by capital flows. Akhil Gupta argues that governmentality has become "unhitched from the nation-state to be instituted anew on a global scale" (1998, 321), and that indeed the modern state has no choice but to be complicit in a larger capitalist order of global assemblage and production. As the Vietnamese state revaluates its diaspora and attempts to reintegrate them into the homeland, motivated in part by a desire to improve its financial bottom line, it is responding to and emulating the neoliberal dynamics of globalism. Bodies become seemingly synonymous with finance, yet they are not.

State attempts to officially manage the global mobility of migrants nonetheless run parallel with financial-sector efforts to manage the return of remittance money through formal channels. As I discussed in the introduction, development policy analysts have emphasized the importance of shifting from informal to formal transfer channels, and this shift has been accompanied by significant political oversight and governance measures. Yet one of the attractions of informal financial channels is the multidirectionality of flows: money departing from Vietnam can be effectively and easily swapped for money arriving there. The most widespread mode of informal remittances is what has been called "hot transfers" (Hernandez-Coss 2005, 43). Hot transfers, which use creative bookkeeping techniques across transnational business and trade operations to transfer value without physically transferring any money, are popular and cost-effective in Vietnam and among Vietnamese communities abroad. Capital controls and restrictions make it difficult and expensive to get money out of Vietnam to facilitate international business and trade operations. In the United States, many Vietnamese working in the informal cash economy (with jobs at restaurants or nail salons, for example) also prefer to keep their money below the tax radar. Informal services step in to provide innovative and under-the-table accounting and invoicing methods that essentially swap remittances from the United States to Vietnam with outgoing investments and payments from Vietnam to the United States, providing needed financial transfer services on both sides of the Pacific that circumvent official governance and oversight. In this case the multidirectional economic flows seem more closely aligned with the circulatory momentum of return migrants than with static notions of homeland cultures and primordial emotional attachments that are used to explain migrant behavior and exploited by states to influence their unidirectional return. As the cases of Catherine, Kim, Đức, and Linh show, their willingness and interest to return to and live in Vietnam is based on their capacity to freely circulate in and out of the country and maintain a transnational sense of home across more than one locale.

The Vietnamese state is in a transitional phase as it decides how to engage its global diaspora, whose members are now lumped under an overarching definitional umbrella of *Người Việt Nam ở Nước Ngoài* and placed under the oversight of a single Committee for Overseas Vietnamese Affairs. The largest and most conspicuous portion of the Vietnamese diaspora is made up of post-1975 refugees and migrants living in the United States, Canada, Australia, and Western Europe. But the diaspora also includes significant populations whose members are not the subject of this book. The Committee for Overseas Vietnamese Affairs also includes in its oversight of *Người Việt Nam ở Nước Ngoài* pre-1975 migrants to destinations such as France and elsewhere in the former French empire; the Chinese Vietnamese who left following the Sino-Vietnamese War; socialist-era worker and student migrants to Eastern Europe and the Soviet Union; current student migrants to Asia, Europe, and North America; Vietnamese populations in neighboring Cambodia and Laos; marriage migrants to nearby countries like Taiwan and South Korea; international scientific experts; and the rapidly increasing number of worker migrants to destinations ranging from Jordan to Malaysia.[10] For each of these populations, the channels, circulatory capacities and directional momentums of bodies and monies are different, and yet the government attempts to develop policies that will address all of their perceived needs.

Vietnam finds itself navigating a new globalized era of state engagements with transnational diasporic subjects. In this sense its diaspora policies parallel the growth of diaspora ministries in other countries across the Global South with histories of extensive overseas migration.[11] Such diaspora ministries—whether in Vietnam, India, Israel, or Haiti—highlight the inescapable primacy and necessity of mobility to nation-state governance in a globally interdependent world. Yet policies to oversee and manage multidirectional and multipurpose migration also face the challenges and limits of such governance. Despite the seemingly straightforward nature of the task (the cultivation of relations between an overseas diaspora and the homeland), there is significant confusion about how to go about it, as *Hội Kiều Bào* representatives shared with me. The most fundamental logistical paradox is the fact there are multiple types of emigrants, with complex corresponding relations to the homeland and thus motivations for return. As Xiang Biao, Brenda Yeoh, and Mika Toyota point out in their work on how and why Asian states encourage return migration, diverse types of migrants may be "treated very differently from each other, and yet are . . . lumped together under the rubric of 'return'" (2013, 4). Biao et al. make the case that "the all-embracing, naturalizing notion of 'return' in public discourse ascribes particular universalistic meanings to diverse return flows" (ibid., 6) and that even differences in the state's power to control such flows are subsumed in interstate agreements and international consensuses on regional and global mobility governance policy. The institutionalization and modeling of diaspora engagement policies without nuanced distinctions that account for the unique economic, geographic, and political circumstances of migration is not a problem in Vietnam alone. But it may be more complicated in Vietnam's case due to the country's particular history of war that violently produced such a significant proportion of its contemporary diaspora.

Money-Gift Embodiments

Returning to Marcel Mauss's observation of the *hau* (or spirit of the giver) that embodies the gift, as well as Bronislaw Malinowski's description of the entanglement of commodities and gifts in the Kula circles of the South Pacific, it appears that controlling modern migrant return channels in the case of financial and migratory repatriation remains an elusive goal that is nonetheless anxiously sought by the state. Mauss reminds us that despite the gift's desire to return home via the affectual momentum of the *hau*, it continues to circulate, passed on again and again and always demanding greater mobility and associations: "the hau that wishes to return to its birthplace . . . which itself moreover possesses a kind of individuality—is attached to this chain of users until these give back . . . the equivalent or something of even greater value" (1967, 12). In this sense its momentum opposes in desire but emulates in practice what Karl Marx observed in the circulation of money, which "continually moves away from its own starting-point . . . as the medium of circulation, [it] haunts the sphere of circulation and constantly moves around within it" (1992, 213). The energy of the monetary gift, embedded among the gifters and the other material exchanges it incorporates and is entangled with in producing and recognizing value, is not easily constrained.

Despite elaborate rules established by societies and categories created by analysts that attempt to domesticate, explicate, and control the boundaries of the gift, its exuberant tendency (particularly in the form of money) is inevitably unleashed in circulation. Refugee migrants, embodying the elusive capital and remittance gifts they seek and continuously earn and pass on in hopes "of even greater value," demonstrate a similar creative mobile momentum. Having fled Vietnam in the aftermath of war to start new lives scattered across the globe, a generation later former refugee migrants are leaving those lives to rediscover opportunities in Vietnam, all the while retaining and managing transnational connections and horizons with "chains" of gifters and giftees on both (indeed, multiple) sides. Their migratory momentums "haunt the sphere of circulation," catalyzing the imaginaries of others who also want to "move around within it" and contributing to the widely observed correlation between remittance reception and migratory desire. Given these ethnographic insights into the circulatory momentum and energy of migrant mobility, the geopolitical naturalization of unidirectional return by the Vietnamese state appears in fact quite unnatural. Significant numbers of overseas Vietnamese are finding their way back to the homeland in a variety of ways and for a variety of motivations, but it is rarely their singular end point. Like the remittance money that circulates in multiple directions to, from, and beyond Vietnam, so do the returnees that send, make, and bring those monies. The only thing that can be said definitively about the contemporary situation in Vietnam is that the amounts of remittances and numbers of returnees are increasing as rapidly as the rationales for and experiences of return. The more significant consequence is that such flows of migrants and monies are contributing to visceral "cultures of migration" (Cohen and Sirkeci 2011) in which the "nerviness and excitement" (Mauss 1967, 38) of the circulatory momentum of bodies and gifts becomes obsessive, pervading contemporary Vietnamese structures of social comparison and aspiration.

Money appears as a paramount factor in the various personal and policy motivations related to return migration discussed in this chapter, which returns us to our basic question: what is money, and how and why does it get entangled in the realm of sociality? By looking at how the state attempts to channel money and bodies and in the process link the two via the notion of the gift, we see once again how the question of money is in part an infrastructural one. While the surface rationale of diaspora return policies may appear affectively nationalistic, encouraging the return of gifts and bodies to the womb, the root of their logic is economic, and it is for this reason that many return migrants may resist calls to set aside personal agendas that do not align with state priorities, as well as feel more generally ambivalent about the sincerity of the nation-state in welcoming them to back to the homeland. This ambivalence is noticeably marked in the case of former refugees, where return and money are caught up with political and social memories of trauma and betrayal. And here we once again see that money—despite its formal definition as a mere unit of account, store of value, means of exchange, and method of payment—is always much, much more. By considering remittances as money in conversation with the gift, including attending to the affectual *hau* that can never be disentangled from it, remittances reveal themselves as complex actants imbricated in the lives of the actors and networks that use and exchange them. Remittances offer insight into the stories, behaviors and motivations of those actors, reveal their networks, and gesture toward even more.

Conclusion

NOT YET ENOUGH: MOBILITY
AND ITS MALCONTENTS

This book began by introducing and contextualizing migration and remittance economies in Vietnam. It has moved ethnographically through different landscapes of mobile persons, monies, commodities, ideas, and imaginaries. These landscapes range from urban Ho Chi Minh City to coastal Quy Nhơn and suburban California and have involved the lives of Vietnamese in Vietnam encountering returning overseas Vietnamese and their gifts, transnational individuals and organizations moving between the United States and Vietnam, and Vietnamese living in ethnic communities on the far side of the Pacific Ocean from Vietnam. This book has also looked at how mobility has been defined, channeled, and capitalized upon by the state: particularly at a moment of widespread return by former refugees and their remittances, as well as how state migrant subject categories are inhabited, experienced, and circumnavigated by overseas Vietnamese as they seek to connect to transnational kin through bodily and financial return. The argument has been made that the particular circumstances of Vietnamese refugees (that is, the origins of their departures, entangled with historical traumas of war and subsequent escape and exile) make for a very different relationship to nations, home communities, and kinship networks than is the case in many situations of contemporary global migration. Most importantly, the ethnographies presented in this book illustrate that in remittances-as-gifts economies, the gift's monetary form displays characteristics that are increasingly individually or collectively desired and embodied by remittance exchange participants—namely, the characteristics of mobility and exchangeable value, which are perceived to enable social transformation in a global economy.

What is to be learned from the varied ethnographic accounts presented in this book? For one thing, I hope that these materials clearly demonstrate that any discussion of remittance economies must recognize the complex actions, reactions, and motivations of the exchange participants. Not surprisingly, the remittance actor, sometimes caricatured for the needs of development policy research, prediction, and implementation, is more complicated than typically assumed. Remittance flows, while certainly an important tool for poverty alleviation in many communities, are also private gifts that carry complex and latent symbolic meanings. Remittances, which most often serve as family support from those who have more economic earning capacity to those with less, are in many ways merely a transnationalization and in some cases a monetization of long-standing traditional modes of kinship support and relationship building. As Peggy Levitt (2001) describes it, the village has become transnational, but it is still a village. To draw such familial rituals of gifting and kinship belonging into the public realm is to risk misunderstanding and to intrude in personal matters that have specific histories, contexts, and complexities that cannot be standardized for the purposes of policy planning and analysis. Remittance participants are not the stereotypical economic actors of rational choice theory, nor do they necessarily respond well to the assumptions and incentives of state homeland promotion campaigns. The gambling proclivities of some remittance recipients detailed in the ethnographies in this book clearly demonstrate that remittances are not always directed toward productive family and community investments, as many economic development policy makers would like to presume is the case.

This is not to say that remittances are not helpful in reducing poverty and meeting basic needs in low-income communities. Remittances provide an important source of household credit and often address critical needs in health and education.[1] Nonetheless, remittance economy participants also use their incomes to support a range of other activities that cannot be generalized but differ widely according to circumstance and individual preference. Even a behavioral-economic lens is unlikely to serve us well in predicting the motivations, actions, and investment strategies of remittance actors, nor is it the intention of this book to offer a predictive or interpretive model of the behavior patterns of remittance actors.

By considering the themes of gifts, mobility, and flows that underlie remittances, one notices how together they contribute to the emergence of an imaginative comparative specter that pervades and influences individual and collective structures of expectation, desire, and satisfaction. Remittance gifts bring vastly different life worlds into intimate encounter, while also drawing attention to the stark limitations of human action in shaping individual and collective efforts to produce human social transformations. International remittances channeled between and across spatial environments molded and differentiated by global and local political and economic factors beyond individual control reinforce an already strong Vietnamese notion of fate (*số phận*) that continues to be an important factor in explaining the conditions and limits of possibility in Vietnam. But also important is the fact that there exist opportunities for gaining access to varying conditions of potential and opportunity through mobility and migration. The strong qualitative correlation found in this research between reception of remittances and migratory desire and planning in households demonstrates a detectable heightening of agential aspiration and expectation in remittance economies.

In some cases, such agential aspirations reflect a desire for and belief in the possibility of systemic change, as in the case of many Vietnamese American charities and NGOs staffed by volunteers like Linh in chapter 5 whose supporters hope through their labor and monetary contributions to bring social justice to and alleviate the poverty of those left behind in Vietnam. But many Vietnamese who have stayed in Vietnam seem primarily to desire access to outward physical bodily mobility. Here the agency enacted often reflects a desire not to change what is seen as a corrupt system but to escape it altogether and begin life anew in a completely different political, economic, and cultural environment with fresh horizons of possibility. Such was the case of Phuong in chapter 1, who sought to escape Vietnam permanently to find a new identity in the United Kingdom that would be free of social obligations and structural obstacles to personal development. While her case reflects a strong individualized desire for mobility, in many other cases migratory aspirations are collective in that they tend to be part of family diversification strategies. This was reflected in many stories throughout this ethnography, such as the case of Hai and his family in chapter 3 who had successfully established a networked trans-Pacific lifestyle, or Thach, also in chapter 3, who had unsuccessfully tried to leave Vietnam during an earlier period to reduce the economic burden on his family. Local histories of migration have infused a sociocultural dynamic of collective migratory yearning and even gendered adventurism in many of the communities where remittances and overseas relations are prevalent, such as Quy Nhơn and its coastal neighbors. Although migration is not personally desired by everyone who stayed behind in Vietnam, especially among a current generation of older people who have settled into familiar lifestyles, it is an option in the basket of choices available to families whose members are planning and making collective decisions about issues of employment, education, social development, financial security, marriage prospects, and kinship networks.

The production of imagined alternative identifications facilitated by remittances from former refugees may also act as a conservative force that preserves long-standing social ties and identities, connecting some of those more elderly participants to older (often pre-1975) life worlds. This is particularly when aspirations for social transformation through migration or full participation in the capitalist economy are frustrated, leaving shrinking remittance streams as a begrudged source of dependency. While the cycles of economic change that have enveloped Vietnam, from the postwar command economy to the reintroduction of capitalism, have forced many of its citizens to rapidly adapt to changing social, economic, and political norms, those who are connected to and sheltered by remittance support networks are less vulnerable to the tumultuous political and economic cycles of Vietnam's ongoing quest for postcolonial stability. In such cases, the imagination can orient one less to a future possibility than to a nostalgic past to which the vestiges of former life worlds and horizons continue to cling. On the one hand, the remittance gift invites the possibility of accessing alternative structural environments. On the other hand, it may resign those unable or too tired to ride the migratory wave of social transformation to familiar but perhaps unsatisfactory life worlds. As suggested, in such worlds dependence on historical support networks, even if now dispersed overseas, discourages one from forging new identifications in the contemporary economy and consigns one to remain on the receiving end of the gifting relationship. This was seen, for example, in the case in chapter 2 of the unemployed man in the coffee shop who complains that Vietnam was once richer than Korea and China. He sees no point of engaging in the local economy to build a life beyond what remittance support makes possible for him, nor does he have the energy to try to leave Vietnam, unlike Phuong.

On the remittance providing side, remittance gifts may sustain relationships and inhibit the exploration of personal horizons, as in the cases of many remittance senders in California who feel burdened by but nonetheless continue their giving patterns. This may be true in the case of domestic remittance providers in Vietnam as well, such as Thuy in chapter 1, who chose not to risk going abroad for education so she could continue working in Saigon to support her extended family in the Mekong Delta. In such cases, by directing one's gaze either to an unknown overseas future or a comfortable familial past, remittance economies may serve to temporally distance participants from the immediacy of their present economic, political, and social conditions, as well as from their individual sense of investment in them.

It is at the intersection of local worlds and migratory imaginations where the notion of the gift as introduced to us in anthropology has been a helpful analytic departure point. In chapter 1 I considered Vietnamese notions of gifting in various circumstances and examined more closely the contextual nuances of Marcel Mauss's argument about the gift. Mauss romanticizes the gift as a non-monetary form of exchange in which personal relations are preserved, cultivated and foregrounded, rather than diminished or eradicated. Gifts draw our attention to the "total social fact" (Mauss 1967, 78; see also Durkheim 1965) of society, which human relations are entangled within and which cannot be abstracted from the broader economy and its institutions—what Karl Polanyi famously termed a "substantive economy" (1968, 124) and Keith Hart expands upon with his framework of a "human economy" (2017, 3). Mauss claims that "it is by considering the whole entity that we could perceive . . . the fleeting moment when society, or men, become sentimentally aware of themselves and of their situation in relation to others" (1967, 80). The non-monetary form of the gift, as represented in the Kula shells, potlatches, and other cultural and ritual forms Mauss presents, elucidates the social significance of the gift medium. Yet it is clear in the case of Vietnamese remittance economies that money is not a replacement for the gift, but rather stands in for it. Transnational remittance gift economies between the United States and Vietnam re-signify the work of money in a capitalist economy. The gift of money is unable to pay off obligations or establish impersonal contracts, in the way that money is intended to work. Rather, in a country that is undergoing rapid capitalist transformation, the anomie of capital flows from abroad observed by Vietnamese residents is re-personalized when they arrive as remittances designated as gifts expressing sentiment between family members. Yet control of the emotional meanings and intentions of the gift highlights its limitation in the case studies presented in this book. The gift, particularly in its monetary form in a long-distance economy, prompts many participants in the gift exchange to contemplate its broader role and the subjectivities it affords in the global capitalist economy from which green dollars flow.

The gift, as commonly interpreted by social analysts, is endowed with a certain force that derives from the giver but that also has power over the giver and the receiver. Mark Osteen explains Mauss's discussion of this force as follows: "Basing his interpretation upon the words of a Maori sage . . . Mauss held that a spirit—named *hau* by the Maori—within the objects given causes them to be passed on" (2002a, 3). In Mauss's own words, the *hau* is "the spirit of things," (67) and "What imposes obligation in the present received and exchanged is the fact that the thing received is not inactive. Even when it has been abandoned by the giver, it still possesses something of him . . . [T]he hau follows after anyone possessing the thing" (1967, 12). Mauss also discusses the *mana* of the gift—the "honor, prestige," and "authority" one gains and can only hold by passing the gift on (ibid., 8). While it is the poesies of the *hau* that humanities scholars often fixate upon, it is also important to consider its entanglement with *mana*. The gift is composed of the spirit of the thing (the *hau*) as well as the social authority (the *mana*) by virtue of its relationship to what the thing bestows upon its possessor. Despite attempts to control its meaning, in the end the gift indexes social recognition of larger forces beyond a person's capacity to control as well as the predication of individual identity on participation, interaction, and comparison with a broader social community. It is the dominance of structural environmental and social factors over the alluring neoliberal faith in individual agency, although individual perceptions often mask that dominance and project the opposite illusion.

Perhaps it is Mauss's implicit Western emphasis on individuality (ironically, the very impulse that he argues against) that results in an analytic exaggeration of the individuality of *hau* or, as has been suggested here, agency, in his analysis of the gift.[2] Of course the remittance sender, as the gift giver, may seek to control the gift and its flow, often directing its use and seeking recognition of the giver's generous intentions. Yet time and again the use of the gift by its receivers in Vietnam differs from the intent of its givers. Overseas Vietnamese senders invoke their authority as gifters to direct what the gift should be used for, but Vietnamese recipients, as I have shown in the ethnographic materials presented in this book, often employ the monies received for other purposes. Meanwhile, attempts by Vietnamese remittance recipients to reciprocate the gift, such as with locally produced nostalgia products as described in chapter 3, often remain underappreciated by overseas Vietnamese. The frustrations and misunderstandings on both sides of the relationship that have lasted over decades of remittance and gift exchanges have been expressed throughout the ethnographies presented in this book.

Yet despite everything, the gift seems to go on. While it has been shown that substantive remittances often taper off within individual families over time, giving continues during holidays and special occasions, and charitable giving to humanitarian causes in Vietnam has risen, especially as overseas Vietnamese become less connected to direct family members with the passage of time and the emigration of close relatives. Despite the frustrations of gifting, and the repeated experiences of gift exchanges falling short of their intended outcomes, giving gifts remains an ongoing mode of maintaining and producing relationships with relatives, a homeland, and personal and collective identity formations. There does indeed seem to be an excessive spirit that drives the need to give, which (even when absent) haunts the discourse of identity and memory surrounding the individuals involved.

In Mauss's descriptions of the potlatch, gift giving does not emphasize relationality with the Other on the other side of the relationship but rather maintenance, transformation, and possession of the self (1967, 46). Again returning to conceptions of authority and pride, Mauss tells us that "the obligation to give is the essence of the potlatch" (ibid, 39). The giver "can only preserve his authority . . . [and] maintain his rank . . . if he can prove he is haunted and favoured by the spirits and by good fortune, that he is possessed, and also possesses it . . . [H]e can only prove this good fortune by spending it out, humiliating others by placing them 'in the shadow of his name'" (ibid.). Mauss goes on to say that "in the things exchanged during the potlatch, a power is present that forces gifts to be passed around, to be given, and returned" (ibid., 43). What is this power that obliges gifts? The impulse to ascribe mystical or magical power to such forces undermines Mauss's more general observation (a truism, really) that one's social identity is exactly that: predicated on the social. Humans depend on the recognition of others outside of themselves to affirm and develop their own being in the world. One might even call such a force "culture," the prism through which we formulate our notions of social identity through relational difference.

Jacques Lacan understands the contingency of identity emerging from a very early stage of human cognition, as he demonstrates in his discussion of the "mirror stage" of child development (2002, 3). The mirror stage is when the child first sees his image reflected back at him. The child in a sense views and identifies himself for the first time as an Other, outside of the interiorized identity that he has allegedly known until that point, and this is the beginning of a lifelong process of alienation from the self. In this critical scene, however, there is also the spectral presence of an exterior onlooker from which affirmation is sought. Lacan writes: "For the total form of his body, by which the subject anticipates the maturation of his power in a mirage, is given to him only as a gestalt, that is, in an exteriority (ibid., 5). Here we come to understand that identity is doubly alienated in that we can know ourself only as a stranger to ourself, and that furthermore we depend on the recognition of those altogether outside of ourself, beyond our human capacity to control or even identify, for ontological affirmation. While the mirror image is alienating, Lacan's subject still hopes to overcome and master that fragmented alienation. An "exteriority" however recognizes the factor of comparative relationality that now exceeds and prevents a retreat to an a priori interiority, that until the point of the mirror stage was unaware of an outside. "This gestalt is also replete with the correspondences that united the *I* with the status onto which man projects himself, the phantoms that dominate him, and the automaton with which the world of his own making tends to achieve fruition in an ambiguous relation" (ibid.). This is the realization that there is much in our sense of identity that remains beyond our ability to influence or control: identity is contingent and dependent on external variables, relationality, recognition, and circumstances of chance. As Lacan says, "the mirror stage is a drama whose internal thrust is precipitated from insufficiency to anticipation—and which manufactures for the subject, caught up in the lure of spatial identification, the succession of phantasies that extends from a fragmented body-image to a form of its totality . . . and lastly, to the assumption of the armour of an alienating identity" (ibid., 6).

Sigmund Freud identifies this strange duality of self-alienation and recognition as a feature of the "uncanny" (1999, Vol. 17, 219), an aesthetic lens I have used repeatedly in this book to consider diaspora-homeland encounters. Freud personifies the condition of the uncanny, a state in which something is both familiar yet strangely alienating and unfamiliar, in the figure of the automaton. The automaton appears human, but its actions are directed by a force outside of itself. The automaton furthermore unconsciously directs the actions of anyone who interacts with it. Freud offers an intriguing account of how one arrives at the state of the uncanny through the realization that a homelike situation has quite suddenly, yet without any noticeable shift, become unhomelike (*unheimlich*). This experience is confirmed by examining the roots of the word itself: "among its different shades of meaning the word '*heimlich*' exhibits one which is identical with its opposite, '*unheimlich*'" (ibid.). In the case of remittance gifts that return home, they are directed by and represent a sender who enacts the agency and free will of gifting. Yet the action of remittance giving and receiving is also strangely automaton-like. One gives out of habit or a sense of obligation, and even when the disappointments that so often characterize the remittance exchange experience arise, one continues to give. The expressions of remittance fatigue by senders reported in this book indicate an obliged process of informal aid that continues long after the original gifting intentions have faded or failed.

Remittances from an overseas migrant return home to a place one has left, an "identity maintaining mechanism" (Najam 2006, 127) intended to keep one's home and family alive in one's memory and emotions and, in the case of younger members of the diaspora, construct home as an imagined but also a material place of origins. At the same time, remittances alter one's home and family to the point that they often are unrecognizable to the migrant upon return. Remittances also represent monetary income that has socially transformed both the sender and receiver, through the consumption patterns that they enable. Money's ability to radically transform competes with its supplementary role of symbolically securing familiarity and stability. In the reencounter with home and the homeland Other in such relationships, the uncanny nature of something "secretly familiar" (Willford 2006) yet changed (a "double," as Freud might call it—homelike but strange) is certainly present. As Mauss describes the state of exchange, "one fraternizes, yet one remains a stranger" (1967, 38). More importantly for this discussion, however, is the observation that the remittance exchange is seemingly directed by circumstances beyond one's control. This is a defining feature of remittance economies, despite the gift's seeming to symbolize an opposite relationality. There is a compelling and defining force that drives but also exceeds the immediate relations and intentions of the remittance participants.

While the intersubjective dimensions of the uncanny can arise in the exchanges of remittance economies, subjecting seemingly familiar parties to the anxiety of reencounter, the force that directs such exchange circulations also deserves attention here. The mediums of gift exchange, if one can indeed ascribe a *hau* that drives it, takes many forms, which have changed over time. The *hau* defined as the spirit of the giver is perhaps most apparent in material gift forms and informal remittance transfers, where the giver has taken the time to select a material gift tailored to the real or imagined circumstances of the receiver, or where the monetary gift is accompanied by a personalized note or delivery. Here we see its meaning in the Durkheimian sense of the social: the social relations between giver and receiver are displaced and represented in the material form of the gift. As Émile Durkheim says, "collective feelings become conscious of themselves only by settling upon external objects . . . in this way, they took on a kind of physical nature; they came to mingle as things" (1965, 422).

Yet in some ways the shift toward formalized and purely financial remittance channels, particularly over the past decade of frenzied economic development, is more reflective of the type of *hau* that appears in Mauss's accounts of gifting. The *hau* is not merely the spirit or agency of the giver but is also indicative of an outside force that compels the giving circulations of remittance economies. This is reflected in the gift itself, which Mauss says is animated and has a "personality" of its own that defines those who exchange it (1967, 46). The *hau*'s intersection with the *mana* of gifting exchange participants can create a disturbing and contentious articulation of the force that increasingly compels one to participate in expanding circulations of giving in which individual and collective identity and sociality are the ultimate stake. Remittance pressures here are not only transnational; they begin within the giving communities. Social circles in which money is the central medium of participation, from Vietnamese credit (*hụi*) rotations to Vietnamese American philanthropic giving circles in collective remittance scenarios (discussed in chapter 4), highlight the fact that the pressures of giving are not necessarily traced only to the expectations of remittance receivers but are also experienced through a broader social gaze that judges one's capacity for generosity and trust as a measure of status within the community.

The contentious cycles of potlatch giving define a significant aspect of the gift's character but also mark the failure of Mauss's attempt to analyze what the gift precisely does and how it might be modeled. While Mauss's hope was that a return to gifting economies would rescue humanity from the increasing anomie and depersonalized exchanges that defined capitalist systems, the agonistic instincts involved in the potlatch reveal a system in which humans also may give not only in search of an exuberant release—"a luxurious squandering of energy in every form," as Georges Bataille described it (1989, 3), but also out of a sense of begrudged and antagonistic obligation. The affective yet automaton-like practices of gift giving are a response to an involuntary force outside of oneself that compels one to give and participate in networks of sociality and exchange, even when such participation is neither productive nor desired and, furthermore, is recognized for its self-destructive tendencies. As Bataille says, the potlatch participant "must waste the excess, but he remains eager to acquire even when he does the opposite, and so he makes waste itself an object of acquisition" (1989, 72). Participation in the potlatch is irresistible, for it is also, in Mauss's words, "a phenomenon of social structure" that "brings about a remarkable state of nerviness and excitement" (1967, 38).

What is the external force that pervades and dominates these remittance exchange economies that are characterized by excessive and incessant excitement and dissatisfaction? To paint with a somewhat broad brush, one might say it is the infrastructural vicissitudes of capitalism itself. As Vietnam is increasingly drawn into the global capitalist system, its citizens experience capital circulations of dizzying scale and speed. The same is true for those overseas Vietnamese communities whose members over time have become increasingly professionally and materially successful in the capitalist-centered geographies where they have resettled. The unfettered flow of capital, upon which capitalist development and accumulation is predicated, is symbolic of a mobility enabled by financial channel infrastructures that have become exponentially faster and more accessible since the launch of Đổi Mới, when the Vietnamese state first decided to reengage with the broader capitalist world. During the years in which money (particularly dollars) has become the primary mode of remittance exchange, the shift toward progressively formalized money transfer services has meant that the medium of exchange has come to in some ways obscure the particulars of the social relations and obligations involved. Georg Simmel's analysis (2004) of a medium of money that masks the entangled desires and sacrifices of those who exchange it (discussed in the introduction and chapter 2) is relevant to the situation of remittance economies in that money has come to stand in for the gifting intentions and meanings it is intended to represent. Yet money not only conceals, it also reveals. In the capitalist system, money symbolizes what Marx describes as ever-expanding and elusive circulations of capital that are increasingly beyond the individual's control to capture and maintain. Remittances as capital index the sender's ability to participate in the global capitalist economy, and in most cases they make possible similar if partial modes of participation on the receiving side.

Yet to participate in a capitalist order is to always already be behind what is deemed sufficient to be social in such a system. The constantly shifting level of material well-being that is deemed to be enough (đủ)—not for physical survival, but for social status—draws one into cycles of dissatisfaction and future-oriented ontologies in which achieving economic and social arrival is constantly deferred. The gift's lack is always at risk of exposure. Like fashion or other trends that mark capitalist modes of social distinction, one participates in a dynamic economy in which identity is always sought but never realized. While the future is never reached, the past and its own elusive horizons are reinvoked through traces of older identities and relationships maintained by remittance exchanges, resulting in a confusing mixture of ontological belonging that is partially mired in history, partially gazing toward the future, and notably disengaged with the present. In the meantime, there lurk silent spectators who are unable to participate in the remittance gift process, let alone the rapidly expanding capitalist economy. They mark the other side of the gift, which must always necessarily exclude at the same time it includes. Nonetheless, the gift's widespread visibility and centrality to everyday social discourse makes it a prevalent marker of social reflexivity. Furthermore, for many remittance participants the future orientation of the gift and the aspiration for social transformation it represents are what drives the gift's continuance and expansion.

If modern identity is, as Immanuel Kant (1955) suggests, predicated on a blank horizon and one never knows what one will be, only that such identity will be radically different than what was in the past, remittance economies represent a particular intersection at which unequal socioeconomic worlds collide in systems of highly intimate international encounter and exchange. Through participation in the highly developed economies of the capitalist West, former refugees in the diaspora are able to earn and save money to send to relatives and communities back home. Reception of remittances in Vietnam are considered a critical source of capital in households, communities, and the national economy and eagerly sought after by those on the receiving side of the relationship. The guilt that drives much remittance giving is based on a starkly obvious economic differential in which the conditions of possibility in the Global North and South are exposed, confronted, and challenged. As I discussed in chapter 4, Vietnamese in the United States give because they have opportunities there that are not (at least, on the same scale) in Vietnam. Yet they also give because of personal connections and empathies, as they realize how dramatically different life would be if such opportunities were not available. Remittance recipients, on the other hand, receive because they must. Yet accepting remittances only reinforces the perception that unequal conditions of possibility are not based on individual capabilities, but rather on political and economic structural environments beyond the individual's control, as observed by Hoang in chapter 2 and Sang in chapter 3 in discussing the limitations of talent.

In every encounter, remittance participants reflect on what their identities would be like if they were on the opposite side of the exchange, with different hypothetical opportunities. Margaret, the Vietnamese American discussed in chapter 5, feels compelled to repeatedly photograph and exchange stories with Vietnamese women her age as she imagines an alternative life in Vietnam, and Lam, the man discussed in chapter 3, sits resignedly drinking beer and staring at the sea as he remembers his multiple failed attempts to cross it to seek social transformation abroad. Thus, the strong correlation between the reception of remittances and the desire to migrate reflects an exchange dynamic where felt external forces compel one to participate in a substantive social economy in which there is heightened awareness of the centrality of mobile circulations and environments to formulations of identity. There is also recognition of the fact that access to such mobility is unevenly distributed and a matter of chance. For the southern Vietnamese I interviewed for this study, participation in remittance economies is also often part and parcel of engaging with a broader global capitalist economy. Just as the "hau follows after anyone possessing the thing" (Mauss 1967, 12), new forms of capitalist subjectivity and desire frequently emerge among participants in transnational U.S.-Vietnam remittance exchange economies.

In Jacques Derrida's discussion of the gift (1992), the very idea of the gift becomes impossible in the naming of it. To give or receive a gift and recognize it as such is to destroy the idea of what it is intended to be. One must give and forget, which makes the origins of any cycle of gifting impossible to trace. The gift's impossibilities have shaped the stereotypes of impoverished Vietnamese American refugees forced to be perpetually grateful for the supposed gift of freedom they received from the United States in the aftermath of the destruction of their homeland by that same gifter, as Mimi Nguyen (2012) has argued, drawing on Derrida. Related to such subject constructions, Derrida has also shown that hospitality, the motivation for the gift, is predicated on Othering and by extension inhospitality, for only in an encounter with a foreigner viewed as different from ourselves are we obliged to offer hospitality. Yet to bring the Other into reciprocal exchange relations is to commit a violence by forcing the Other to "speak our language"—to respond on our terms to the expectations we have of Others and, most likely, to be disappointed and even angered when they fall short. According to Derrida, "this is where the question of hospitality begins: must we ask the foreigner to understand us, to speak our language, in all the senses of this term, in all its possible extensions, before being able to welcome him into our country?" (2000, 15).

If the desired gift medium and language of hospitality and generosity is money, then in situations of gift reciprocity Vietnamese remittance receivers are effectively rendered mute by their inability to return the equivalent monetary form within a shared emerging framework of capitalist subjectivity and value. Yet despite the rational impossibility of the gift and the deconstruction of the hospitality it invokes, we know it goes on and on. Derrida's focus, of course, is on the epistemology of analysis rather than the object itself. Naming the gift gives it an illusion of stability, but it is always already deconstructed the moment we begin to place it within a predictive or interpretive frame. Therefore, the gift has both been the subject and not been the subject of this study. It is an entry but also departure point that offers insight into the many other social forces that aspire but ultimately fail to keep the gift concept together as a Weberian ideal type of category.

The gift as remittance also goes on, and as records of total remittance flows indicate, remittance-gifts are on the rise. This runs parallel with increasingly deeper societal engagements with a capitalist economy that have already begun to defy state-imposed controls on its particular national and ideological character, reflected in the common but seemingly contradictory hybrid label of a "market economy with a socialist orientation" (*Kinh tế thị trường theo định hướng xã hội chủ nghĩa*) used to describe Vietnam's political economy. At the same time, economic interests in capital flows have made remittances a visible policy issue, highlighting financial and gift flows across international family networks that once remained largely below the radar of inputs to the formal economy (Callon 1998). Remittances have become named and capitalized upon by the capitalist order and its forms of governance. In the course of their establishment as a language and medium of emerging capitalist subjectivities and social relations—a monetary stand-in that maintains geographically and temporally distant relationships— remittances have also come to reflect and define the characteristics and desires of remittance senders and receivers alike. Money represents and becomes a socially transformative and affective force on all those who encounter and participate with it.

Throughout this book, I have presented various ethnographic examples of how remittance gift exchanges and the channels through which they are mobilized bring givers and receivers into intimate encounters. In these encounters money (and through it, imagination) is central. It is helpful to return again to Arjun Appadurai's description of the imagination as "an organized field of social practices . . . and a form of negotiation between sites of agency and global defined fields of possibility" (1996, 31). Lisa Lowe (1996) has demonstrated how differentials in transnational labor spaces and regimes not only draw attention to the inclusions and exclusions of global capitalism but also present new transnational opportunities for imagined belonging and action. Nguyen-Vo Thu Huong (2008) illustrates how neoliberalism produces gendered Vietnamese bodies that are imagined and classed across transnational lines, from sex to garment workers. Kimberly Hoang (2015) argues that increasing investment flows from East Asia have reoriented Vietnamese desires away from the West and toward East Asia. And Allison Truitt makes the case that dreams of money in Vietnam serve as an "infrastructure for reassembling the self and nation" (2013, 153). If we further examine these suggestions to identify the particulars of how the imagination acts as an infrastructure and field of belonging, desire, and negotiation, remittance economies offer a revealing example. In such economies the site of negotiation between local agency and global possibility is money, as a medium of the social relations it represents through gift exchange. As remittance economies have become increasingly monetized over time, money has come to represent the life world of the givers and the social transformation and enabling environments of agency they are perceived to have access to overseas.

Here the imaginary is shaped not only by money, but also by the apprehension of bodies and things. As postwar refugees escaped the borders of Vietnam's socialist state they passed, as many of the Vietnamese I interviewed perceived, into a capitalist lifeworld seen as an idealized neoliberal environment for social identity transformation. This spectral "capitalocentric" (Gibson-Graham 2006, 56) fantasy world in which not only money but also bodies and things reside is overwhelmingly located in the West due to the sheer size of diasporic populations permanently resettled there. Social transformation in economic cores of Western capitalism, epitomized by the United States, is imagined and described by Vietnamese as being structurally enabled by unfettered accumulation and flows of capital, and visually and experientially represented by diasporic subjects who not only live in America but also become Americans. A distinct theme has emerged through the various ethnographies presented in this book of the imagined role of money in enabling Vietnamese who have gone overseas to transform themselves into idealized neoliberal subjects and, in many cases, realize or at least perform new forms of capitalist personhood as indexed by the things and money they send back to Vietnam. This perceived transformation is confirmed whenever overseas Vietnamese bodies return to the homeland, even if only occasionally.

The environment (*môi trường*) of Western life overseas is understood to be critical in exposing Vietnamese to opportunities for material betterment and character improvement that are unavailable in Vietnam. Such was the view of numerous informants such as Ha, the woman in chapter 3 who sought educational opportunities abroad for her daughter. Central to these opportunities is money. Money funds material well-being, education, and health care; memorializes loss; purchases real estate; and creates marriage opportunities. As seen in the cases of the gamblers and spenders interspersed throughout this book, money also funds gamble and play—the character of which is always, as Bataille (1989) suggests, escapist from and resistant to broader societal limitations and impositions of particular and narrowly constructed forms of identity and personhood.[3] The generation of money makes a plethora of imagined socially transformative opportunities possible, and the general perception in Vietnam is that money can be earned in the simplest of occupations abroad, from restaurant and janitorial work to jobs in nail salons.

A central root of this possibility, as imagined by many of the interlocutors presented in this book, is the perceived difference in value ascribed to labor between Vietnam and a Western capitalist economy. Whereas such jobs provide only a pittance in Vietnam, labor is deemed to be generously rewarded in places like America. The imagined reason for this, in the view of numerous Vietnamese I spoke with, is not only that "Americans are lazy and don't want these jobs" but also that "the government there is good." In Vietnam Vietnamese are also derided by remittance senders and receivers alike for being "lazy," but this is because their character has not been sufficiently "developed" through opportunities for work overseas. Such was the view of Trang, the woman in chapter 2 who criticized the Vietnamese cultural, political, and economic environment for discouraging individual incentive and hard work. The door to labor opportunities is deemed to remain open to people lucky enough to migrate and willing to do basic manual work, in an environment where the government (playing a capitalist management rather than a rent seeking or even ideological role) facilitates the structural production of new opportunities. Such labor opportunities are rewarded by money, and labor and money are equated with the development of socially mobile immigrant personhoods in the capitalist West. One is socially transformed by money in a Western country of resettlement and migration, and one demonstrates this through the subsequent performance of remittance sending made possible by such labor opportunities. Money, it should be obvious by now, represents much more than money.

Labor is also entangled with money in this process of social transformation. Many post-1975 Vietnamese migrants risked their investments and lives to undertake dangerous journeys from Vietnam. Arriving in the West with few resources, they took entry-level jobs and began the process of earning money, leading to opportunities for betterment and transformation for themselves and their families. When such money is channeled back to Vietnam, however, both senders and receivers believe it is unable to bring about the same social transformation, unless it is invested in sending another family member overseas. The money sent back to Vietnam represents the labor performed by the remittance senders, but it does not lead to new labor opportunities or, by extension, further monetary accumulation and financial independence for the remittance recipients. The economies of dependency and migratory yearning that settle into "Dollar Village (*Xóm Đô*)" communities are blamed by remittance senders and receivers alike on the systematic lack of labor valuation within Vietnam's limited capitalist political economy. One can work locally, but doing so never brings about the economic returns possible in an idealized capitalist environment abroad. In such a situation, one becomes less rather than more inclined to seek work. "Vietnam is poor, and so its people are too," remarked one of my informants. Poverty in this case does not merely describe a state of material deprivation but also refers to personal character and access to global opportunities and networks.

Therefore, international remittance flows cannot, in the eyes of remittance economy participants, bring about widespread social transformation in Vietnam, for they do not produce new valued labor opportunities there. This remains the perception despite the well-intentioned capacity building work of many Vietnamese American NGOs. Work and money do not seem to be equated in Vietnam for many of my informants, and therefore they cannot cooperate to produce new identities. International remittances entering Vietnam are only money, the signifier of what labor is in another distant place but not within the borders of the Vietnamese state when devoid of transnational connections. Labor, or the work of the human body, is understood by those who reflect on the remittances they give and receive to be the ontological foundation of any possibility for radical social transformation.[4] Money earned abroad through labor performed there becomes evidence of this lay wisdom.

In the end the gift continues to trump money in its formal sense because it arrives, performs, and transforms differently depending on the environment of the holder and must always repeat itself in search of a social meaning that continually escapes it. It remains personally and socially entangled in a way that money—with its contractual boundaries—is not. The gift of money teases one to imagine what more it could do or could have done, if only one was somewhere else, contributing to long distance imaginaries directed toward distant worlds populated by familiar diasporic bodies that nonetheless remain intangible. Here again, the histories of migratory chance lead givers and receivers to reflect on the vicissitudes of fate, which the gift (with its characteristics of unpredictability, alterity, and unintentional displacements) continues to index. Frustrated subcultures of in situ displacement and heightened desires for mobility, in which hopes for migration and social transformation seem to be consistently deferred, are represented by the characteristics of the gift as money, reminding remittance recipients of the limitations of their agency in the face of broader structural obstacles. Yet the stories of those who overcame the odds loom large in the collective memory of Vietnam's out-migration communities and cultures.

Such frustrations play out in a variety of consumption patterns in which aspirations for social and physical mobility, as imaginatively enabled in an idealized American capitalist economy, may be symbolically and materially manifested and valued in mobile consumer commodity forms such as the motorcycle. The multiple occasions when I was invited by (mostly male) informants to "*đi chơi*," "*đi vòng vòng*," or "*đi giam giam*" (go around in circles for fun) on the back of a new motorcycle purchased with overseas money, cruising Vietnam's towns and cities with no particular destination in mind, seem to reflect the general circulations of bodies and capital regularly experienced by remittance economy participants and their spectators in Vietnam. In Vietnam, however, such circulations can become frustratingly contained, familiar, repetitive, and ultimately clogged, rather than expanding to and explorative of unknown horizons.

If the gift falls short of achieving its aspirations to establish social symmetry through exchange, this is also because in its monetary form it has taken on a life of its own beyond those of its givers and receivers. Money alone cannot transform personhood; rather, it must represent a process of embodied labor and structurally enabled opportunities that can bring about social transformations. Yet when money symbolically comes to stand outside of the labor and personhood that produced it, when remittances are seen as ends in themselves and objects that must be given and received for transnational sociality to exist, then sociality itself fails. It does so because the sign and the signifier—the remittance and the work that produced it—are revealed to no longer be in relationship to one another despite the rational and emotional impulses that attempt to keep them connected. Furthermore, the symmetry between the two is predicated on histories of chance and gambles in which the limits of human agency and reflections on failed personal histories in the face of larger structural barriers and the vicissitudes of fate are exposed. Yet the recognition of failure is only partial. Thus, the remittance gift becomes animate and fetishized and indeed emerges as a principal subject of social discourse in remittance economies. Two characteristics of money that my informants reflected on time and again are its ephemerality and its shortage.

FIGURE 13.   An abandoned boat, Bình Định Province.

Money becomes an incessant topic in everyday discussions, from its characteristics of elusiveness to its promise of future economic potential and sociocultural transformation.

In standing in for the sociality of exchange, money and its mobile and transformative characteristics as channeled in a global economy become a medium for and language of social relations in remittance economies and ultimately are fundamental to changing notions and measures of personal and collective identities vis-à-vis increasing encounters with a once uncanny diasporic Other. While exchange between selves and Others has always been central to the production of social identities, in the case of international remittance economies, the Other is traditionally familiar yet removed by distance (although this is changing with increased migratory returns and technological innovations). In the Other's place the gift takes on heightened symbolic meaning, offering the imagination extra rein to run wild. The imagination, seeking to reembody the gift in the participants who exchange it, journeys to the landscapes of the gift's imagined origins and across those that it travels. Alternative versions of the self supplant the Other, as one imagines what one could, should, or would be on the other side of the exchange relationship. Most notably the imagination becomes distracted by and entangled in the monetary medium of the gift, playing a critical role in the arbitrage of relational subjectivities in and across global Vietnamese remittance economies and communities. Yet the work of arbitraging meaning never quite reaches its mark. As we have seen, the resultant ontological dynamics that characterize transnational migration and remittance cultural economies seem to produce a great deal of nerviness and excitement, as Mauss might say, but the energy of exchange can never be traced to either an origin or an arrival point. Indeed, the frenzied sociocultural dynamics that emerge from and drive histories and futures of transnational remittances and migration between the United States and Vietnam seem to reflect a momentum that is always excitable but never contented, constantly aspirational yet continuously dissatisfied, perpetually circulating away, back and beyond, and invariably obsessed with what is always already, not yet enough (*chưa đủ*).[5]

Afterword

> **The canoe is made for a certain use, and with a definitive purpose; it is a means to an end, and we, who study native life, must not reverse this relation, and make a fetish of the object itself. In the study of the economic purpose for which a canoe is made, of the various uses to which it is submitted, we find the first approach to a deeper ethnographic treatment. . . . Even this, however, does not touch the most vital reality of a native canoe. For a craft, whether of bark or wood, iron or steel, lives in the life of its sailors, and is more to a sailor than a mere bit of shaped matter . . . a craft is surrounded by an atmosphere of romance, built up of tradition and of personal experience. It is an object of cult and admiration, a living thing, possessing its own individuality.**

–Bronislaw Malinowski, *Argonauts of the Western Pacific*

It is a cold gray New England day in March 2016. The bells on the door jingle as I enter a travel and tax service office, tucked inconspicuously into a suburban Vietnamese shopping center, to meet Kelly. A Vietnamese American friend had introduced her to tell me more about the financial practices of the local Vietnamese community. And of course, with the April 15 deadline looming, she could do my taxes. Kelly's store provided travel and visa services to Vietnam, as well as delivery services for boxes and financial remittances. Kelly told me about her years of experience providing services to the Vietnamese community in the area. Gesturing to the wall behind us, which was covered with children's photographs, she explained that they were passport photos of her customers' children, many of whom had grown up and become customers of her shop themselves. "We know our customers well," Kelly said. "They are our friends and neighbors. We've been helping to keep them in touch with, and travel and send money to, friends and family in Vietnam for many years." As we moved on to talk about remittances, however, she explained how it was becoming more difficult for a small business like hers to facilitate financial transfers between the United States and Vietnam. In the past she used to do it herself, via a bank account. Now, she said, "banks don't allow it—I'm not sure why." As an informal remittance provider, operating in a gray market to facilitate small transfers, her cross-border services had become visible to the expanding financial world and potentially risked being labeled a black market operation. She had recently outsourced her financial transfer services to an external provider, but she noted: "It's hardly worth it for me anymore. I only get $1.25 per transaction. But our customers need to send money and expect us to provide the service, so we continue to do so. It is very important for them."

Kelly's office in New England and my fieldwork sites in Vietnam and California are far apart in both distance and time, and quite a bit has changed in recent years. In this afterword I begin by reflecting back on the temporal and infrastructural context of the research I conducted for this book. My original fieldwork coincided with a critical transformation in the global economy: the financial crisis of 2008. At the time I was narrowly focused on my research in Vietnam and not well attuned to news back in the United States. Yet what was happening in the U.S., the core of global capitalism, was having reverberations in Vietnam. They were small at first: rising food prices and rents, inflation, and downturns in real estate prices and the stock market. I recall being slightly annoyed when I found, in paying my rent in May 2008, that the dollar-*đong* exchange rate had suddenly gone up quite dramatically. I noted that my neighbors were complaining about rice shortages at the market, and I listened to Vietnamese friends grumbling about losing money in land and real estate investments. But ironically, these economic shifts seemed tangential to my investigation of remittances. This was in part because family-to-family remittances tend to remain steady even in times of economic instability (D. Yang 2005). Remittance flows were not yet declining, and the effect of the recession on financial flows was not yet commonly mentioned in the discussions I was having with my informants—although this started to change once I arrived in California.

As I returned to my field notes and interview transcripts in revising the manuscript for this book, I thought about how I had been in Vietnam during a period of critical global economic transformation, yet it had not struck me as calamitous as all of the subsequent analyses have described. If anything, I had felt that Vietnam's 2007 accession to the World Trade Organization was the primary macroeconomic event that shaped my time there—and indeed that was accompanied by a brief spike in overseas investments and remittances that continued through much of the time when I lived in Ho Chi Minh City. Yet as I have continued to visit Vietnam on a regular basis to pursue new research and study projects, the country does strike me as radically different place from what it was a decade ago, including the contours of its "finance-scapes" (Appadurai 1996, 34). Money and the imaginaries and manifestations of its transformative powers flow and often become congested, but (as with Saigon's incessant traffic) in slightly different patterns and with different felt effects than before. When and how exactly did these changes take place? Why is it that such shifts are so much more apparent to me as I come and go every one or two years but seemed less immediate when I was living there for nearly two straight years? Importantly in relation to all of this, what macro global transformations structured the regulation of international finance that shapes and reflects such flows?

Of course, what I was observing in 2008 was still was still an "emergence," while now it is history—even if still relatively recent.[1] History, as often narrated by historians, tends to be demarcated and defined by distinct political and economic events and periods. But in lived experience, the transitions in behavior and cognition that accompany such events are usually not as marked or apparent at the moment of occurrence; rather, they unfold slowly and indistinctly. There have been many changes in the Vietnamese financial sector since 2007–2009, when I conducted my study, and indeed such transformations are ongoing. Many are gradual infrastructural shifts that eventually affect and modify economic and monetary behaviors, but not necessarily in immediately noticeable or disruptive ways. Ultimately, however, as the anthropologist Brian Larkin contends, shifts in "infrastructures produce [new] ambient conditions of everyday life" (2013, 336).

The everyday phenomena and ambient conditions of international remittances in Vietnam have undoubtedly changed since 2008. These transformations are connected to infrastructural shifts in banking, payments, technology, and financialization, as Vietnam not only further integrates itself into the global economy but also establishes itself as one of its fastest growing hubs. To understand these developments as they relate to this study, we must first consider the regulatory responses to the global financial crisis originating in the United States, and how corresponding policy changes have modified the channels by which remittances flow to Vietnam and the actors who mediate them. Bill Maurer has encouraged economic anthropologists to think "orthogonally" (2012, 17) when it comes to analyzing the seemingly apparent nature of exchange and capital flows. This means also attending to the mundane procedures of payment, or the "act and infrastructure of value transfer," (ibid., 19) that make those exchanges and flows possible. In thinking about infrastructure on both the macro and micro levels, I cannot help but think of the canoe, analyzed by Bronislaw Malinowski in the anthropological classic *Argonauts of the Western Pacific* (1984), as an apt metaphor. The material gifts, ritualized social exchanges, and reciprocities of the infamous Trobriand Kula rings written about by Malinowski and highlighted by Marcel Mauss in *The Gift* (1967) are widely recognized in anthropology. Less attention however has been paid to the details, also meticulously documented by Malinowski, of sailing technologies and dugout canoe preparations that made such expeditions and transport of valuables and goods possible. In the case of financial infrastructure, it is helpful to also attend to the "canoes," or the channels and services that have facilitated the transfer of money and gifts between the United States and Vietnam. In particular, how have these changed over time, and what practical, technical, and affective roles do they play in framing the economic and social relations that they maintain and produce?

In the case of Vietnam there has been a growing monetization of remittances as channels for sending them have become increasingly available. It is striking to compare today's financial remittance practices to those in the immediate postwar period, when most remittances took the form of boxes of material goods that were sent by mail for exchange on the black market. As we have seen, following Vietnam's economic reforms and the reestablishment of U.S.-Vietnam relations, monetary remittances to Vietnam rapidly increased. This was particularly the case after 2002, when the Vietnamese government expanded the range of financial institutions permitted to deliver them. Then in 2008 the global financial crisis happened. For Vietnam, the quantitative impact came in 2009, when remittances declined for the first time since the start of recording their amounts. However, the decline did not last long, and remittances were on the rise again by 2010. In recent years remittances have increased up to 15 percent annually, reaching a high of $13.2 billion in 2015. There was a slight decline again in 2016, to $11.9 billion, which has been partially blamed on a stronger dollar and lower interest rates in Vietnam. But estimates are that they will recover (World Bank 2016). Transferring remittances is a profitable business, fueled by fees and exchange rate differentials. These days most banks provide international remittance services, and global money transfer companies such as Western Union and MoneyGram are aggressively seeking to expand their share of the remittance market.

Since the financial crisis I have been speaking to remittance service providers in the informal and formal sectors in both the United States and Vietnam, to learn how they adapt to and strategize about market shifts and futures shaped by changing financial regulations. Many of these regulations were put in place in response to the crisis to stabilize and track the more exuberant circulations and accumulations of money in the previously and still relatively unfettered global capitalist system. From subprime mortgages and derivatives trading to deceptively flexible "economies of appearances" that disguised global corporate fragilities (Ho 2009, 308), the unexpected and rapid collapse of the world economy in 2008 drew attention to the need for reform and oversight in the centers of global capitalism. Managers of money transfer operations I interviewed noted that since the crisis, and since 2013 in particular, a new market is emerging for outbound international remittances from the United States, in large part due to regulatory reforms in the

Dodd-Frank Wall Street Reform and Consumer Protection Act of 2010 (Dodd-Frank) that, according to them, make it difficult for small remittance players to afford to stay in the business. These include oversight and regulatory measures meant to enhance transparency and protection for customers, as well as requirements of know-your-customer due diligence to prevent money laundering, which hold remittance service providers to a higher standard of liability. Compliance can be bureaucratic, requiring significant additional paperwork; legally complicated, requiring additional expertise on staff; and costly to pay the salaries of such staff.

Mainstream money transfer organizations and banks are still figuring out how to take advantage of the changing legal and business climate, but in general there is confidence that, given their economy of scale, new regulations will eventually allow them to tap deeper into the informal sector's base of customers. In Vietnam the share of the population with bank accounts remains relatively low, at 31 percent (World Bank 2016), and many Vietnamese Americans continue to prefer alternative nonbank financial services for transferring money to family members in Vietnam. A variety of corporate strategies are emerging to tap this significant group of customers. One consultant hired by a money transfer organization told me about a marketing campaign focused on capturing workers in nail salons, who send to Vietnam a high proportion of their earnings. Wells Fargo and other banks offer a monthly allotment of free international remittance transfers connected to personal checking and savings accounts, with a marketing focus on California, where over one-third of Vietnamese Americans live (in addition to many other remittance-sending immigrant populations). I discovered that many financial market consultants are doing research very similar to mine as they try to understand how to enter the U.S.-Southeast Asia remittance corridor and woo customers to the formal sector, sometimes offering opportunities for para-ethnographic collaboration (Holmes and Marcus 2010). One of the main questions that many industry researchers have is why small Vietnamese money transfer companies, such as the one I discussed at the start of this afterword that began with more informal gift service offerings, continue to be extremely trusted and popular. Beyond competitive rates, most informal money transfer organizations in the Vietnamese community offer special services tailored to the particular dynamics of Vietnamese customers' remittance needs, such as home delivery to recipients so they do not have to travel to a brick-and-mortar bank—preferences that the formal sector is coming to understand but is still limited in catering effectively to.

The informal transfer sector has been significant in the Vietnamese community—ten years ago, it was estimated to account for at least half of the remittance market, and today the figure is about one-third—comprised of a creative

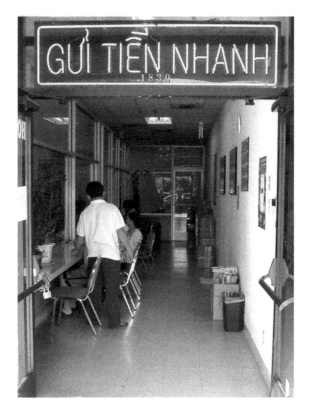

FIGURE 14. Vietnamese American remittance shop,
San Jose, California.

collage of community trusted "mom-and-pop" money transfer businesses often
called "ethnic services," jewelry shops, courier services, family networks, and
hawala ("hot transfer") operations.[2] Many of these services have small yet
trusted staffs, and they have traditionally operated in a gray market, officially reporting some transfers while facilitating others under the table. Know-your-
customer requirements were sometimes ignored due to the cost and paperwork
involved in complying with them. However, recent legal changes are moving some
of these semi-informal gray operators into the black market or out of the market
altogether. The financial and legal infrastructure for international remittances sent
from the United States (from which the highest amount of remittances in the
world flow) has been transformed significantly since the global financial crisis,
and in particular since the passage of Dodd-Frank. Specifically, regulations associated with Dodd-Frank require that any transfer of more than $15 comply with
disclosure, consumer protection, and error resolution rules, which require remit-

tance providers to take more steps and fill out more paperwork to arrange a financial transfer. Formal and informal services and channels now compete for shares of a lucrative remittance market that is actually quite mature in the informal sector but just emerging in the formal one, but in which the latter now has a comparative advantage.

Vietnam's postwar history of remittances and migration highlights the important infrastructural role of the payment as well as gift medium in framing the meanings, expectations, and relationships involved in transfers. If remittances arguably stand in for gifts in the Maussian sense, then the creative and often homemade Kula canoes (an appropriate metaphor for the innovative local ethnic remittance channels and informal financial practices that have faithfully and often creatively transferred money, gifts, and messages across transnational kin, social, and business networks for the past forty years) are by now tried and trusted, as members of both sender and recipient communities time and again attested in interviews. In all of my discussions for this study, I never came across a story of a lost remittance transfer. Were such an occurrence to ever happen, there is a limited degree of separation between customer and provider in closely knit Vietnamese American communities where professional and social lives often overlap, in which case the provider's reputation would quickly be tarnished. The "mom-and-pop" segment of the remittance provider business is aging, however. The founders of many of the smaller ethnic Vietnamese remittance operations in the United States still run them despite reaching retirement age and are now competing with much larger, more savvy, and better resourced financial institutions, technologies, and service providers. There has been an air of change in the financial worlds of Vietnam and Vietnamese communities abroad, and in the international remittance sector more broadly. As one agent working in a remittance operation in Little Saigon, California, told me, "it's definitely harder to work in this business now. There's more oversight since the financial crisis, and you can get in trouble for accounting practices that were previously commonplace." A number of agents of smaller remittance service providers say that perhaps the long-term goal should not be to keep the business running in the same way as in the past, but rather to find new partnerships and adapt to a changing market. Nowadays the big banks that benefit from legal teams and economies of scale can provide services more effectively, but as one ethnic remittance service agent pointed out, "we still have the customer base, and those customers trust us." When I visited Kelly again in 2017, she noted that the future of the international remittance landscape was again in flux, as the new administration of President Donald Trump talks about scaling back Dodd-Frank reforms while also cracking down on undocumented migrants, leaving her to have to anticipate yet another business model and customer base reorientation.

Besides navigating regulations, new remittance players also aspire to tap into the Vietnamese remittance market through innovations in financial technology (Fintech), such as from Wells Fargo account add-ons; prepaid gift cards offered by Mastercard; digital wallets; and emerging and anticipated mobile upload, transfer, and payment applications. Blockchain technologies like Bitcoin are also on the remittance horizon in Vietnam. By avoiding bank fees, along with its rapid recent rise in value, Bitcoin can be an attractive solution for intermediaries offering remittance services to migrants eager to reduce transaction costs. Bitcoin allows remittance providers to undercut formal bank and money transfer operator costs while still charging migrants a percentage on each transaction and thus ensuring comfortable profit margins. This is particularly true in the current Korea-Vietnam remittance corridor, where transfer fees are significantly higher than for remittances between the United States and Vietnam. This is in part due to the unidirectionality to Vietnam of financial flows from short-term Vietnamese workers in South Korea that diminishes opportunities for hot transfer/*hawala* arbitrage that are more common with U.S.-Vietnamese transfers. But with new regulatory reforms on the horizon, it remains to be seen how blockchain technologies serving remittance transfer platforms will play out.

In the last decade significant global attention has been paid to mobile phone technologies that would allow people without a bank account but with a mobile phone to use it to store and remit money, potentially increasing financial access for the unbanked poor, lowering transaction costs, and eventually paving their way to becoming banked (Maurer, Musaraj, and Small 2018). Mobile value remittance practices are starting to emerge in Vietnam where the mobile penetration rate is 130 percent (Tellez 2011), as users within the same telecommunications provider network are able to transfer airtime credit via phone. There has also been experimentation with electronic kiosks, where users can deposit money and input a phone number to which the credit will be sent. Some companies like Momo have moved from airtime credit transfer to mobile wallet and e-payment services. The Vietnam Bank for Social Policies, in partnership with Mastercard and the Asia Foundation, ran a feasibility study and implemented a pilot project for mobile banking in 2014, clarifying the technological and banking potential but remaining vague on the specifics of official regulatory support for mobile money. The range of payment options within mobile value ecosystems is rapidly expanding, from games to bills and transport payment. Unlike countries such as Kenya or the Philippines where mobile money is widespread, however, there is not yet a way to cash out such credit person-to-person (p2p) in Vietnam without a bank account.[3] Legally allowing telecommunications operators to cash in and cash out credit as banks do would open up a new domestic remittance channel, potentially linked to international payments. Mobile money services need gov-

ernment regulatory approval and cooperation between banks and telecom operators, which has not yet happened in Vietnam. Nonetheless, there is change in the
air, as the Vietnamese government has advanced policy decisions to promote
greater cashlessness by 2020 (Vietnam News 2017), and many tech start-ups are
jockeying for an anticipated place in Vietnam's increasingly digital economy.

Besides managing new services, regulations, and technologies, banks and
money transfer operations penetrating the Vietnamese remittance market are also
attuned to existing cultural sentiments and practices to lure customers. These
range from incentive rewards to recipients from Western Union (which has offered Tết gifts to families in Vietnam as add-ons to remittances received) to Wells
Fargo's sponsorship of diasporic community celebrations. For example, the long-
standing Vietnamese International Film Festival in California was renamed the
Wells Fargo Viet Film Fest in 2013, in part as a result of corporate sponsorship
by the bank and its connections in the community. Bank executives shared with
me some of their insights from marketing research, finding among other things
that targeted community engagement activities are more effective in cultivating
brand recognition and loyalty than generic marketing and information campaigns.
While culturally immersed marketing strategies may appear appropriated from
the mom-and-pop services menu, banks employ these strategies while also maintaining financial and legal platforms that are fully compliant with know-your-
customer regulations—ironically poaching remittance senders from entrenched
ethnic operations whose staff members have already known their customers intimately for years.

International remittances to Vietnam have clearly gone beyond family-to-
family subsistence gifts and now include investments in business, real estate, and
philanthropy. However, U.S.-Vietnam remittances flowing in the other direction
are also increasing, earmarked for everything from business and real estate investment to college tuition payments. Remittance and migration channels appear
to increasingly fall on one side or the other of the stiffening formal-informal divide. Diversified formal financial channels—as well as a range of official U.S. migration visa programs such as for family visitors, tourists, and students, and the
EB-5 visas that provide pathways to green cards and citizenship through investment (discussed in chapter 4)—are becoming mainstream, as Vietnam leaves its
boat refugee exodus past behind. In the meantime, informal financial transfer and
undocumented migratory arrangements are becoming more complicated, as
those who facilitate hot transfers or overstay visas are increasingly visible and
liable.

The traditional directions, meanings, and symbols of remittances as payments,
obligations, gifts, or something else may be changing with the introduction of a
range of new service platforms and practices from providers eager to persuade

FIGURE 15. Vietnamese bank with remittance services.

remittance senders and recipients to trade in the trusty old homemade "canoe" for a sleek modern yacht, so to speak. In this afterword I have momentarily stepped back from ethnographic stories of remittance exchange among participants to consider more broadly how financial regulatory reforms in the United States as well as emerging technologies are changing the international remittance landscape. These shifts are affecting remittance service providers and, by extension, their customers. The formalizing of informal cross-border value transmission practices in a globalized world draws our attention to the multiple manifestations of money's forms and influences, as well as the channels by and through which money flows. While there have been a plethora of savvy financial inclusion and transfer ecosystem expansions within the formal banking and money transfer operator sector, it is important to also recognize and appreciate the informal financial practices that still continue alongside them. Community-based ethnic remittance service providers have been working to facilitate and maintain kinship and community relations between the United States and Vietnam (and other countries) for a very long time. And here we return our attention to ethnographies of exchange and why they matter. As the wall of cherished customer photos in the remittance shop described at the start of this afterword attests, the service of financial channeling is infrastructural but also affective. Many anthropologists have recently called for greater attention to infrastructure (Star 1999; Larkin 2013) or, as in the case at hand, the issue of payment channels (Maurer, Nelms, and Rea 2013). However, it is worth remembering that while we attend metaphorically to Malinowski's canoes, he also cautioned against overly focusing on such channels, as they were in his words merely "a means to an end": "The canoe is made for a certain use, and with a definitive purpose . . . [W]e . . . must not reverse this relation, and make a fetish of the object itself" (1984, 105). Malinowski went on to call for further ethnographic data about the canoe's "ownership, accounts of who sails in it, and how it is done; information regarding the ceremonies and customs of its constructions, a sort of typical life history of a native craft—all that bring us nearer still to the understanding of what his canoe truly means to the native" (ibid.). As we have seen, remittances, in their entanglement with gifts and money, arbitrage across their diverse characteristics and capacities in their hope to extend and recover meaning through exchange.[4] Attending to the global financial infrastructures and actors that channel these remittances is important, but doing so does not diminish the participants' accounts of exchange and meaning making that those infrastructures enable. Indeed, it is these ethnographic accounts that have been at the heart of this book.

Nonetheless, considering the role of international financial architectures (including, in this case, the particular histories of informal sector remittance services as well as the shifting consequences of formal regulations governing them) draws our attention to another important component of the remittance equation. Ethnic remittance providers have served a critical role that is not merely abstract and technical, but in many cases quite personally and emotionally entrenched. It is only by appreciating the affective labors of those who channel money and their contributions to transnational communication that one can understand why informal services continue to flourish and command trust and respect, in the face of the formal financial sector's intrusion. Backgrounded infrastructures are also manned by people who are entangled with the foregrounded personal experiences examined in this book. Examining their messy and complex histories and connections offers further insights into the transnational socioeconomic relations that are affectively shaped by money, emotionally framed by gifts, and logistically mediated by remittance flows.

POSTSCRIPT

I began this afterword by reflecting on my tunnel vision at the end of my primary fieldwork in Vietnam in 2009, and the need not only to update but also to step back in order to take a broader temporal and infrastructural view of all that has unfolded in the context of Vietnam's incredible growth over the past decade. In many ways I now feel that I am tunnel-visioned on the other side of the ocean and country, caught up in the details of my busy professional and personal life and with less time to return to, let alone explore, Vietnam or even California. The kind of slow-cooked day-to-day ethnography that I participated in for nearly two years, unfolding in all of its sumptuous, surprising and even mundane details, seems a distant memory and privilege. Yet Vietnam is far from removed in my mind, and a repetitive compulsion to return continues. A decade after I started my initial fieldwork as a doctoral candidate, and a generation after my arrival there as a wide-eyed study-abroad student, I still find Vietnam to be a country that intrigues and beguiles, both within and beyond its borders, and that—as my most recent visit, in 2017, reminded me—never ceases to surprise.

If the standard Western narrative about Vietnam was once about a war, nowadays it is about an economy. The 2017 Asia-Pacific Economic Cooperation forum was appropriately held in Danang, Vietnam's emerging new economic and technological center. Situated on the coast midway between Hanoi and Ho Chi Minh City, but also between Thailand, Laos, and the South China Sea, the city has been developing itself as a hub for north-south and east-west trade. Danang is a key port city and is investing heavily in infrastructure, with ambitious plans in the works to expand its population and metropolitan reach. It has also attracted a burgeoning start-up culture, in which overseas Vietnamese venture capital has been an important factor ("Da Nang Determined to Build Startup City" 2017; Quek 2017). Over the past few years whenever I return to Vietnam, and increasingly Danang, I encounter ambitious young entrepreneurs eager to promote their visions of the next mobile or technological advance, from transportation to phones and remittance applications.

I mention this in closing only to reflect my amazement, undiminished over the past twenty years since my first extended engagement with the country as a student in Saigon in 1998, of how Vietnam continues to transform itself in ever new directions and at ever more astounding speeds. One of my clearest memories from my first visit to Saigon in 1993 was waiting in line at a post office for nearly an hour to use a telephone booth. The second time, only three years later, there was one house phone that was shared by the entire neighborhood I was staying in. I would walk down the street and knock on the neighbor's door to make or receive a call, leaving a small wad of cash afterward for using the service. Two years after that I enjoyed the luxury of having an individually assigned house phone, a phenomenon that was increasingly widespread at least in the city. Then came the cell phone and texting, then the smart phone and apps, and then . . . ? It is incredible to reflect on how advances in a technology as simple as the telephone has dramatically transformed Vietnamese networks of communication and knowledge—including the hardware itself, which can now potentially be used to send and receive remittances.

Technology compels the imagination to mobilize in creative and unexpected ways. From print technologies facilitating imagined communities across reading publics sharing the same language (Anderson 2006) to emerging relations between technology and science that are reshaping knowledge and personhoods (Fischer 2009), the role of technology in human life is profound and unbound. This is especially true when it comes to migrants and homelands where technology mediates loss and transformation of the familiar, as various examples throughout this book have shown. These have ranged from phone calls and e-mail messages to check on a relative in the homeland or to ask for assistance from an empathetic diasporic acquaintance abroad; sending photographs from afar that depict unimaginable things and lives in other lands; and using social media applications where real-time connections convey illusions of immediacy. Were I to continue this study into the next decade, I would probably make technology (as it intersects with both migration and finance, as well as with conceptions of mobility more broadly) a more specific theme of inquiry in my conversations with remittance senders and receivers and in the resulting analysis.

The latter part of this Afterword has outlined some of the directions these techno-mobile intersections are moving toward from the perspective of remittance providers, who also play a key background role in linking the senders and receivers that were the main subject of this study. I have chosen to conclude by gesturing to the role of technology in part because of its potential to critique the examination of the imagination that has been central to this book, including the limits of its applicability to other contemporary migration cases. I have suggested that the disjunctures between bodies and money and between past and present produce spaces for imaginaries that aspire to supplement the felt gaps between experience and apprehension. As I observed in the introduction, "the remittance relationship . . . continually confronts gaps in understanding and transgressing differences, which were always present but have been more clearly revealed as a result of the long historical, political, social, and mnemonic divide experienced by the participants in remittance exchanges. It is in this space of difference that new forms of imagination and agency emerge, with corresponding sociocultural formations and affects." Technology, admittedly, can change the contours of this space. Just as canoes connected the Trobriand islands, bringing parties into encounter and exchange, so do simple technological advances, such as the expansion of digital connectivity, narrow the gap within which imaginaries of the Other once grew unchecked during long years of exile and limited communication.

Technologies compel the imagination of radically different futures. They transgress the limitations of the past and transcend the physical limitations of borders. These are the very temporal and geographic orientations that have been so central to tensions arising from gift origins and returns. Like the gift, technology also offers a vehicle for the imagination that gestures toward alluring if not elusive horizons. Further examining the emerging affordances of new communicative and financial technologies as they inevitably change the contours of diaspora-homeland imaginaries and linkages going forward promises to be a fascinating ethnographic arena to follow.

Notes

INTRODUCTION

1. "Việt Nam" will be referred to following the American spelling, "Vietnam," throughout this book.

2. The war is commonly called the American War (*Chiến Tranh Mỹ*) in Vietnam.

3. Christopher Goscha terms the string of military conflicts between and within Vietnam, and different outside actors (ranging from Japan, France, the United States, Cambodia and China) the "30-Years War" (2016b)

4. According to the United Nations, a refugee is defined as a person who "owing to well-founded fear of being persecuted for reasons of race, religion, nationality, membership of a particular social group or political opinion, is outside the country of his nationality and is unable or, owing to such fear, is unwilling to avail himself of the protection of that country" (1951 Convention Relating to the Status of Refugees). Although people fleeing for economic reasons are generally considered migrants, consideration of dire structural economic conditions from which one has little choice but to flee has led to development of the term "economic refugee," the use of which is advocated by many humanitarian organizations.

5. North-South core-periphery remittances are widely recognized, but South-South remittances are also significant and often occur between semiperiphery and periphery countries. "Core," "semiperiphery," and "periphery," terms derived from Immanuel Wallerstein's 1974 study of the structural causes of inequality of the world system, will be at times used in this study to emphasize global economic hierarchies revealed and navigated by remittances.

6. In the case of the United States, the Federal Deposit Insurance Corporation and the Automated Clearing House are part of the banking system.

7. Bohannan 1955 identified three distinct spheres of exchange with rules of how goods could be traded within and across spheres among the Tiv in Nigeria that were disrupted and effectively dismantled by colonialism and the introduction of money. For a critique of the geographic and temporal boundaries of this analysis, see Guyer 2004.

8. For a general review essay on anthropological studies of money, see Maurer 2006.

9. The International Monetary Fund (2009) provides updated guidelines on what to count as and how to track remittances. Changing calculation mechanisms have resulted in capturing previously unrecorded remittance flows, which are reflected in reports reflecting significant quantitative increases.

10. On the productivity of mess as data and analytic, see Manalansan 2014.

11. See, for example, Bourdieu 1977; Strathern 1988; Derrida 1992; Weiner 1992; Godelier 1999; Miyazaki 2010; Graeber 2011.

12. Review essays of the gift in anthropology include Miyazaki 2012, Hann 2006, and Osteen 2002b.

13. The relational designations of Vietnamese pronouns highlights and complicates this all the more.

14. Guyer's (2004) critique of Bohannan, showing that in fact the Tiv had long been connected to broader trading networks, is an empirical one. The point here is that Bohannan's

discussion of money conceptually constructs its function as emphasizing the connectivity of parties across geographic distances.

15. The one period of slight increase was just after the Cold War. This was primarily to the breakup of the Soviet Union into a number of independent countries, which turned formerly internal migrants into international ones. Nonetheless, the global migration rate has hovered close to 3 percent: in 1990, at the end of the Cold War migrants accounted for 2.9 percent of the global population, compared to 2.6 percent in 1960 and 3.3 percent in 2015. The vast majority of the world's population does not migrate across borders. For a more detailed analysis of these numbers, see Connor 2016.

16. Since 1980 the proportion of GDP that moves across borders in the form of foreign investment has increased roughly 500 percent. Focusing on percentages, rather than numbers, allows for a more representative comparison of the difference between global capital and migrant flows, since of course quantitative increases are significant for both.

17. Pseudonyms for informants are used throughout the book.

18. Saigon is still the name used by most residents to refer to the urban core of the city, and it will therefore be used interchangeably with Ho Chi Minh City throughout this book. Ho Chi Minh City consists of a much larger geographical area (including rural districts) than pre-1975 Saigon.

19. Ho Chi Minh City has a significant population of families with histories of rural-urban migration from the adjacent Mekong Delta, in which ongoing kinship linkages are easily maintained due to relative proximity. Some of these are discussed in chapter 2.

1. THE "DANGEROUS" GIFT

1. The overseas Vietnamese I interviewed for this study varied considerably in terms of their travels to Vietnam. Some made regular business and family trips, while others never went back. Some families sent one member back in periods of downtime, such as during the summer break for a schoolchild or slow seasons for a husband or wife who were business owners. However, the majority of informants reported that their return trips to Vietnam were typically spaced two to three years apart and lasted approximately one month. Return travel accompanied by remittances to Vietnam from the diaspora was thus described neither as regular or as irregular, but rather as when one can or occasional.

2. For relatively comprehensive overviews of gifting literatures and conceptualizations, see Osteen 2002a; Hann 2006; Miyazaki 2010.

3. Although under French colonial rule. Annam was the official name for only the central Vietnamese protectorate, with Tonkin to the north and Cochinchina to the south. However, Annam, where the Vietnamese emperor continued to hold nominal power, was commonly used to refer to all three Vietnamese regions, and Annamese referred to the people living in all three. Vietnam had also been called Annam when it was a province under Chinese rule. The name in Chinese (安南) is sometimes translated as "Pacified South."

4. In the late nineteenth and early twentieth centuries, armchair anthropology was the disciplinary norm, with anthropologists collecting accounts of the customs of distant cultures coming into contact with colonial expansion from travelers, traders, missionaries, soldiers, and others. These anthropologists did not necessarily visit those societies themselves. The practice of fieldwork often associated with contemporary cultural anthropology is commonly attributed to Bronislaw Malinowski, a Pole who was a citizen of the Austro-Hungarian Empire. During a visit to Papua New Guinea at the start of World War I, he was detained for the duration of the war. Papua New Guinea was part of the British Empire and therefore on the other side in the conflict. During his forced stay he developed and outlined the practice of field ethnography, described in his 1922 publication *Argonauts of the Western Pacific* (1984).

5. The above mentioned trader Dupuis, for example, describes how his arrival in Hanoi in 1872, as part of an attempt to secure passage up the Red River to Yunnan, was met with both agitation by local mandarins and welcome by the Chinese colony there; both cases involved receptions for and gifts to dignitaries (1910, 31).

6. The localized social impacts of broader "cultures of migration" have been explored by, among others, Cohen and Sirkeci 2011.

7. R. Lacombe, l'interprete stagiaire, charge du controle (trainee interpreter, in charge of control); Marseilles, October 6, 1917, Centre des Archives d'Outre Mer Fonds Ministeriels Indo/NF/263, Aix-en-Provence, France. The French original is: "Si l'esprit de nos protégés est généralement bon; leur conduire privée, telle que nous la souhaiterions ici pour garder intact en Indochine le prestige de l'Européenne, laisse de plus en plus à désirer. Nos moeurs il faut bien le reconnaître, ce prêtent admirablement a leur lubricité naturelle. La prostitution dans les grands villes leur offre des plaisirs charnels qui sont d'autant plus goûtés que les prix en sont souvent inférieurs à ceux de la colonie et que le confort toujours [est] pour eux incomparable. Les arrivants ne tarrissent pas d'éloges à ce qu'illustrent avec une grande indécence les cartes postales et l'on continue à trouver sur les nudités qui viennent nombreuses des bataillons indochinois, la phrase sacramentelle 'il n'y rien de beau, de joli, d'intéressant ici si ce n'est ça.'"

8. Derrida discusses the potentially threatening and destabilizing nature of communication via the open nature of the postcard, which "falls into anyone's hands . . . once intercepted . . . .the message no longer has any chance of reaching any determinable person, in any (determinable) place whatever." (1987, 51).

9. It is common for many Vietnamese to refer to their days in the Army of the Republic of Vietnam (ARVN) as being in the American army (*Quân đội Mỹ*).

10. For an anthropological analysis of the roles of sacrifice and filial piety in Vietnam, see Shohet 2013.

11. For more on discourses related to culture and civilization in Vietnam, see Harms 2011 and 2016.

12. About 70 percent of Vietnam's population is estimated to be Buddhist, with the majority following the Mahayana tradition.

13. My own translation from Nguyễn Huy Thiệp 1988. This differs somewhat from the 1992 English translation (by Lockhart) in emphasizing fidelity to word choices, structure, and tone.

14. On the microfinance landscape in Vietnam, see Vietnam Microfinance Working Group 2013.

2. SÀI GÒN, OVERLAID BY HỒ CHÍ MINH

1. Internal migration has been severely underestimated in Vietnam, where difficulties in registration (*Hộ khẩu*) and state efforts at controlling urban growth have resulted in many migrants' having to live and work illegally in the informal sector. It is estimated that over 86 percent of households in Vietnam receive some form of domestic remittances from family members who are internal migrants (Pfau and Giang 2009).

2. Saigon was the capital of the French colony of Cochinchina. The other regions of central and northern Vietnam (Annam and Tonkin), along with Cambodia and Laos, were administered by France as protectorates rather than colonies.

3. Quite a few overviews of Vietnamese history have been published. Three recent ones that provide a relatively comprehensive chronological overview from premodern times up through the Vietnam War are K. Taylor 2013, Goscha 2016 and Kiernan 2017.

4. Gainsborough 2003, appendix A1.2. On postwar urban management of Ho Chi Minh City, see Turley 1976.

5. For discussions of the city's rapid geographic expansion over the last generation, see Harms 2011 and 2016.

6. Imaginaries of capitalist fantasy lands are not unique to Vietnam and have been observed elsewhere in the socialist world (Borneman 1992; Berdahl 2009)

7. In Vietnam, people are often called by the appropriate pronoun in relation to the caller (in this case loosely translated as grandmother), followed by the order of their birth in the family—with the caveat that the number "1" is never used. It is said that this is out of fear that the first child, being the most valued, might be snatched by harmful spirits.

8. On the difficulty of accessing microcredit in rural Vietnam, see Barslund and Tarp 2008. For a discussion of rotating credit arrangements in Ho Chi Minh's urban petty trader markets, see Leshkowich 2014. On comparative examples of rotating credit initiatives and other monetary practices in developing economies, see among many other studies Bajracharya's work on *dhukuti* in Nepal, as well as other chapters in Maurer, Musaraj and Small (2018).

9. Before the division of Indochina into Vietnam (South and North), Cambodia, and Laos in 1954, a significant proportion of Phnom Penh's urban population was Vietnamese, with many members of that group holding civil- service positions in the colonial government. A large Vietnamese population remains in Cambodia today, and its members often face discrimination. For more on the ethnic population formations, divisions, and dispersals within Indochina, see Goscha 2012.

10. Children of Vietnamese mothers and American GI fathers were sometimes called the "dust of life (*bụi đời*)" in the 1980s, as many were abandoned by their parents. See McKelvey 1999.

11. Zhou and Bankston 1998 categorize the different migrant generations as follows: 1st generation designate those who were adults at the time of leaving Vietnam, 1.5 generation designate those who moved to the U.S. between 5 and 12 years of age, and 2nd generation designate those who moved to the U.S. before 5 years old.

12. On policy initiatives and research to incentivize increased formal banking participation, see World Bank Global Financial Development Report (2014) among others.

13. Saigon South is a new residential district on the outskirts of Saigon. For an ethnographic study of this development, see Harms 2016.

14. Until recently there was also anticipation about the Trans-Pacific Partnership, the future of which now (April 2018) remains in uncertain flux.

15. The street was named *Tự Do* (Freedom) Street under the Saigon government and Rue Catinat under the French colonial regime.

16. This information is based on interviews with researchers, consultants, and staff members of market research firms that serve as consultants for international money transfer organizations.

17. This information is based on interviews with staff members of the Transnational Institute for Grassroots Research and Action in July 2008. For more on the institute, see Transnational Institute for Grassroots Research and Action n.d.

18. The B-2 tourist visa in the United States is good for a period of six months to one year.

19. For a further discussion of the changing roles of sentiment and emotion in Vietnam's neoliberal economy, see A. Tran 2015.

3. COASTAL FLOWS AND HYPOTHETICAL HORIZONS

1. On refugee camps in Southeast Asia and the work of memory, see Q. Tran (2012). In 1989 the international Comprehensive Plan of Action limited asylum for Vietnamese boat people, and those who were identified as economic migrants rather than political ref-

ugees were returned to Vietnam under the auspices of the United Nations High Commissioner for Refugees.

2. For a historiographical discussion of Vietnamese narratives of this southward movement of the Viet people into Cham and later Khmer territories, see Ang 2013.

3. The Vietnamese name for the South China Sea, *Biển Đông*, is translated as Eastern Sea. There has been a long conflict between Vietnam and China over who owns these waters (see Hayton 2014).

4. On South Korea's military presence in South Vietnam as a U.S. ally during the war, see H. Kwon 2006.

5. In Ho Chi Minh City, a prevalence of other economic activities often results in remittances being only one comparatively minor flow of income among others for households with working-age members.

6. Upgrading in most cases involved the destruction of the previous structure and rebuilding on top of it, typically costing $15,000 to $20,000, whereas I was told that buying a new house with its land ranges from $60,000 to $80,000 (in 2009).

7. Quy Nhơn fell to North Vietnamese troops at the beginning of April 1975, and many of its residents fled south to Saigon. The first wave of Vietnamese left by airplane in the final days of the South Vietnamese regime at the end of April 1975. Flows of boat refugees followed through the late 1970s and 1980s. Later refugees who wanted to leave Vietnam applied to the U.S. Orderly Departure and Humanitarian Operation Programs. If accepted they could fly directly to a sponsoring country of resettlement. However, many continue to wait years after submitting their paperwork requesting emigration. See the introduction.

8. Officials in the Binh Định Province People's Committee estimated in discussions with me in May 2008 that at least 40 percent of the residents of Quy Nhơn have members of their extended family living abroad, although there has been no official count.

9. This case reflects what the geographer Ronald Skeldon (2006) has observed in the apparent linkage between internal and international migration, with the former potentially being the first step to achieving the latter.

10. Vietnamese nail-salon entrepreneurs have done well, making up 45 percent of licensed manicurists in the United States, and 80 percent in California (Bates 2012). However, this was also a sector that experienced some flux after the financial crisis.

11. Such incidents did occur. For a review of Duc Nguyen's 2008 documentary *Bolinao 52* exploring memories of this, see Small 2014.

12. My informants generally remembered that the standard fee for passage on a boat was three to five bars.

13. This joking comment was a deliberate play on the similar sounds of the words: *Việt Kiều* / *Việt Cộng.*

14. For an ethnography and analysis of Vietnamese petty market traders adapting to Vietnam's burgeoning economy, see Leshkowich 2014.

15. On the challenges of medium-size enterprises and the growth of a middle class in Vietnam, see Van Arkadie and Mallon 2003; Gainsborough 2003 and 2010; Drummond, and Belanger 2012; Earl 2014; Le Thu Huong 2016.

16. In Vietnamese: *Kinh tế thị trường theo định hướng xã hội chủ nghĩa.*

17. The inability to identify common patterns in overseas visa interview questions, despite a pooling of knowledge, was a widespread frustration among many would-be migrants. In informal conversations with me, consular officials acknowledged that this was an intentional strategy.

18. Ông Nam Hải (the South Sea god) is also known as Cá Ông or Ông Cá in Vietnam (literally, Lord Fish); generally translated as the whale (*cá voi*) god but also, according to my informants, sometimes inclusive of dolphins (*cá heo*).

19. In Vietnam there are a variety of terms used for religious and memorial worship sites specific to the religion, belief, or context, including Buddhist pagodas (*chùa*), Christian churches (*nhà thờ*), memorial temples to Confucian leaders or political heroes (*đền*), communal house (*đình*), and mausoleum (*lăng*).

20. Mạc (2008) categorizes whale worship as one of seven forms of "popular belief" in southern Vietnam. For more on the whale god, see Lantz 2009 and T.L. Nguyễn Thanh Lợi 2014.

21. Remittances as gratitude for divine assistance extend to other religious practices as well. In Vung Tau a towering statue of Jesus stares out to sea, and the pathway up to it is lined with stone chairs commemorating donations from overseas Vietnamese Catholics. Similar commemorative chairs are found at the Linh Ung Buddhist Pagoda in Danang, where a statue of Quan Am gazes at the Pacific Ocean from atop a mountain, as well as at many smaller temples, pagodas, and churches across coastal southern Vietnam where boat refugee emigration was significant.

22. For an extended anthropological discussion on the gendered relationality of gifts, see Strathern 1988.

23. On the translation, "*phù*" is a Chinese word root (浮) meaning "floating" or "drifting," and "*du*" is a Chinese word root (游) meaning "meandering" or "wandering." In its colloquial usage, the phrase was explained as an ephemeral situation in which money is always on the move and seemingly always just out of reach, unable to be controlled but nonetheless sought after. "Money is ephemeral" may be a more concise translation, but "money wanders everywhere, one cannot control it" perhaps better captures the socially transient and elusive qualities of money reflected upon in this context.

24. As discussed earlier, the global marriage market has opened up new migration channels, particularly for Vietnamese women. It is now common for *Việt Kiều* men to return to marry local women (see Thai 2008). Thai (2014) also argues that achieving status is a key motivation for low-income migrants who return to Vietnam, because they generally lack social capital in the United States.

25. Remittance senders have much to say on this issue, as I will discuss in more detail in chapter 4.

26. Berlant describes cruel optimism as "the condition of maintaining an attachment to a significantly problematic object . . . if the cruelty of an attachment *is* experienced by someone/some group, even in a subtle fashion, the fear is that the loss of the promising object/scene itself will defeat the capacity to have any hope about anything" (2011, 24).

4. THE BEAUTIFUL, TIRED COUNTRY

1. 美国, with the first character coming from a transliteration of "America."

2. On the naming, see discussion later in this chapter.

3. This number does not include the Vietnamese Americans I interviewed in Vietnam.

4. On the practice of earmarking as analyzed in economic sociology, see Zelizer 1989.

5. For recent analyses of the disconnects experienced by Asian Americans traveling to so-called ancestral homelands, see, for example, Yamashiro 2017; Pido 2017.

6. There were such controversies about the 2014 establishment of a sister-city relationship between Riverside, California, and Can Tho, Vietnam; the Vietnamese American Arts and Letters Association's "FOB II: Art Speaks" exhibition in 2009; David Thomas's 2000 exhibition of portraits of Ho Chi Minh at the Pacific Bridge Gallery in Oakland, California; and the 1997 performance in Los Angeles of the Thang Long water puppet troupe from Hanoi.

7. It was pointed out to me that a visual material marker of Vietnamese households, often dispersed through ethnically diverse communities, is a preference for Japanese cars parked in the driveways—particularly Hondas and Toyotas.

8. Elliott and Urry define "network capital" as "the capacity to engender and sustain social relations with . . . people not necessarily proximate, which generates emotional, financial and practical benefit" (2010, 59).

9. On Vietnamese consumer obsessions with quality and origins connected to a very different commodity, motorcycles, see Vann 2006.

10. For example, Bao Nguyen, a Vietnamese American Democrat, was elected mayor of Garden Grove, California (part of Little Saigon) in 2014, despite his Republican opponent's attempt to paint him as a communist sympathizer in Vietnamese-language campaign materials. However, Nguyen's popularity suffered when he refused to criticize nearby Riverside's sister-city arrangement with Can Tho, Vietnam, an arrangement that led to some protests in the Vietnamese community. Nguyen was defeated in the next election.

11. Such a visa requires an investment of a million dollars, or of half a million dollars if the money is invested in targeted U.S. areas with high unemployment, plus the creation of ten jobs. For more on the EB5 visa, see U.S. Department of Homeland Security n.d.

12. On anti-communism and Vietnamese American diasporic formations, see T. Hoang 2016, N. Ong and Meyer 2008, Vo Dang 2005.

13. Collet and Furuya note that anticommunist activism in the Vietnamese American community, or what they call "Saigon nationalism" (2010, 19), contributes to shaping community self-conceptions and advancing the political goal of "collective membership and incorporation in American society" (2010, 22).

14. Omi and Winant point to the exceptionalism of ethnic consciousness in the United States, where "from the very inception of the Republic to the present moment, race has been a profound determinant of one's political rights, one's location in the labor market, and indeed one's sense of 'identity'" (1994, 1).

15. For a creative reflection on this phenomenon, see G. B. Tran's graphic memoir, *Vietnamerica* (2011).

5. CROSSING THE BRIDGE . . . HOME?

1. These expatriates are sometimes called "VKs." For recent ethnographic studies that focus on these return *Việt Kiều* communities, see Nguyen-Akbar 2014 and 2016; Koh 2015; Thai 2014.

2. "*Người Việt Nam ở nước ngoài*" is the official state term for overseas Vietnamese, as reflected in the name of the state ministry that overseas them, the *Ủy Ban Nhà Nước Về người Việt Nam ở Nước Ngoài* (State Committee for Vietnamese in Foreign Countries).

3. For an analysis of the lack of transparency and general illegibility of Vietnamese government bureaucracy, see MacLean 2013.

4. See the Vietnamese government's "homeland" website for an English translation of Resolution 36 (quehuong).

5. The Chinese radical in *qiao* 僑 (overseas sojourn) is the character for person, while the radical in *qiao* (bridge 橋) is the character for wood. In Sino-Vietnamese the word is *kiều* or, in the vernacular, *cầu*. Despite the different characters, the semantic links nonetheless suggest a shared word family. On old Chinese word families, see Laurent Sagart 2004. See also Li 1994; Chu 2010.

6. For a discussion of the "Washington consensus" on global trade and financial liberalization and promoting free capital flows, see Williamson 1990. See also Williamson 1993 and 2004.

7. Chu also notes the visceral relation between bodies, money, and the imagination in her discussion of the "Inappropriate(d) Other," drawing on the work of Trinh T. Minh-Ha. Chu discusses her own subjectivity in this analysis, reflecting: "As a first-generation Chinese American, I was probably not so different from what aspiring Longyan migrants imagined they might become once they crossed the South China Sea" (2010, 16).

8. Vietnam's 2008 Nationality Law allowing dual citizenship extended a five-year period for people who were Vietnamese "citizens" by virtue of blood to officially register as such, but as of 2014 only 6,000 had done so, the majority of members of the diaspora preferring to maintain single citizenship in their country of resettlement (Tuoi Tre 2014). Some overseas Vietnamese who had taken up the offer of citizenship have had it revoked in response to political activism. For example, Pham Nguyen Hoang, a dissident blogger critical of Vietnam's one-party rule, environmental degradation, corruption, and relations with China, held dual French and Vietnamese citizenship but was stripped of the latter and deported from Vietnam in 2017.

9. Data on 1987, 1992 and 2002 retrieved from staff at the Vietnam State Committee for Overseas Vietnamese office in Ho Chi Minh City in 2008. On 2015 figure see Gribble and Tran 2016.

10. On pre-1975 migrations to France, see Bousquet 1991; McConnell 1989; Hill 2011; Rettig 2012. On socialist-era migrations, see Schwenkel 2014. On the Chinese exodus, see Chan 2011. On marriage migrants, see H. Lee 2014; L. Hoang and Yeoh 2015. On Southeast Asia worker migrants, see T. Le 2010.

11. For more on diaspora ministries, see Mendoza 2009.

CONCLUSION

1. For more on the limitations of credit access in Vietnam, see Barslund and Tarp 2008. I was told by several informal high-interest moneylenders that most of their clients are not from remittance-receiving households, as overseas relatives usually provide loans to such families. Relevant to a more general discussion of credit and gifting, Mauss (1967, 111) cites Boas as discussing potlatch gifting as an advanced system of credit, in which collective trust supports an otherwise artificial and unsustainable expansion of capital as well as future-oriented subjectivities.

2. A key ethical concern for Mauss in *The Gift* is the dehumanization of social relations through the individuality and competition inherent in capitalism (see the last section of chapter 4).

3. Tangentially, Mauss mentions the "Asiatic" nature of gambling in a footnote and asserts that the practice of gambling is an integral "form of the potlatch and of the gift system" (1967, 112).

4. There is a broad range of literature on embodiment in relation to work (see, for example, Foucault 1977; Bourdieu 1977), and it was also a key site of inquiry for Mauss. For an ethnography on the affective transformation of the body and identity through labor, see Schattschneider 2003. For one on the absence of work, see J. Kwon and Lane 2016.

5. The expression "not yet enough" occurred repeatedly in my interviews with remittance economy participants. It not only referred to amounts of gifts and money sent and received but also served as a critical commentary on general states of societal satisfaction, national development, and the capacity of global capitalism to sufficiently deliver on its idealized promises of sufficient socioeconomic transformation—"sufficient" being the key word in question and another translation of *đủ*.

AFTERWORD

1. What are called ethnographic emergences in anthropology are understood to be situations still taking shape and therefore presenting intriguing new possibilities for analysis. The concept of ethnographic emergences and corresponding analytic approaches of para-ethnography in anthropology require open-ended observations and collaborative methods that defer meeting the demand for analytical understanding (Maurer 2005; Holmes and Marcus 2008).

2. The term *hawala* originally comes from Arabic but in monetary studies is a general term applied to any informal transfer system that circumnavigates official banking channels through account-swapping methods. This has been called "hot transfer" in the context of this study.

3. Safaricom's M-Pesa in Kenya was one of the first mobile money services in the world, and the domestic remittances it enables has become a global success story. In 2011, Safaricom also partnered with Western Union to facilitate international remittances. In Southeast Asia mobile money has been successfully used in the Philippines, particularly the GCash service now in partnership with PayPal. The significant overseas and domestic migrant worker population in the Philippines (which has the largest in-bound remittance flow in the region), along with corresponding government regulatory cooperation to facilitate both banked and unbanked financial transfers, has made the country a model to study and a site of future possibilities for policy makers, regulators, and financial entrepreneurs in Southeast Asia.

4. On the concept of arbitrage in economic anthropology, see discussion in Introduction.

Bibliography

AAPIP: Asian Americans / Pacific Islanders in Philanthropy. "Giving Circles." Accessed April 15, 2018. https://aapip.org/what-we-do/national-giving-circle-network/our -community.

Adams, Richard H., and John Page. 2005. "Do International Migration and Remittances Reduce Poverty in Developing Countries?" *World Development* 33(10):1645–1660.

Aguilar-San Juan, Karin. 2009. *Little Saigons: Staying Vietnamese in America*. Minneapolis: University of Minnesota Press.

Anderson, Benedict. 1998. *The Spectre of Comparisons: Nationalism, Southeast Asia, and the World*. London: Verso.

——. 2006. *Imagined Communities: Reflections on the Origin and Spread of Nationalism*. London: Verso.

Ang, Claudine. 2013. "Regionalism in Southern Narratives of Vietnamese History: The Case of the 'Southern Advance' [Nam Tiến]." *Journal of Vietnamese Studies* 8 (3): 1–26.

Appadurai, Arjun. 1986. *The Social Life of Things: Commodities in Cultural Perspective*. Cambridge: Cambridge University Press.

——. 1996. *Modernity at Large: Cultural Dimensions of Globalization*. Minneapolis: University of Minnesota Press.

——. 2011. "The Ghost in the Financial Machine." *Public Culture* 23 (3): 517–39.

——. 2013. *The Future as Cultural Fact: Essays on the Global Condition*. London: Verso.

Axel, Brian K. 2002. "The Diasporic Imaginary." *Public Culture* 14 (2): 411–428.

Bachelard, Gaston. 1994. *The Poetics of Space*. Boston: Beacon Press.

Barslund, Mikkel, and Finn Tarp. 2008. "Formal and Informal Rural Credit in Four Provinces of Vietnam." *Journal of Development Studies* 44 (4): 485–503.

Bataille, Georges. 1989. *The Accursed Share: An Essay on General Economy*. New York: Zone Books.

Bates, Karen Grigsby. 2012. "Nailing the American Dream, with Polish." NPR, June 14. Accessed September 30, 2017. https://www.npr.org/2012/06/14/154852394/with -polish-vietnamese-immigrant-community-thrives.

Benjamin, Walter. 1969. *Illuminations*. Edited by Hannah Arendt, translated by Harry Zohn. New York: Schocken.

Berdahl, Daphne. 2009. *On the Social Life of Postsocialism: Memory, Consumption, Germany*. Indianapolis: Indiana University Press.

Beresford, Melanie, and Phong Dang. 2000. *Economic Transition in Vietnam: Trade and Aid in the Demise of a Centrally Planned Economy*. Cheltenham, UK: Edward Elgar.

Berlant, Lauren. 2011. *Cruel Optimism*. Durham, NC: Duke University Press.

Biao, Xiang, Brenda Yeoh, and Mika Toyota. 2013. *Return: Nationalizing Transnational Mobility in Asia*. Durham, NC: Duke University Press.

Boas, Franz. 1898. *Twelfth and Final Report on the North-Western Tribes of Canada*. London: British Association for the Advancement of Science.

Boellstorff, Tom. 2012. *Ethnography and Virtual Worlds: A Handbook of Method*. Princeton, NJ: Princeton University Press.

Bohannan, Paul. 1955. "Some Principles of Exchange and Investment among the Tiv." *American Anthropologist* 57 (1): 60–70.

Borneman, John. 1992. *Belonging in the Two Berlins: Kin, State, Nation*. New York: Cambridge University Press.

Bourdieu, Pierre. 1977. *Outline of a Theory of Practice*. Translated by Richard Nice. New York: Cambridge University Press.

Bousquet, Gisèle. 1991. *Behind the Bamboo Hedge: The Impact of Homeland Politics in the Parisian Vietnamese Community*. Ann Arbor: University of Michigan Press.

Boyer, Dominic, James D. Faubion, and George E. Marcus, eds. 2015. *Theory Can Be More Than It Used to Be: Learning Anthropology's Method in a Time of Transition*. Ithaca, NY: Cornell University Press.

Bracken, Christopher. 1997. *Potlatch Papers: A Colonial Case History*. Chicago: University of Chicago Press.

Brocheux, Pierre, and Daniel Hemery. 2009. *Indochina: An Ambiguous Colonization, 1858–1954*. Translated by Ly Lan Dill-Klein, with Eric Jennings, Nora Taylor, and Noémi Tousignant. Berkeley: University of California Press.

Callon, Michel. 1998. *The Laws of the Markets*. Oxford: Blackwell.

Cao, Lan. 1997. *Monkey Bridge*. New York: Viking Penguin Books.

Carruthers, Ashley. 2008. "Saigon from the Diaspora." *Singapore Journal of Tropical Geography* 29 (1): 68–86.

Castles, Stephen. 1993. *The Age of Migration: International Population Movements*. New York: Guilford Press.

Chakrabarty, Dipesh. 2000. "Universalism and Belonging in the Logic of Capital." *Public Culture* 12 (3): 653–678.

Chan, Yuk Wah, ed. 2011. *The Chinese/Vietnamese Diaspora: Revisiting the Boat People in Hong Kong*. New York: Routledge.

Chu, Julie. 2010. *Cosmologies of Credit: Transnational Mobility and the Politics of Destination in China*. Durham, NC: Duke University Press.

Clifford, James. 1997. *Routes: Travel and Translation in the Late Twentieth Century*. Cambridge, MA: Harvard University Press.

——, and George E. Marcus. 2010. *Writing Culture: The Poetics and Politics of Ethnography*. Berkeley: University of California Press.

Cohen, Jeffrey, and Ibrahim Sirkeci. 2011. *Cultures of Migration: The Global Nature of Contemporary Mobility*. Austin: University of Texas Press.

Collet, Christian, and Hiroko. Furuya. 2009. "Enclave, Place, or Nation? Defining Little Saigon in the Midst of Incorporation, Transnationalism, and Long Distance Activism." *Amerasia Journal* 36 (3): 1–28.

Connor, Phillip. "International Migration: Key Findings from the U.S., Europe and the World." Pew Research Center. Accessed December 15, 2017. http://www.pewresearch.org/fact-tank/2016/12/15/international-migration-key-findings-from-the-u-s-europe-and-the-world/.

Constante, Agnes. 2017. "Advocates Warn Vietnamese-American Community of Possible Immigration Detentions." NBC News, November 7. Accessed November 15, 2017. https://www.nbcnews.com/news/asian-america/advocates-warn-vietnamese-american-community-possible-immigration-detentions-n818596.

Corbin, Alain. 1995. *The Lure of the Sea*. London: Penguin.

Coutin, Susan. 2007. *Nations of Emigrants: Shifting Boundaries of Citizenship in El Salvador and the United States*. Ithaca, NY: Cornell University Press.

Crapanzano, Vincent. 2004. *Imaginative Horizons: An Essay in Literary-Philosophical Anthropology*. Chicago: University of Chicago Press.

"Da Nang Determined to Build Startup City." 2017. *Da Nang Today*, July 24. Accessed December 30, 2017. http://baodanang.vn/english/business/201707/da-nang -determined-to-build-startup-city-2563482/.

Đang, Nguyen Anh. 2005. "Enhancing the Development Impact of Migrant Remittances and Diaspora: The Case of Vietnam." *Asia Pacific Population Journal* 20 (3): 111–122.

Đang, Phong. 1999. *Viet Kieu Va Su Nhap Cuoc Voi Kinh Te Viet Nam*. Hanoi, Vietnam: Vien Kinh Te.

——. 2000. "The Vietnamese Diaspora: Returning and Integrating into Vietnam." *Revue Européenne des Migrations Internationales* 16 (1): 185–203.

Davis, Bradley. 2016. *Imperial Bandits: Outlaws and Rebels in the China-Vietnam Borderlands*. Seattle: University of Washington Press.

Derrida, Jacques. 1987. *The Post Card: From Socrates to Freud and Beyond*. Chicago: University of Chicago Press.

——. 1992. *Given Time. I, Counterfeit Money*. Translated by Peggy Kamuf. Chicago: University of Chicago Press.

——. 2000. *Of Hospitality*. Translated by Rachel Bowlby. Stanford, CA: Stanford University Press.

Đinh Linh. 2004. *Blood and Soap: Stories*. New York: Seven Stories Press.

Dodd Frank Wall Street Reform and Consumer Protection Act 2010. Accessed April 15, 2018. https://www.congress.gov/111/plaws/publ203/PLAW-111publ203.pdf.

Duong, Lan. 2012. *Treacherous Subjects: Gender, Culture, and Trans-Vietnamese Feminism*. Philadelphia: Temple University Press.

Dupuis, Jean. 1910. *Tonkin de 1872 à 1886: Histoire et politique*. Paris: A. Challamel.

Durkheim, Émile. *The Elementary Forms of the Religious Life*. New York: Free Press, 1965.

Dutton, George, Jayne Werner, and John Whitmore. 2012. *Sources of Vietnamese Tradition*. New York: Columbia University Press.

Earl, Catherine. 2014. *Vietnam's New Middle Classes: Gender, Career, City*. Copenhagen: Nordic Institute of Asian Studies Press.

Elliott, Anthony, and John Urry. 2010. *Mobile Lives*. New York: Routledge.

Elyachar, Julia. 2005. *Markets of Dispossession: NGOS, Economic Development and the State in Cairo*. Durham, NC: Duke University Press.

Escobar, Arturo. 1995. "Anthropology and the Future: New Technologies and the Reinvention of Culture." *Futures* 27 (4): 409–421.

Espiritu, Yen Le. 2006. "Towards a Critical Refugee Study." *Journal of Vietnamese Studies* 1 (1–2): 410–433.

Feldman, Shelley, Charles Geisler, and Louise Silberling. 2003. *Moving Targets*. Oxford: Blackwell.

Fischer, Michael. 2009. *Anthropological Futures*. Durham, NC: Duke University Press.

Foucault, Michel. 1977. *Discipline and Punish: The Birth of the Prison*. Translated by Alan Sheridan. New York: Pantheon Books.

Freud, Sigmund. 1999. The "Uncanny". Translated by James Strachey. In Sigmund Freud, *The Standard Edition of the Complete Psychological Works of Sigmund Freud*, Volume XVII (of 24) (1917–1919): An Infantile Neurosis and Other Works, pp. 217–256. London: Vintage.

Gainsborough, Martin. 2003. *Changing Political Economy of Vietnam: The Case of Ho Chi Minh City*. New York: Routledge.

——. 2010. *Vietnam: Rethinking the State*. London: Zed Books.

Geertz, Clifford. 1973. *The Interpretation of Cultures: Selected Essays*. New York: Basic Books.

Genin, E. 1882. *J. Dupuis et Francis Garnier Au Tongkin*. Nancy: Berger-Levrault et Cie.

Gibson, James. 1979. *The Ecological Approach to Visual Perception*. Boston: Houghton Mifflin.

Gibson-Graham, J. K. 2006. *A Post Capitalist Politics*. Minneapolis: University of Minnesota Press.

Gilroy, Paul. 1993. *The Black Atlantic: Modernity and Double Consciousness*. Cambridge, MA: Harvard University Press.

Glick-Schiller, Nina, and Georges Fouron. 2001. *Georges Woke Up Laughing: Long-Distance Nationalism and the Search for Home*. Durham, NC: Duke University Press.

Godelier, Maurice. 1999. *The Enigma of the Gift*. Chicago: University of Chicago Press.

Goldring, Luin. 2004. "Family and Collective Remittances to Mexico: A Multi-Dimensional Typology." *Development and Change* 35 (4): 799–840.

Goscha, Christopher. 2012. *Going Indochinese: Contesting Concepts of Space and Place in French Indochina*. Honolulu: University of Hawai'i Press.

——. 2016a. *Vietnam: A New History*. New York: Basic Books.

——, 2016b. "The 30-Years War in Vietnam." February 7, 2017. *New York Times*. Accessed April 12, 2018. https://www.nytimes.com/2017/02/07/opinion/the-30 -years-war-in-vietnam.html.

Graeber, David. 2001. *Toward an Anthropological Theory of Value: The False Coin of Our Own Dreams*. New York: Palgrave.

——. 2011. *Debt: The First 5,000 Years*. Brooklyn, NY: Melville House.

Gribble, Cate and Ly Thi Tran. 2016. "Connecting and Reconnecting with Vietnam: Migration, Vietnamese Overseas Communities and Social Media". In Gomes, Catherine. *The Asia-Pacific in the Age of Transnational Mobility*. London: Anthem Press.

Gupta, Akhil. 1998. *Postcolonial Developments: Agriculture in the Making of Modern India*. Durham, NC: Duke University Press.

GSO Vietnam (General Statistics Office of Vietnam). Accessed July 10, 2016. www.gso .gov.vn.

Guyer, Jane. 2004. *Marginal Gains: Monetary Transactions in Atlantic Africa*. Chicago: University of Chicago Press.

Hann, Chris. 2006. "Gifts and Reciprocity." In *Handbook of the Economics of Giving, Altruism and Reciprocity*, vol. 1, *Foundations*, edited by Serge-Christophe Kolm and Jean Mercier Ytier, 207–223. Amsterdam: Elsevier.

Harmand, François-Jules. 1997. *Laos and the Hill Tribes of Indochina: Journeys to the Boloven Plateau, from Bassac to Hue through Laos, and to the Origins of the Thai*. Bangkok: White Lotus Press.

Harms, Erik. 2011. *Saigon's Edge: On the Margins of Ho Chi Minh City*. Minneapolis: University of Minnesota Press.

——. 2016. *Luxury and Rubble: Civility and Dispossession in the New Saigon*. Berkeley: University of California Press.

Hart, Keith, 2017. "Introduction." In Keith Hart, ed. *Money in a Human Economy*. Oxford: Berghahn.

Harvey, David. 1989. *The Condition of Postmodernity: An Enquiry into the Origins of Cultural Change*. Cambridge: Blackwell.

Hayton, Bill. 2014. *The South China Sea: The Struggle for Power in Asia*. New Haven, CT: Yale University Press.

Hegel, Georg. 1977. *Phenomenology of Spirit*. Translated by Arnold Miller. Oxford: Clarendon Press of Oxford University Press.

Heidegger, Martin. 1977. *The Question Concerning Technology, and Other Essays.* Translated by William Lovitt. New York: Harper and Row.

Hernandez, Ester, and Susan Biber Coutin. 2006. "Remitting Subjects: Migrants, Money and States." *Economy and Society* 35 (2): 185–208.

Hernandez-Coss, Raul. 2005. *The Canada-Vietnam Remittance Corridor: Lessons on Shifting from Informal to Formal Transfer Systems.* Washington: World Bank.

Hill, Kim Loan. 2011. *Coolies into Rebels: Impact of World War I on French Indochina.* Paris: Les Indes Savantes.

Ho, Karen. 2009. *Liquidated: An Ethnography of Wall Street.* Durham, NC: Duke University Press.

Hoang, Kimberly. 2015. *Dealing in Desire: Asian Ascendency, Western Decline, and the Hidden Currencies in Global Sex Work.* Berkeley: University of California Press.

Hoang, Lan Anh, and Brenda Yeoh. 2015. "I'd Do It for Love or for Money." *Gender, Place and Culture* 22 (5): 591–607.

Hoang, Tuan. 2016. "From Reeducation Camps to Little Saigons: Historicizing Vietnamese Diasporic Anticommunism." *Journal of Vietnamese Studies* 11 (2): 43–95.

Holmes, Douglas, and George Marcus. 2008. "Collaboration Today and the Re-Imagination of the Classic Scene of Fieldwork Encounter." *Collaborative Anthropologies* 1 (1): 81–101.

Hoskins, Janet. 2015 *The Divine Eye and the Diaspora: Vietnamese Syncretism Becomes Transpacific Caodaism.* Honolulu: University of Hawai'i Press.

——, and Viet Nguyen. 2014. *Transpacific Studies: Framing an Emerging Field.* Honolulu: University of Hawai'i Press.

Human Rights Watch. 2009. "Vietnam: Sharp Backsliding on Religious Freedom." Accessed August 15, 2016. https://www.hrw.org/news/2009/10/18/vietnam-sharp -backsliding-religious-freedom.

Hunt, David. 2014. "'Modern and Strange Things': Peasants and Mass Consumer Goods in the Mekong Delta." *Journal of Vietnamese Studies* 9 (1): 36–61.

International Monetary Fund. 2008. "Globalization: a Brief Overview." Accessed July 16, 2017. https://www.imf.org/external/np/exr/ib/2008/053008.htm.

——. 2009. *International Transactions in Remittances: Guide for Compilers and Users.* Accessed March 27, 2017. https://www.imf.org/external/np/sta/bop/2008/rcg/pdf /guide.pdf.

Kant, Immanuel. 1955. *Critique of Pure Reason.* Translated by J.M.D. Meiklejohn, Thomas Kingsmill Abbott, and James Creed Meredith. Chicago: Encyclopedia Britannica.

Kaufmann, Vincent, Manfred Max Bergman, and Dominique Joye. 2004. "Motility: Mobility as Capital." *International Journal of Urban and Regional Research* 28 (4): 745–756.

Kerkvliet, Benedict. 2005. *The Power of Everyday Politics: How Vietnamese Peasants Transformed National Policy.* Ithaca, NY: Cornell University Press.

Ketkar, Suhas and Dilip Ratha. 2010. "Diaspora Bonds: Tapping the Diaspora During Difficult Times." *Journal of International Commerce, Economics and Policy* 1(2): 251–263.

Kiernan, Ben. 2017. *Viet Nam: A History from Earliest Times to Present.* Oxford: Oxford University Press.

Koh, Priscilla. 2015. "You Can Come Home Again: Narratives of Home and Belonging among Second-Generation Việt Kiều in Vietnam." *Sojourn* 30 (1): 173–214.

Kwon, Heonik. 2006. *After the Massacre: Commemoration and Consolation in Ha My and My Lai.* Berkeley: University of California Press.

——. 2007. "The Dollarization of Vietnamese Ghost Money." *Journal of the Royal Anthropological Institute* 13 (1): 73–90.

——. 2008. *Ghosts of War in Vietnam*. Cambridge: Cambridge University Press.

Kwon, Jong Bum, and Carrie Lane, Introduction, pp 1–18. In Kwon and Lane, eds., 2016, *Anthropologies of Unemployment: New Perspectives on Work and Its Absence*. Ithaca, NY: Cornell University Press.

International Organization for Migration. 2005. *Labour Migration in Asia: Protection of Migrant Workers, Support Services and Enhancing Development Benefits*. Geneva: International Organization for Migration.

Lacan, Jacques. *Ecrits: a Selection*. 2002. Bruce Fink, trans. New York: Norton.

Lantz, Sandra. 2009. *Whale Worship in Vietnam*. Uppsala: Swedish Science Press.

Larkin, Brian. 2013. "The Politics and Poetics of Infrastructure." *Annual Review of Anthropology* 42:327–43.

Le Thu Huong. 2010. "A New Portrait of Indentured Labour: Vietnamese Labour Migration to Malaysia." *Asian Journal of Social Science* 38:880–896.

——. 2016. "Vietnam Needs a Policy for its Growing Middle Class." *Kyoto Review of Southeast Asia* 19. Accessed October 1, 2017. https://kyotoreview.org/yav /vietnams-urban-middle-class-rapidly-growing-slowly-awakening.

Lee, Don. 2009. *Los Angeles Times*. "Multinationals Take a Longer View of Vietnam."

Lee, Hyunok. 2014. "Trafficking in Women? Or Multicultural Family?" *Gender, Place and Culture* 21 (10): 1249–1266.

Lee, Jonathan H. X., and Kathleen M. Nadeau, ed. 2011. *Encyclopedia of Asian American Folklore and Folklife*. Santa Barbara, CA: ABC-CLIO.

Lefebvre, Henri. 1991. *The Production of Space*. Translated by Donald Nicholson-Smith. Oxford: Blackwell.

Leshkowich, Ann Marie. 2014. *Essential Trade: Vietnamese Women in a Changing Marketplace*. Honolulu: University of Hawai'i Press.

Levitt, Peggy. 1998. "Social Remittances: Migration Driven Local-Level Forms of Cultural Diffusion." *The International Migration Review* 32(4): 926–48.

——. 2001. *The Transnational Villagers*. Berkeley: University of California Press.

Li, Victor Hao. 1994. "From Qiao to Qiao." In *The Living Tree: The Changing Meaning of Being Chinese Today*, ed. Tu Wei-ming, 213–220. Palo Alto, CA: Stanford University Press.

Lindley, Anna. 2010. *The Early Morning Phone Call: Somali Refugees' Remittances*. Oxford: Berghahn Press.

Lindquist, Johan. 2009. *The Anxieties of Mobility: Migration and Tourism in the Indonesian Borderlands*. Honolulu: University of Hawai'i Press.

Long, Lynellyn, and Ellen Oxfeld. 2004. *Coming Home? Refugees, Migrants, and Those Who Stayed Behind*. Philadelphia: University of Pennsylvania Press.

Lowe, Lisa. 1996. *Immigrant Acts: On Asian American Cultural Politics*. Durham, NC: Duke University Press.

Luong, Hy Van. 2003. *Postwar Vietnam: Dynamics of a Transforming Society*. Lanham, MD: Rowman and Littlefield.

Lý, Thiên. 2016. "Foreign Investors Change Their Minds about Oil Refineries." Viet Nam News. Accessed August 1, 2017. http://vietnamnews.vn/economy/talking -shop/300777/foreign-investors-change-their-minds-about-oil-refineries .html#LhefoWu7rhwU5t3F.97.

Mạc, Đường. 2008. "Characteristics of Belief and Religion in the Southern Region of Vietnam in the Ethnological-Religious Approach." *Religious Studies Review* 3 (2): 16–21.

MacLean, Ken. 2013. *The Government of Mistrust: Illegibility and Bureaucratic Power in Socialist Vietnam*. Madison: University of Wisconsin Press.

Maimbo, Samuel Munzele, and Dilip Ratha. 2005a. "Remittances: An Overview." In *Remittances: Development Impact and Future Prospects*, edited by Samuel Munzele Maimbo and Dilip Ratha, 1–16. Washington DC: World Bank.

——, eds. 2005b. *Remittances: Development Impact and Future Prospects*. Washington DC: World Bank.

Malinowski, Bronislaw. 1984. *Argonauts of the Western Pacific*. Prospect Heights IL: Waveland Press.

Malkki, Liisa H. 1995. *Purity and Exile: Violence, Memory, and National Cosmology among Hutu Refugees in Tanzania*. Chicago: University of Chicago Press.

Manalansan, Martin. 2000. *Cultural Compass: Ethnographic Explorations of Asian America*. Philadelphia: Temple University Press.

——. 2014. "The 'Stuff' of Archives: Mess, Migration and Queer Lives." *Radical History* 120:94–107.

Marcus, George. 1995. "Ethnography in/of the World System: The Emergence of Multi-Sited Ethnography." *Annual Review of Anthropology* 24:95–117.

Marcus, George, and Michael Fischer. 1999. *Anthropology as Cultural Critique: An Experimental Moment in the Human Sciences*. Chicago: University of Chicago Press.

Mariano, L. Joyce Zapanta. 2017. "Doing Good in Filipino Diaspora: Philanthropy, Remittances, and Homeland Returns." *Journal of Asian American Studies* 20 (2): 219–244.

Martin, Philip. 2017. "The Impression of Power—Memory, Affect and Ambivalent Masculinities in Vietnam." *NORMA* 12(3–4): 256–269..

Marx, Karl. *Capital*. 1992. Edited by C. J. Arthur. Translated by Ben Fowkes. London: Lawrence and Wishart.

Massumi, Brian. 2002. *Parables for the Virtual: Movement, Affect, Sensation*. Durham, NC: Duke University Press.

Maurer, Bill. 2005a. "Introduction to 'Ethnographic Emergences.'" *American Anthropologist* 107 (1): 1–4.

——. 2005b. *Mutual Life, Inc.: Islamic Banking, Alternative Currencies, Lateral Reason*. Princeton, NJ: Princeton University Press.

——. 2006. "The Anthropology of Money." *Annual Review of Anthropology* 35:15–36.

——. 2012. "Payment: Forms and Functions of Value Transfer in Contemporary Society." *Cambridge Anthropology* 30 (2): 15–35.

——. 2015. *How Would You Like to Pay?: How Technology is Changing the Future of Money*. Durham NC: Duke University Press.

——, Smoki Musaraj, and Ivan Small. 2018. *Money at the Margins: Global Perspectives on Technology, Financial Inclusion and Design*. New York: Berghahn Press.

Maurer, Bill, Taylor Nelms, and Stephen Rea. 2013. "Bridges to Cash: Channeling Agency in Mobile Money." *Journal of the Royal Anthropological Institute* 19 (1): 52–74.

Mauss, Marcel. 1967. *The Gift: Forms and Functions of Exchange in Archaic Societies*. Translated by W.D. Halls. New York: Norton.

McConnell, Scott. 1989. *Leftward Journey: The Education of Vietnamese Students in France, 1919–1939*. New Brunswick, NJ: Transaction.

McElwee, Pamela. 2016. *Forests Are Gold: Trees, People, and Environmental Rule in Vietnam*. Seattle: University of Washington Press.

McKelvey, Robert. 1999. *The Dust of Life: America's Children Abandoned in Vietnam*. Seattle: University of Washington Press.

McLeod, Mark W., and Thi Dieu Nguyen. 2001. *Culture and Customs of Vietnam*. Westport, CT: Greenwood Press.

Mendoza, Dovelyn Rannveig. 2009. *Closing the Distance: How Governments Strengthen Ties with Their Diasporas*. Washington: Migration Policy Institute.

Merli, M. Giovanna. 1997. "Estimation of International Migration for Vietnam, 1979–1989." Center for Studies in Demography and Ecology, University of Washington, Working Paper No. 97-04.

Merz, Barbara, Lincoln Chen, and Peter Geithner. 2007. *Diasporas and Development.* Cambridge, MA: Global Equity Initiative, Asia Center, Harvard University Press.

Meyers, Dean. 1994. *French in Indo-China: With a Narrative of Garnier's Explorations in Cochin-China, Annam and Tonquin.* Bangkok: White Lotus.

Michaud, Jean. 2007. *"Incidental" Ethnographers: French Catholic Missions on the Tonkin-Yunnan Frontier, 1880–1930.* Boston: Brill.

Miller, Karl. 2015. "From Humanitarian to Economic: The Changing Face of Vietnamese Migration." Migration Policy Institute. Accessed November 1, 2017. https://www.migrationpolicy.org/article/humanitarian-economic-changing-face-vietnamese-migration.

Mills, C. Wright. 1959. *The Sociological Imagination.* Oxford: Oxford University Press.

Miyazaki, Hirokazu. 2004. *The Method of Hope: Anthropology, Philosophy, and Fijian Knowledge.* Stanford, CA: Stanford University Press.

——. 2006. "Economy of Dreams: Hope in Global Capitalism and Its Critiques." *Cultural Anthropology* 21 (2): 147–172.

——. 2010. "Gifts and Exchange." In *The Oxford Handbook of Material Culture Studies,* edited by Dan Hicks and Mary Beaudry, 246–264. Oxford: Oxford University Press.

——. 2013. "The Gift in Finance." *NatureCulture* 2:38–49. Accessed April 10, 2018. http://natureculture.sakura.ne.jp/wp/wp-content/uploads/2015/09/PDF-natureculture-02-04-the-gift-in-finance.pdf.

Morice, Albert. 1876. *Voyage en Cochinchine Pendant les Annees 1872-1873-1874.* Lyon: H. Georg.

Morris, Rosalind C. 2000. *In the Place of Origins: Modernity and Its Mediums in Northern Thailand.* Durham, NC: Duke University Press.

Mydans, Seth. 1994. "To Vietnamese in America, the Homeland Beckons." *New York Times,* February 12.

Najam, Adil. 2006. *Portrait of a Giving Community: Philanthropy by the Pakistani-American Diaspora.* Cambridge, MA: Harvard University Press.

Nguyễn, Du. 1983. *The Tale of Kieu.* Translated and annotated by Huỳnh Sanh Thông. New Haven CT: Yale University Press.

Nguyen, Duy Lap. 2017. "Sovereignty, Surveillance and Spectacle in *the Saigon Fabulous Four.*" In *Surveillance in Asian Cinema: Under Eastern Eyes,* edited by Karen Fang, 128–155. New York: Routledge.

Nguyễn, Huy Thiệp. 1988. *Tướng Về Hưu: Truyện Ngắn Chọn Lọc.* Đà Nẵng, Vietnam: Tuần báo Văn Nghệ.

——. 1992. translated by Greg Lockhart. *The General Retires and Other Stories.* Singapore: Oxford University Press.

Nguyen, Mimi. 2012. *The Gift of Freedom: War, Debt and Other Refugee Passages.* Durham, NC: Duke University Press.

Nguyễn, Thanh Lợi. 2014. *Mot Goc Nhin Ve Van Hoa Bien.* Ho Chi Minh City: Nha Xuat Ban Tong Hop Thanh Pho Ho Chi Minh.

Nguyen-Akbar, Mytoan. 2014. "The Tensions of Diasporic 'Return' Migration in the Transnational Family." *Journal of Contemporary Ethnography* 43 (2): 176–201.

——, Mytoan. 2016. "Finding the American Dream Abroad? Narratives of Return Among 1.5 and Second Generation Vietnamese American Skilled Migrants in Vietnam." *Journal of Vietnamese Studies* 11 (2): 96–121.

Nguyen-Marshall, Van, Lisa Drummond, and Daniele Bélanger. 2012. *The Reinvention of Distinction: Modernity and the Middle Class in Urban Vietnam.* New York: Springer.

Nguyen-Vo, Thu Huong. 2008. *The Ironies of Freedom: Sex, Culture and Neoliberal Governance in Vietnam.* Seattle: University of Washington Press.

Nhất Hạnh. 1997. *Living Buddha, Living Christ.* New York: Riverhead Books.

Ninh, Erin Khuê. 2011. *Ingratitude: The Debt-Bound Daughter in Asian American Literature.* New York: New York University Press.

Omi, Michael, and Howard Winant. 1994. *Racial Formation in the United States: From the 1960s to the 1990s.* New York: Routledge.

Ong, Aihwa. 1999. *Flexible Citizenship: The Cultural Logics of Transnationality.* Durham, NC: Duke University Press.

———. 2003. *Buddha Is Hiding: Refugees, Citizenship, the New America.* Berkeley: University of California Press.

Ong, Nhu-Ngoc, and David Meyer. 2008. "Protest and Political Incorporation: Vietnamese-American Protests in Orange County, 1975–2001. " *Journal of Vietnamese Studies* 3 (1): 78–107.

Orozco, Manuel. 2000. "Latino Hometown Associations as Agents of Development in Latin America." Inter-American Dialogue and the Tomás Rivera Policy Institute Working Paper. Accessed March 14, 2018. http://www.centralamerica.thedialogue.org/PublicationFiles/Orozco%20Assoc%20-%20HTAs.pdf.

———. 2013. *Migrant Remittances and Development in the Global Economy.* Boulder, CO: Lynne Rienner.

Osius, Ted. 2018. "Respect, Trust and Partnership: Keeping Diplomacy on Course During Troubling Times," *The Foreign Service Journal.* Accessed April 15, 2018. https://www.afsa.org/respect-trust-and-partnership-keeping-diplomacy-course-troubling-times.

Osteen, Mark. 2002a. "Introduction: Questions of the Gift. In *The Question of the Gift: Essays across Disciplines*, edited by Mark Osteen, 1–42. New York, Routledge.

———, ed. 2002b. *The Question of the Gift: Essays across Disciplines.* New York: Routledge.

Paerregaard, Karsten. 2015. *Return to Sender: the Moral Economy of Peru's Migrant Remittances.* Berkeley: University of California Press.

Palumbo-Liu, David. 2012. *The Deliverance of Others: Reading Literature in a Global Age.* Durham, NC: Duke University Press.

Parreñas, Rhacel Salazar. 2001. *Servants of Globalization: Women, Migration and Domestic Work.* Stanford, CA: Stanford University Press.

Parry, Jonathan. 1986. "The Gift, the Indian Gift and the 'Indian Gift.'" *Man* 21(3): 453–473.

Parry, Jonathan, and Maurice Bloch, eds. 1989. *Money and the Morality of Exchange.* Cambridge UK: Cambridge University Press.

Pedersen, David. 2013. *American Value: Migrants, Money and Meaning in El Salvador and the U.S.* Chicago: University of Chicago Press.

Pedraza, Silvia, and Ruben G. Rumbaut. 1996. *Origins and Destinies: Immigration, Race, and Ethnicity in America.* Belmont: Wadsworth.

Pfau, Wade Donald., and Long Thanh Giang. 2009. "Determinants and Impacts of International Remittances on Household Welfare in Vietnam." *International Social Science Journal* 60 (197–198): 431–443.

Pido, Eric. 2017. *Migrant Returns: Manila, Development, and Transnational Connectivity.* Durham, NC: Duke University Press.

Pike, Douglas. 1998. *Viet Kieu in the United States: Political and Economic Activity.* Lubbock: Texas Tech University Vietnam Center.

Pine, Frances. 2014. "Migration as Hope: Space, Time, and Imagining the Future." *Current Anthropology* 55 (Supplement 9): 95–104.

Polanyi, Karl. 1957. *The Great Transformation*. Boston: Beacon Press.

Polanyi, K. 1968. *The Economy as Instituted Process*. in LeClair, Edward, Harold Schneider, and Melville Herskovits eds. 1968. *Economic Anthropology; Readings in Theory and Analysis*. New York: Holt, Rinehart and Winston.

Pribilsky, Jason. 2008. "Sending Energias from the Andes: The Social Efficacy of Traveling Medicines." *Anthropology News* 49 (5): 13–14.

Quek, Christopher. 2017. "Vietnam through the Eyes of Local Startups." Tech in Asia, March 21. Accessed December 30, 2017. https://www.techinasia.com/talk/vietnam-eyes-local-startups.

Quehuong. Accessed April 15, 2018. http://quehuongonline.vn/van-kien-nghi-quyet/nghi-quyet-36-cua-bo-chinh-tri-ve-cong-tac-doi-voi-nguoi-viet-nam-o-nuoc-ngoai-6493.htm.

Rafael, Vicente L. 2000. *White Love: And Other Events in Filipino History*. Durham, NC: Duke University Press.

Rao, Vijayendra, and Michael Walton, eds. 2004. *Culture and Public Action*. Stanford, CA: Stanford University Press.

Ratha, Dilip, and Munzele Maimbo. 2005. *Remittances: Development Impacts and Future Prospects*. Washington: World Bank.

Ratzel, Friedrich, translated by Arthur John Butler. 1896. *The History of Mankind*. 3 vols. London: Macmillan and Co.

Reid, Anthony. 1993. *Southeast Asia in the Early Modern Era: Trade, Power, and Belief*. Ithaca, NY: Cornell University Press.

Rettig, Tobias. 2012. "From Subaltern to Free Worker: Exit, Voice, and Loyalty among Indochina's Subaltern Imperial Labor Camp Diaspora in Metropolitan France, 1939–1944." *Journal of Vietnamese Studies* 7 (3): 7–54.

Roy, Ananya, and Aihwa Ong. 2013. *Worlding Cities: Asian Experiments and the Art of Being Global*. Oxford: Wiley-Blackwell.

Rydstrom, Helle. 2003. *Embodying Morality: Growing up in Rural Northern Vietnam*. Honolulu: University of Hawai'i Press.

Sagart, Laurent. 2004. *Roots of Old Chinese*. Shanghai: Shanghai Jiao Yu Chu Ban She.

Salazar, Noel B., and Alan Smart. 2011. "Anthropological Takes on (Im)mobility." *Identities* 18 (6): i–ix.

Schattschneider, Ellen. 2003. *Immortal Wishes: Labor and Transcendence on a Japanese Sacred Mountain*. Durham, NC: Duke University Press.

Schlund-Vials, Cathy. 2014. "Re-Sighting and Re-Imagining Southeast Asian American Studies." In *Southeast Asian Diaspora in the United States: Memories and Visions, Yesterday, Today and Tomorrow*, edited by Jonathan Lee, 317–326. Newcastle upon Tyne, UK: Cambridge Scholars.

Schwenkel, Christina. 2013. "Post-Socialist Affect: Ruination and Reconstruction of the Nation in Urban Vietnam." *Cultural Anthropology* 28 (2): 252–277.

———. 2014. "Rethinking Asian Mobilities." *Critical Asian Studies* 46 (2): 235–258.

Scott, James C. 1998. *Seeing Like a State: How Certain Schemes to Improve the Human Condition Have Failed*. New Haven, CT: Yale University Press.

Segal, Uma, Nazneen Mayadas, and Doreen Elliott. 2006. "A Framework for Immigration." *Journal of Immigrant and Refugee Studies* 4 (1): 3–24.

Shipton, Parker. 2007. *The Nature of Entrustment: Intimacy, Exchange and the Sacred in Africa*. New Haven, CT: Yale University Press.

Shohet, Merav. 2013. "Everyday Sacrifice and Language Socialization in Vietnam: The Power of a Respect Particle." *American Anthropologist* 115 (2): 203–217.

Siegel, James T. 1997. *Fetish, Recognition, Revolution*. Princeton, NJ: Princeton University Press.

——. 2011. *Objects and Objections of Ethnography*. New York: Fordham University Press.

Simmel, Georg. 2004. *The Philosophy of Money*. Edited by David Frisby. Translated by Tom Bottomore and David Frisby. New York: Routledge.

Singer, Barnett. 2004. *Cultured Force: Makers and Defenders of the French Colonial Empire*. Madison: University of Wisconsin Press.

Skeggs, Beverley. 2004. *Class, Self, Culture*. London: Routledge.

Skeldon, Ronald. 2006. "Interlinkages between Internal and International Migration and Development in the Asian Region." *Population, Space and Place* 12:15–30.

Small, Ivan. 2014. "Betwixt and Between: Tragedies and Memories of the Vietnamese Exodus, in Film and Audience." *Visual Anthropology* 27 (1–2): 197–200.

Smith, Robert. 2005. *Mexican New York: Transnational Lives of New Immigrants*. Berkeley: University of California Press.

Sorensen, Ninna Nyberg. 2004. *The Development Dimension of Migrant Transfers*. Copenhagen: Danish Institute for International Studies.

Soucy, Alexander. 2012. *The Buddha Side: Gender, Power and Buddhist Practice in Vietnam*. Honolulu: University of Hawai'i Press.

Spyer, Patricia. 2000. *The Memory of Trade: Modernity's Entanglements on an Eastern Indonesian Island*. Durham, NC: Duke University Press.

Star, Susan Leigh. 1999. "The Ethnography of Infrastructure." *American Behavioral Scientist* 43 (3): 377–391.

Strathern, Marilyn. 1988. *The Gender of the Gift: Problems with Women and Problems with Society in Melanesia*. Berkeley: University of California Press.

Tai, Hue-Tam H. 2001. *The Country of Memory: Remaking the Past in Late Socialist Vietnam*. Berkeley: University of California Press.

Takaki, Ronald T. 1998. *Strangers from a Different Shore: A History of Asian Americans*. Boston: Little, Brown.

Taylor, Charles. 2004. *Modern Social Imaginaries*. Durham, NC: Duke University Press.

Taylor, Keith W. 1998. "Surface Orientations in Vietnam: Beyond Histories of Nation and Region." *Journal of Asian Studies* 57 (4): 949–78.

——. 2013. *History of the Vietnamese*. Cambridge: Cambridge University Press.

Taylor, Philip. 2001. *Fragments of the Present: Searching for Modernity in Vietnam's South*. Honolulu: University of Hawai'i Press.

Tellez, Camillo. 2011. "Momo: a new mobile offering in Vietnam." Accessed April 15, 2018. https://www.gsma.com/mobilefordevelopment/programme/mobile-money /momo-a-new-mobile-money-offering-in-vietnam/.

Thai, Hung Cam. 2014. *Insufficient Funds*. Stanford, CA: Stanford University Press.

Thai, Hung Cam. 2008. *For Better or for Worse: Vietnamese International Marriages in the New Global Economy*. New Brunswick, NJ: Rutgers University Press.

Thomas, Mandy. 1999. "Dislocations of Desire: The Transnational Movement of Gifts within the Vietnamese Diaspora." *Anthropological Forum* 9 (2): 145–61.

Thompson, Maddy. 2017. "Migration Decision-Making: A Geographical Imaginations Approach." *Area* 49:77–84.

Tran, Allen. 2015. "Rich Sentiments and the Cultural Politics of Emotion in Postreform Ho Chi Minh City, Vietnam." *American Anthropologist* 117 (3): 480–492

Tran, G. B. 2011. *Vietnamerica*. New York: Villard.

Tran Khe Nu. 1989. "Les Travailleurs Indochinois en France de 1939 a 1948." Universite de Nanterre, Bulletin du Centre d'histoire de la France Contemporaine, no. 10.

Tran, Quan. 2012. "Remembering the Boat People Exodus: A Tale of Two Memorials." *Journal of Vietnamese Studies* 7 (3): 80–121.

Transnational Institute for Grassroots Research and Action. N.d. "TIGRA Mission."
    Accessed March 10, 2018. http://transnationalaction.org/.
Truitt, Allison. 2013. *Dreaming of Money in Ho Chi Minh City*. Seattle: University of
    Washington Press.
Truong, Kim Chuyen, Ivan Small, and Diep Vuong. 2008. "Diaspora Philanthropy in
    Vietnam." In *Diaspora Giving: An Agent of Change in Asia Pacific Communities?*,
    edited by Paula Jones, 251–293. Manila: Asia Pacific Philanthropy Consortium.
Tuổi Trẻ. 2008. "Tiền ở Mỹ, gửi tại Việt Nam."
Tuoi Tre News. 2014. "Millions of Viet Kieu Risk Losing Vietnamese Nationality as
    Registration Deadline Nears." Accessed April 15, 2018. https://tuoitrenews.vn
    /society/18813/millions-of-viet-kieu-risk-losing-vietnamese-nationality-as
    -registration-deadline-nears.
Turley, William. 1976. "Urban Transformation in South Vietnam." *Pacific Affairs* 49 (4):
    607–24.
Turner, Victor. 1969. *The Ritual Process: Structure and Anti-Structure*. Chicago: Aldine.
UNAVSA: Union of North American Vietnamese Associations, collective philanthropy
    project. Accessed April 15, 2018. http://cpp.unavsa.org/about/.
United Nations High Commissioner for Refugees. 2000. *The State of the World's Refugees
    2000: 50 Years of Humanitarian Action*. Accessed May 1, 2016. http://www.unhcr
    .org/afr/publications/sowr/4a4c754a9/state-worlds-refugees-2000-fifty-years
    -humanitarian-action.html.
U.S. Department of Homeland Security. N.d. "EB-5 Immigrant Investor Program."
    Accessed March 13, 2018. https://www.uscis.gov/eb-5.
——. 2016. "Entry/Exit Overstay Report: Fiscal Year 2015." Accessed December 15,
    2017. https://www.dhs.gov/sites/default/files/publications/FY%2015%20DHS%20
    Entry%20and%20Exit%20Overstay%20Report.pdf.
Ủy Ban Nhà Nước Về người Việt Nam ở Nước Ngoài. 2006. *Kiều Bào và Quê Hương*.
    Ho Chi Minh City: Nhà xuất bản Trẻ. Valverde, Kieu Linh. 2012. *Transnational-
    izing Viet Nam: Community, Culture and Politics in the Diaspora*. Philadelphia:
    Temple University Press.
Van Arkadie, Brian, and Raymond Mallon. 2003. *Viet Nam: A Transition Tiger?*
    Canberra: Asia Pacific Press.
Vann, Elizabeth F. 2006. "The Limits of Authenticity in Vietnamese Consumer Markets."
    American Anthropologist 108 (2): 286–296.
Verdery, Katherine. 1996. *What Was Socialism, and What Comes Next?* Princeton, NJ:
    Princeton University Press.
Viet Fellows. 2011. "Meet the 2011 Fellows." Accessed March 14, 2018. http://www
    .vietfellows.org/.
Vietnam Microfinance Working Group. 2013. Accessed March 9, 2018. http://www
    .microfinance.vn.
Vietnam News. 2017. "Deputy PM Signs no Cash Policy". Retrieved April 21, 2018.
    http://vietnamnews.vn/economy/349425/deputy-pm-signs-no-cash-policy
    .html#RfhpfDv8b4csp6Hi.97.
Vietnamese American Non-Governmental Organization Network. N.d. "About Us."
    Accessed March 14, 2018. http://va-ngo.org/about/.
Voice of Vietnam World. 2016. "Mobilising Overseas Vietnamese to national develop-
    ment." Accessed April 16, 2018. http://vovworld.vn/en-US/current-affairs
    /mobilizing-overseas-vietnamese-to-national-development-487207.vov.
Vo Dang, Thuy. 2005. "The Cultural Work of Anticommunism in the San Diego
    Vietnamese American Community." *Amerasia Journal* 31 (2): 65–85.
Wallerstein, Immanuel. 1974. *The Modern World System*. New York: Academic Press.

Weiner, Annette. 1992. *Inalienable Possessions: The Paradox of Keeping-While-Giving.* Berkeley: University of California Press.

Westermarck, Edward. 1924–1926. *The Origin and Development of the Moral Ideas.* 2 vols. Second edition. London: Macmillan and Co.

Westminster City Council, Resolution 3750, 2/19/03. "A Resolution of the City Council of the City of Westminster Recognizing the Flag of the Former Republic of Vietnam as the Official Flag of the Vietnamese People Overseas."

Williams, Raymond. 1983. *Culture and Society, 1780–1950.* New York: Columbia University Press.

Willford, Andrew. 2006. "The "Already Surmounted" yet "Secretly Familiar": Malaysian Identity as Symptom." *Cultural Anthropology* 21(1): 31–59.

Williamson, John, ed. 1990. *Latin American Adjustment: How Much Has Happened?* Washington DC: Institute for International Economics.

——. 1993. "Democracy and the 'Washington Consensus.'" *World Development* 21(8):1329–1336.

——, 2004. "A Short History of the Washington Consensus." Accessed April 15, 2018. https://piie.com/publications/papers/williamson0904-2.pdf.

Woodside, Alexander 1988. *Vietnam and the Chinese Model.* Cambridge, MA: Council on East Asian Studies, Harvard University.

World Bank Vietnam. Accessed April 1, 2018. http://www.worldbank.org/en/country /vietnam.

World Bank. 2014. "Global Financial Development Report." Accessed April 10, 2018. http://siteresources.worldbank.org/EXTGLOBALFINREPORT/Resources /8816096-1361888425203/9062080-1364927957721/GFDR-2014_Complete _Report.pdf.

World Bank. 2016. "Migration and Remittances Data." Accessed December 30, 2017. http://www.worldbank.org/en/topic/migrationremittancesdiasporaissues/brief /migration-remittances-data.

Wucker, Michele. 2004. "Remittances: The Perpetual Migration Machine." *World Policy Journal* 21 (2): 37–46.

Yamashiro, Jane. 2017. *Redefining Japaneseness: Japanese Americans in the Ancestral Homeland.* New Brunswick, NJ: Rutgers University Press.

Yang, Dean. 2005. *International Migration, Human Capital, and Entrepreneurship: Evidence from Philippine Migrants' Exchange Rate Shocks.* Washington, D.C.: World Bank, Development Research Group, Trade Team.

Yang, Mayfair. 1994. *Gifts, Favors, and Banquets: The Art of Social Relationships in China.* Ithaca, NY: Cornell University Press.

Zelizer, Viviana A. 1989. "The Social Meaning of Money: 'Special Monies.'" *American Journal of Sociology* 95 (2): 342–77.

Zhou, Min, and Carl Bankston. 1998. *Growing Up American: How Vietnamese Children Adapt to Life in the United States.* New York: Russell Sage Foundation.

Zong, Jie, and Jeanne Batalova. 2016. "Vietnamese Immigrants in the United States." Migration Policy Institute. Accessed July 18, 2016. http://www.migrationpolicy .org/article/vietnamese-immigrants-united-states.

Index

Page numbers followed by n or nn indicate notes.